A HANDBOOK
OF
DEFENCE ECONOMICS

A HANDBOOK
OF
DEFENCE ECONOMICS

Col. (Retd.) S. C. Narang

PRASHANT PUBLISHING HOUSE
DELHI-110094

Published by:
Prashant Publishing House
C-34, 28 Foota Road, Gali No.-3,
West Karawal Nagar, Delhi-110094
Phone : 011-22963970, Mob. : 9810396373

A Handbook of Defence Economics

First Published 2012

ISBN 978-93-80565-27-9

PRINTED IN INDIA
Published by Mr. R.K. Jha M/s Prashant Publishing House and Published at **Dynamic Printers, Delhi**

Preface

Defence economics is defined to embrace all aspects of the economics of defence, disarmament, conversion and peace. This definition needs to be modified to include the economics of wars, conflict and non-conventional conflicts. Defence economics has made a number of pioneering contributions, many of which were from US academics. There is a developing field in the economics of conflict: an area traditionally the preserve of political scientists. Here, one contribution by economists is to focus on the costs of conflict. Wars are costly. However, there is a lack of empirical work on the costs and benefits of conflict (Sandler and Hartley, 2003). For example, a cost-benefit framework for considering a possible conflict with Iraq.

Defence economics is essentially the application of economic principles and analysis to defence issues, including formulation of defence policy. Contributions to the field of defence studies have historically brought analysis and expertise to bear on strategic concerns, international relations and issues relating to the organisation of the military. Only very recently has an attempt been made to systematically encourage discussion of defence economics. The public and the political leadership in India and most other countries by and large subscribe to a "holy cow" status of matters relating to defence. There is a presumption that the needs of defence must be met, and these needs are generally met without serious political debate. Defence budgets attact limited scrutiny even in advanced countries like the USA. The accurate measurement of defence expenditures is also notoriously difficult. For example, paramilitary forces in a military role not being accounted for; merging defence pensions in the civilian budget; and intelligence gathering. With all these hurdles, it is reasonable to ask whether it is worthwhile delving into defence economics in India at all.

Post Kargil, Indian defence imports had been ranging between three to six billion dollars annually whereas defence exports had been stagnating at meagre 50 million dollars an year. Despite India's best efforts very little headway was being made on the export front. As a last resort, a proposal was mooted in 2004 to coerce foreign sellers to compulsorily buy Indian defence goods in exchange. While the proposal was being debated, an article titled "Offsets in Arms Trade: Need for a National Policy" appeared in Indian Defence Review. It had suggested that India should have a national offset policy and all major defence deals must carry mandatory offset obligations. Defence Public Sector Undertakings (DPSU) and the Ordnance Factory Board (OFB) were quick to grasp the significance of offsets and modified their proposal from one of counter-trade to that of offsets. As India has no national offset policy, Ministry of Defence (MoD) took the initiative to evolve its own defence offset policy. Initially announced in early 2005, the policy was made a part of Defence Procurement Procedure-2005. As the primary aim of the policy was to boost exports from the public sector, it allowed discharge of offsets either through FDI in Indian public sector undertaking for defence industrial infrastructure or direct purchase of products/components/services from DPSU/OFB/other industry identified by MoD. Interestingly, the task of monitoring implementation of every offset contract was to be assigned to a DPSU or OFB.

This book makes an interesting reading for historians, defence and policy analysts, researchers and general readers alike.

—*Editor*

Contents

1

Introduction

Defence economics is essentially the applications programme of economic principles and analysis to defence issues, including formulation of defence policy. Contributions to the field of defence studies have historically brought analysis and expertise to bear on strategic concerns, international relations and issues relating to the organisation of the military. Only very recently has an attempt been made to systematically encourage discussion of defence economics. The public and the political leadership in India and most other countries by and large subscribe to a "holy cow" status of matters relating to defence. There is a presumption that the needs of defence must be met, and these needs are generally met without serious political debate. Defence budgets attack limited scrutiny even in advanced countries like the USA. The accurate measurement of defence expenditures is also notoriously difficult. For example, paramilitary forces in a military role not being accounted for; merging defence pensions in the civilian budget; and intelligence gathering. With all these hurdles, it is reasonable to ask whether it is worthwhile delving into defence economics in India at all.

SIZE OF ECONOMIC SYSTEM

The sheer size and scale of the defence sector and its significant share in world economy and trade compel attention. The world spent more than a trillion (1000 billion) US dollars on military expenditures in 2005. Nearly half of this was spent by the USA alone. Globally, arms sales (defence production) were of the order of $ 268 billion in 2004, of which about $ 170 billion was accounted by the USA. In international arms trade in 2004, the top exporting countries were Russia and the USA, and the top two importers were China and India. Arms imports by India in the 2001-05 period are estimated at over $ 9 billion at constant 1990 prices.

For a developing country like India, the opportunity cost (in terms of alternatives foregone) of the marginal defence rupee would tend to be greater than it may be for relatively more developed countries, and the imperative to seek its optimal utilisation accordingly greater.

Core Consequences

Defence economics has been emerging, mainly in the USA and UK, as a distinct branch of economics since the Second World War. While there are many studies on developing countries, rarely do these contain developing country perspectives.

The five sets of issues are as under:

- The Demand for Defence (expenditure), encompassing the "Guns versus Butter" debate, and arms races
- Defence and Economic Growth, including issues of impact and sustainability
- Military Manpower
- Arms Procurement and Trade
- Defence Industry, including "Make versus Buy" issues, and those related to Research and Development.

The Demand for Defence (expenditure): National security is highly valued by most populations, judging by the sacrifices that many countries seem willing to make when territorial integrity is threatened. Perceptions are important in determining the demand. India is no exception to this phenomenon. We have seen that the biggest spikes in defence expenditure tend to occur after a major conflict e.g., 1962 war. Some determinants of demand that may be relevant for India:

- Confrontations with neighbours due to territorial and sovereignty disputes, instability of a neighbouring country, hostile trans-border infiltration, managing bordering ethnic peoples.
- Multilateral and treaty obligations, cooperative efforts with the United Nations and other coalitions and countries, including peacekeeping operations, humanitarian assistance, and disaster relief.
- Impact of trans-national issues such as terrorism, drug-trafficking, and environmental issues.
- Protection of coastal fisheries, marine resources, and Exclusive Economic Zones (EEZs).
- Protection of market access to trade, investment, energy, food, and other vital resources.
- Maintaining domestic law and order, counter-insurgency.

In order to assess demand, we need to have clarity on objectives. In India, there has traditionally been a reluctance to define the country's vital long-term security interests and/ or threat perceptions in any formal way. These objectives, defined in terms of global, regional and internal security interests, could form a sound basis for projecting demand and planning for optimum levels of defence expenditure.

Secrecy requirements should not get in the way. Other countries have found ways to set out their objectives. For example, the UK's Defence White Paper of 2003. France's Law on Military Planning 2003-08. China's Defence White Papers 1998-2004. Canada's Strategy 2020. Most well organised countries attempt to set out their defence objectives and the means to be employed to achieve these objectives. Given that the demand has been determined, by whichever manner, there is the issue of meeting the demand. Typically, there would be competing claims for funds, and inevitably resource constraints. Development programmes in social sectors such as education and health have highly valued ends. If a country has 'too much' defence, it is wasting its resources, and if it has 'too little' defence, its security is at risk. India's defence budget is a substantial Rs 89,000 crores. Another estimate puts it at Rs 104,000 crores, representing a 40 per cent real increase since 2002.

Because the numbers are big, the potential allocation trade-offs are also substantial. For example, just one-third of the $3.5 billion (approx Rs 16,000 crores) proposed to be spent on procuring and building advanced Scorpene submarines from France would be enough to obviate the need for the Government to seek a $1 billion loan from the World Bank to help finance the Bharat Nirman programme aimed at upgrading rural infrastructure. It has proved difficult in practice even to finalize a five-year defence plan before the end of the plan period.

The historical resource allocation strategy has appeared to be incremental, driven and dominated by the felt need by the individual services. It is interesting to note that despite its maritime presence and ambitions, China is managing without an aircraft carrier even today.

DEFENCE AND ECONOMIC PROCESS

The defence sector has a major share of the budget in most countries. The perceived adverse effects of higher defence spending on economic growth are due to the following:

- Purchase by the defence sector of domestic goods, or the use of foreign exchange to purchase imported goods.
- The government sector shows no measurable productivity increases. Thus, an enlargement in defence spending shifts resources from the productive sector to the non-productive sector.
- A shift of resources to defence reduces the resources available for the rest of the economy and in particular

"crowds out" private investment as well as diverts skilled workers from civilian sectors.

The dominant view among economists has been that defence is a drag on economic growth. A contrary view was brought out strongly for the first time in a study of developing countries on this topic by Benoit in 1973. Of the favourable effects of defence spending, Benoit lists many, of which the following seem relevant for the Indian situation: Security effects—To the extent that the military provides security to the country, it enables an atmosphere conducive to investment and long-term planning decisions.

Training effects—Military manpower receives training even at the rudimentary level and this can be beneficial if the recruits come in substantial numbers from the subsistence economy and if the military programmes introduce people to 'modern' methods and social skills and general inculcation of 'national' values.

Infrastructure effects—The military may create infrastructure, such as roads, airports, docks and communications, which can be used by the civilian sector, especially 'up country'.

Consumable effects—The services provide substantial numbers of people with food, clothing, shelter and medicines. They also engage in 'civic action' programmes and in 'hearts and minds' campaigns. The existing research by and large seems to indicate that certain groups of developing countries derive positive benefits from military spending.

The sustainability of the defence budget is a function of the health of the economy. A glaring example of this in recent times has been the inability of the Soviet Union to sustain high levels of defence spending in superpower competition with the USA, in the face of a faltering economy. Defence expenditure in India has benefited from higher growth rates in the recent past. In real dollar terms, the Indian defence budget has more than doubled in the past decade. The ratio of defence expenditure to GDP is well below 3% today, which is a healthy sign. On the flip side, internal security is adversely impacted by social and economic backwardness and regional balance issues seems to be needed for the sustainability both of growth-fostering reformist economic policies as well as a stronger defence.

Military Work Force

The human resource dimension of defence economics is a relatively neglected field. US studies dominate the theoretical, empirical, and policy literature on military manpower. Two issues have been pre-eminent. First, studies of conscription versus an all-volunteer force. Second, the concern with downsizing and its implications for military manpower. In India, the structure of military manpower has changed little since British times. Reliance continues on a large, conventional force with over 1.3 million men in uniform in the armed forces and another nearly 1.7 million paramilitary personnel with about 400,000 of these in organisations directly performing a defence role. In addition, entities like the Border Roads Organization (employing about a lakh) and defence civilians (estimated to be of the order of another four lakhs) perform a support role. There probably is a case for looking at overall numbers in the context of modernization; even the Chinese People's Liberation Army has apparently made conscious manpower reductions in recent times. Putting a price to the manpower input into defence would also be instructive in taking a call on these issues.

Arms Control and Trade

Arms imports by India in the 2001-05 period are estimated at over $9 billion at constant 1990 prices. Defence markets are large, government regulated, and generally non-transparent in their functioning. Economic factors are relevant in understanding and dealing with defence markets. For example, the post-Cold War situation and disarmament in

NATO and in the former Warsaw Pact countries has made their defence contractors seek export sales to compensate for declining domestic procurement. As a result, disarmament in one part of the world might actually promote arms exports, regional arms races, and possibly instability elsewhere in the world. Similarly, major technical advances result in new products and fuel demand from buyers who need to "catch up."

The Indian Context

Issues relating to arms imports are important for India, which has only a 30% rate of self-reliance in arms procurement, despite a sizable arms industry. By their very nature, arms import deals tend to involve large amounts of money, and are politically highly sensitive. It is possible to work out the costs and benefits of a procurement alternative in quantitative terms, and such exercises should be encouraged, so that better decisions are made. The putting in place a new, more transparent Defence Procurement Procedure in India in 2006 has drawn attention to the issue of "offsets". As the arms trade takes place in a buyers' market, it follows that arms importing countries are in a dominant position to extract compensatory investment. The new procedure in India requires direct offsets of 30% of the value of the contract to be made for all defence capital contracts of over Rs 300 crores. This is expected, according to the Defence Minister, to result in gains for the country of over Rs 45,000 crores ($10 billion) in investments over the Eleventh Plan period (2007-12). The limited international research on the subject, however, tends to cast doubt on the net benefits of defence offsets to national economies. As has been pointed out in this context, "there are no free lunches."

Defence Mechanism and Industry

Strategic motivations apart, indigenous arms production efforts have been justified on the economic grounds that (a) It will spur generalized industrialisation by means of spillover or spin-off effects; and; (b) It will permit foreign-exchange earnings. The reference point for determining the value of any defence-industry relationship is its contribution to the ability of the defence forces to meet their key responsibilities. Joint production or collaborative ventures should be expected to lead to cost savings and greater scales of output. But international collaboration is only one form of work sharing: alternative forms are licensed production and offsets; these also need to be evaluated as alternatives.

Economics of Defence Production

A substantial defence production capability has been developed in India, and inevitably some of the issues that surround defence industries in other parts of the world are relevant for India. Efficiency issues exist. The recent award of two $20 million contracts for rocket launchers to be used in the Pinaka missile system to the Indian engineering companies Tata Power and Larsen & Toubro is noteworthy in this context, since it is the first time that private-sector Indian companies have been appointed as prime contractors on a defence project. We should also be concerned that while two decades back, an estimated 40% of weapons and equipment requirements was met by outright imports, today this figure is around 70%. In the case of India's Defence Research and Development Organisation (DRDO), the development time taken is in many cases said to be so long that before an item reaches the prototype stage, the specifications and performance parameters aimed at are obsolete by contemporary standards. Such things are known to happen in more advanced countries also.

The Economics of Insurgency and Extremism

Left wing extremism in India happens to have arisen in the most backward regions of the country, lending support to the argument that economic solutions in terms of raising the levels of development and improving economic prospects for the unemployed have to be a major factor in arriving at long-term solutions to the conflict. At the same time, it has been estimated that "10-20% of development funds" in militancy affected areas in India end up in the hands of the insurgents, major investments committed to the resource-rich but less developed states of central India are at risk due to insurgent attacks on economic targets.

Defence Technology

Technological advances occur today at a breathtaking pace. Economists can contribute in helping identify least cost solutions consistent with security imperatives, using the potential offered by technological changes. The trends outlined are part of the global landscape today, and for the Indian defence forces, it is only a question of whether they will allow the changes to pass them by or will seek to stay ahead of the curve by factoring them into defence strategies. We can begin here and now. The rapidly evolving global scenario will have no mercy on laggards. Would it be prudent to deny ourselves the benefit of information, techniques and analysis that are currently available? Don't we want to squeeze the maximum "bang for the buck", so that the best decisions on strengthening of national security can be made, for any given level of resources allocated? These are the questions that we need to reflect upon. In the answer to these questions lies the road ahead.

DEFENCE ECONOMICS DIRECTION

Defence economics, field of national economic management concerned with the economic effects of military expenditure, the management of economics in wartime, and the management of peacetime military budgets.

OPPORTUNITIES DEPARTED: THE COST OF WAR

There is no such thing as an inexpensive war. First, there is the human cost in loss of life and in the physical and psychological maiming of healthy people. While the personal cost of such loss is immeasurable, the economic cost to society can be estimated. This measure was first proposed by a French economist, Jean-Baptiste Say, in 1803. He asserted the principle that war costs more than its direct expenses, for it also costs what its casualties (military and civilian) would have earned throughout their lifetimes if they had never participated in war. Second, war has economic costs arising from the destruction of buildings, productive farmlands and forests, public services such as waterworks, electricity-generating and distribution systems, roads, bridges, harbours, and airfields, and all manner of personal and corporate property such as homes, possessions, factories, machinery, vehicles, and aircraft. War, therefore, destroys physical capital that has been created by previous economic activity.

Reconstruction after war is a particular economic burden because the finance, imported capital goods, and labour used in reconstruction merely restore the losses a country has sustained, rather than adding to the stock of capital available to its economy.

Thus, even if it manages to restore all its physical losses, it uses scarce resources that would otherwise have been available for extending and improving economic activity. As most wars since 1945 have occurred in the Third World, some of the world's poorest countries have suffered the most from the economic losses of war.

War also costs a great deal in goods and services to create the weapons of war and to supply the people engaged in the war effort. The diversion of these goods and services—which range from the metals and chemicals transformed into weapons to the food, clothing, and shelter for the armed forces—reduces current civilian consumption, which lowers the population's living standards. Metal used to make a tank cannot be used to build bridges, fuel used to transport military supplies cannot be used on school buses, cement used to construct ammunition dumps cannot be used in house construction. This constitutes the opportunity cost of war—

that is, the extent to which the economy foregoes the opportunity to commit these resources to alternative peaceful uses.

The opportunity cost of war is also felt in the future. In addition to allocating resources to consumption (the satisfaction of current needs), an economy allocates resources to investment (the new factories and machinery that produce tomorrow's goods and services). Resources diverted to war cannot be used to create new productive capacity for future consumption, and this reduces the living standards of the population below what they otherwise would have been in the future.

In summary, the total costs of war include the cost of the foregone use of the economic resources used up in the conflict. These include the cost of the foregone lifetime earnings of those killed in the war, the cost of lifetime medical care for those permanently incapacitated by the war, the cost of replacing the physical capital destroyed or damaged by the war, the cost of supplying the armed forces with the weapons of war, the cost of sustaining the armed forces and those in support functions (including their pay and pensions), and the losses to the economy caused by the diversion of resources from peaceful investment in future economic capacity.

COMPARISON BURDENS

International comparisons of how governments arrange their defence spending are fraught with conceptual discrepancies. The defence burden of a country is measured by the d/GDP ratio, which indicates how much of the nation's resources are being allocated to defence each year, but different estimates of both d and GDP are possible, each giving a different d/GDP ratio. Capitalist economies, which use the GDP, measure economic activity differently from communist economies, which use a net material product (NMP) system. The NMP excludes many expenditures, including state administration and defence, normally included under GDP.

This complicates comparisons between these systems. Defence expenditures themselves are subject to controversy.

The North Atlantic Treaty Organization (NATO) has agreed on a measure of defence activity to which it adheres when making comparisons of its members' defence burdens, but other countries follow different conventions. Some, largely low-income countries, exclude internal security expenditures, which can be relatively high, thus lowering their official d/GDP ratio. Others, such as the Soviet Union, exclude defence-related research and development, frontier guards, and paramilitary reserves, thereby reducing the nominal defence expenditure by up to 30 percent.

Even if agreement could be reached on what constitutes defence expenditure, this would still leave countries with a measure denominated in their domestic currencies. For meaningful comparisons of the absolute amounts spent on defence, every country's defence expenditures would have to be reduced to a common currency. But the act of converting each currency into, for example, U.S. dollars could lead to distortions, because official exchange rates reflect official policies and not existing realities. Thus, two countries with similar amounts in dollars spent on defence, and therefore in balance in their defence capabilities, could face a growing imbalance in their dollar-based defence expenditures purely because one of their currencies has changed its exchange rate with the U.S. dollar.

Comparisons of the absolute amounts each country spends on defence are prone to error and must always be used with caution. Nevertheless, because each country measures its defence spending and its GDP in its own currency, the d/GDP ratio is an acceptable measure of a country's defence burden. Ratios can be compared across countries and in different time periods. The d/GDP ratio rises rapidly during a major war—in Britain in 1944 the d/GDP ratio reached 60 percent—and it falls in periods of prolonged peace. A country raising its d/GDP ratio signals that it is concerned with security, in turn causing concern among countries likely to be affected.

Defence Burdens Universal

Security expenditures for both external defence and internal law and order account for major shares of government expenditures. In many low-income countries, these expenditures often exceed 20–30 percent of the state budget and more than 10 percent of the country's GDP. The higher-income countries, while spending higher absolute amounts on defence, tend to spend smaller proportions of state expenditure (under 15 percent) and smaller proportions of GDP (under 5 percent). Given the perilous security situation in the lower-income regions of the world, these discrepancies are understandable (if also regrettable in view of their other pressing needs).

By looking at the actual defence burden of an individual country and comparing it with the norm for similar economies, analysts can infer localized circumstances that may be influencing the government's perceptions of security. For instance, a poor country with a very low d/GDP, or a rich country with a very high d/GDP, is behaving differently from the norm for similar economies. An economist would seek explanations for this in the perception of a threat indicated by the public statements of the government concerned. In the absence of such statements, or where public statements are contrary to the behaviour of the government (for example, if it is raising its d/GDP but publicly proclaiming its peaceful intentions and denying that it is threatened by, or is threatening, any other country), the economist would rely on the d/GDP as an indicator of true intentions. It is likely that the intelligence services of neighbouring countries would draw similar conclusions from the economic data. Within the higher-income countries there are notable differences in the amounts spent on defence. The United States and Britain have spent relatively high proportions (5 to 10 percent) of their GDP on defence since 1955, compared with Japan, which has spent less than 1 percent of GDP over the same period. Germany and France also have tended to spend a smaller proportion of their GDPs than Britain on defence.

The Japanese case is interesting because of the differences in economic achievement between Japan and the big defence spenders. Many economists believe that there is a connection between the amount of GDP spent on defence and a country's economic growth, investment, and living standards. Japan's limit of d/GDP to under 1 percent was a result of its defeat in World War II. There is no doubt that it benefited enormously from limited defence spending (particularly while it could free ride under the military protection of the United States), since resources not allocated to defence went into economic investment, to the direct benefit of civilian employment and output. However, at the same time Japan also spent much less (about half as much) of its GDP on general government expenditure (g) than the United States and western Europe. Whether it was the low d/GDP (1 percent) or the low g/GDP (9 percent) that allowed the resources for Japanese economic successes to be mobilized is arguable. A low g/GDP ratio implies a lower level of taxation than a high g/GDP. This releases a higher flow of savings into the economy, enabling higher investment ratios to be maintained. High rates of investment, which are associated with higher growth rates of GDP, characterized the Japanese post-war economy and are a more likely explanation for the Japanese economic success than its low d/GDP.

The Soviet Union has long spent a high proportion of its national resources on defence. Estimates vary, but the consensus among Western economists is that Soviet d/GDP for much of the postwar period was around 14 percent. (The official Soviet d/GDP was 6 percent.) If defence spending competes with economic growth in the capitalist economies, contributing to inflation, low investment, and lower living standards, then it must have a devastating impact on poorer economies such as the Soviet Union. The need to compete with the United States at all technological levels across the weapons spectrum has been met at the cost of heavy distortions in the rest of the Soviet economy. This has compelled the Soviet Union to review its priorities and to consider whether its security is best assured by continually raising the military ante with the West or by living at some lower level of military tension with a reduced offensive military capability.

DEFENCE MANAGEMENT: BUDGETING DETERMENT

"How much defence is enough defence?" is the great unanswerable question of defence economics. Those charged with preparing a defence capability tend to be more cautious about the level of capability than those who eventually have to pay for it. In fact, the very success of deterrence—a high probability of nonattack throughout a long period of peace—tends to reduce the amount of defence spending that the electorate considers necessary to achieve deterrence. Judging the appropriate level of military preparedness is not a science; it is a mixture of intelligent response to credible threats and of judicious, cautious preparation "just in case" this or that should arise. The managers of the armed forces tend to increase the contingencies they wish to prepare for, while skeptical taxpayers tend to question whether certain preparations are absolutely essential. In democracies this tension forms the permanent agenda of the defence debate.

Stocks and Flows

Defence expenditures are made on an annual basis, the government allocating so much of its total budget to personnel costs, so much to the procurement of weapon systems, and so much to general support. The pay and allowances of defence personnel are consumed within the year; that is, they spend their wages, allowances, and pensions on consumer goods and, in so doing, add to total demand in the economy. Procurement, on the other hand, is somewhat different. A tank lasts much longer than the single year in which it is purchased. Because it is supposed to last as long as it takes to become obsolescent, the tank becomes part of the country's permanent defence capability. That defence capability is, in economic terms, a stock, while the annual expenditure is called a flow. Even if, for some reason, a defence budget is reduced in a single year, a country's defence capability need not be reduced. The government can still draw on the stock paid for by previous defence budgets, which is manifested in its tanks, aircraft, ships, communications systems, trained personnel, and expertise in military affairs. Clearly, if the defence budget continues to be reduced every year, there will come a point at which the country's defence capability will decline through attrition as items of equipment become obsolete or beyond repair.

The analogy is with a bath that is filling with water while the plughole is open. As water pours into the bath, water also drains from the plughole. It is the difference between the rates at which water flows in and out that determines whether the bath fills or empties. If the flows in and out are equal, the water level will remain constant. Likewise with defence capability: if the additions (flow in) to the stock of weapons matches the attrition (flow out) of the stock from all causes, then the country's defence capability will remain constant.

Measuring a Threat: the Example of NATO

Budgeting a nation's defence capability is complicated, however, because defence capability is not determined unilaterally; it depends on the capability of the potential aggressor. The gap in military capability between any two countries is known as the threat, and estimates of the threat constitute the major input into defence planning. If a potential aggressor develops an advanced weapon system that effectively counters a weapon stocked by the defender, it will eventually threaten to overwhelm the latter's defenses. Likewise, a growth in the stock of weapons deployed by a potential aggressor can eventually have a similar effect in threatening to overwhelm the defender's smaller stocks. If the defending country does not invest in overcoming each new threat to its capability—by technology, new types of weapons, increasing the stock of current weapons, or all three options simultaneously—it will risk a reduction in the probability of nonattack—that is, its deterrence capability will be compromised.

The Economics of Nuclear Disincentive

Estimates of the threat of a Soviet invasion across the German border determined the nature of NATO's response for more than 40 years. While NATO planners considered their own forces to be technologically superior to the Soviet forces, they were nevertheless mindful that the Soviet Union had a decisive quantitative superiority in conventional forces (more tanks, armoured vehicles, artillery, combat aircraft, and troops). The threat of a land-based invasion by Soviet forces, which the planners considered to be virtually unstoppable, led directly to the decision to deploy nuclear weapons as the ultimate deterrent against an invasion of western Europe.

Nobody could survive a major nuclear war in Europe. The damage to the Soviet Union from an American nuclear strike would be matched only by the damage to the United States from a Soviet nuclear strike. Because each country has maintained sufficient nuclear forces to respond in kind to a first strike by the other, a nuclear exchange would be suicidal for both. Whatever the rhetoric, therefore, both countries have a strong interest in preventing war of any kind from breaking out on the continent of Europe. Literally, they are hostage to each other's behaviour, making Europe an unsafe place to start a war. This doctrine, known as "mutual assured destruction," was given the appropriate acronym MAD.

The consequences of MAD led NATO to adopt a policy known as "flexible response." Rather than an all-or-nothing nuclear exchange, this envisaged a staged escalation of NATO's response to a Soviet invasion, based on containing the initial thrust of the Soviet forces and warning them of the consequences of further encroachment on NATO's territory. To underline the credibility of the threat of nuclear retaliation, NATO commanders were issued battlefield nuclear weapons, which NATO governments might or might not release for immediate use, with or without warning. Uncertainty about NATO's policy of probable first use of nuclear weapons was regarded as sufficient to make Europe an unsafe place for the Soviet Union to risk the consequences of a conventional war. As long as the risk of the horrendous consequences of a nuclear war exceeded the prospects of potential gain from launching an attack, the probability of nonattack on western Europe by the Soviet Union remained at an acceptable level.

Choosing Weapon Systems

Since the 1960s there have been several attempts to impose some rationality upon defence planning. The complexity of weapons development has few parallels in civilian development. Working close to technological frontiers (sometimes having to think beyond them) under management systems imbued with a public-sector rather than a commercial ethos, under government budgetary constraints and shifting political priorities, and subject to ever-changing estimates of the threat the system is designed to counter, has produced an expensive and time-consuming procurement system. Lead times of 18 to 25 years from initial concept to in-service production are not unknown in defence procurement.

The need for more rational choices in weapon programs and in the deployment of scarce resources increased as the defence budgets grew in absolute size (though falling as a proportion of a growing GDP). The cost of errors in choice increases as the cost of a single weapon platform escalates, so that, with a new weapon system costing $10–40 billion, it is crucial not to find that it is not needed by the time it is in service, that the technology cannot be made to work, or that it has been made obsolete by new developments. The

Polaris submarine-launched ballistic missile program, begun by the United States in 1956, was the first highly complex system that required new management techniques to be brought to successful completion. One technique—called program evaluation and review technique (PERT)—found civilian applications after it was invented by the U.S. Navy to build Polaris on time and under budget. Similarly, earlier techniques such as cost–benefit analysis (invented to cope with submarine hunting problems during World War II) and input–output analysis (a technique developed by the U.S. Air Force for identifying the critical parts of an economy to develop or damage) rapidly spread into civilian use and into most academic management programs.

The first attempts to bring rational choice to the management of a defence budget coincided with the U.S. involvement in Vietnam. Terms such as systems analysis, as well as planning, programming, and budgeting systems (PPBS) and functional costing, became common in defence management. Much of the intellectual capital invested in these techniques came from economists, whose discipline in costing options and marginal analysis provided them (if not always the defence managers they advised) a set of tools appropriate to the task.

When decisions are made solely by the lobbying of special interests—such as the navy, air force, and army—the result is likely to be a constant compromise under which programs remain in the budget because of political considerations. Defence analysts attempt to force the military lobbyists to set specific objectives for their programs and to accept criteria by which the military value of the programs can be judged. Like many management fashions, PPBS and its associated techniques did not survive in their earliest forms, but they did establish the belief that analysing, evaluating, and choosing rationally was superior to lobbying by bureaucrats and, sometimes, by corrupting commercial interests.

This can be illustrated by the technique of functional costing. Ordinarily, most budgets are a listing of expenditures under various main headings—personnel, equipment, and supplies—and the total is approved through the political process. This type of budget is called an accountability budget because it accounts for defence expenditure, but it cannot inform the defence planner (or the taxpayer) how efficiently the defence department has spent the budget. Under functional costing, the objectives of a proposed military program are shown along with the costs of all the resources needed to fulfil each objective, irrespective of which armed service contributes to the activity.

For example, under functional costing there is no navy budget that costs everything spent by the navy. There is instead a maritime defence budget, a deep-sea navy budget, a coastal defence budget, and so on. These budgets may include costed contributions from units of the navy, air force, and army, plus an assessment of the costs of support functions used to carry out the activities. If, for instance, it is proposed to add a longer-range aircraft to the maritime defence role, this can be costed, and, depending upon the importance of extending maritime defence compared to other objectives, an informed decision can be made on whether to allocate the incremental funds to the upgraded aircraft or to some other project supporting some other military activity. Deciding between marginal increases or decreases in expenditures across different functions, all of them linked to specified objectives, is an improvement over buying aircraft simply because it is the turn of the air force to get a big project approved by the government.

War Finance: when Deterrence Fails

War is too serious, and too expensive, to be left to the whim of chance, yet throughout history many governments have been willing to engage in war if it suited their interests as they perceived them, and many have also been dragged into wars when cooler calculations might have encouraged them to remain at peace. It was out of the need to raise the finance to conduct wars that the earliest systems for collecting public finance developed.

Taxation

The practice of taxing the population to pay for war has a long history. In early nomadic societies, wars could be fought with little expense other than time and casualties. Nomadic horsemen engaged in war as an extension of their normal activities as herdsmen. If successful, the warriors plundered the defeated, who were either killed, sold, or scattered. With more-settled agricultural societies, wars could be fought between planting and harvest, the armies living off of the land or the pay of the king. In the feudal system each man had an obligation to fight if required by the lord of the manor, to whom the vassal owed his livelihood. Weapons were often the personal possessions of the warriors and were fashioned by themselves, their forebears, or craftsmen. As weapons improved in quality and ingenuity, special efforts to produce them had to be made—for which their producers were paid out of public funds, as were the soldiers to whom they were distributed. These expenses necessitated the collection of special funds, and thus the government turned to levies on the population to provide the resources.

Where taxation alone was not sufficient to pay for a war, the king could resort to selling relief from feudal obligations (usually to prosperous cities), and to borrowing from rich individuals (who risked confiscation if they refused and not being paid back if they agreed). Most political crises in European history up to the 19th century arose from disputes over public finance, usually to pay for wars. The English Civil Wars of 1642–51 were a typical example of a bitter dispute between king and parliament over which had the powers of taxation. By the time of the French Revolution in 1789, warfare had ceased to be a localized affair with a few thousand soldiers engaged in a single decisive battle. Warfare had become a massive undertaking, often lasting months and years and involving armies of hundreds of thousands. The expense of war reached levels unheard of previously. The Royal Navy, for instance, employed 200,000 men in the 1790s alone. Out of the need to find new sources of revenue for the long war between Britain and France from 1793 to 1815, the British government introduced a temporary income tax to be levied on all persons earning above a high minimum income. The advantages of the system soon became evident, and income taxes were widely adopted as permanent sources of government revenue.

Borrowing

The British government also discovered another source of revenue, the national debt. Whereas previous borrowings by monarchs were a great risk to the lender, under the national debt scheme the government agreed to guarantee regular payment of interest to all persons who lent to it, either in perpetuity or for a fixed term. Holders of government bonds were also permitted to sell them, passing the right to the guaranteed income to the buyer. Again, the system was so successful that it was soon copied by other governments, not all of them as scrupulous in their repayments as they promised. War bonds featured strongly in the two world wars, and it was regarded as patriotic to use personal savings to purchase them—though most of the borrowing came from institutions.

The new sources of war finance enabled the increased expense of war to be met—and, in the opinion of some economists, made it more likely that a government would embark on a war for less than good reason. If war had to be financed out of the current consumption of the population, natural limits would be set on war being undertaken lightly, but borrowing removed these limits. Though the population would be saddled with interest payments for decades to come, this cost was small and of long duration compared to the immediate cut in living standards that would have to be made to pay for a war in full.

War's Consequences: Inflation and Recession

A major modern war can divert from 40 to 60 percent of a country's GDP, and one object of war finance is to release within the economy the resources needed for the war effort without causing inflation. If the government merely prints money to pay for the resources it requires, it will bid up prices in competition with civilians. The alternative is to reduce civilian consumption by imposing taxes at levels sufficient to force consumers to forego bidding for goods and services. The income from taxes can then be applied by the government to bid for the resources released by its program. Taxation acts both to raise necessary finance and simultaneously to reduce aggregate demand, which releases the resources needed for the war effort. The war effort represents a substantial expansion of production, for which producers receive wages and profits. When these same producers attempt to spend their incomes, they face a diminished quantity of civilian goods available for purchase. They must either face rapidly rising prices (caused by excess money chasing insufficient goods), or they must restrain—or be restrained—from spending. A war economy therefore imposes higher taxes on wages and profits to reduce demand. War bonds and taxes provide finance for the war effort and reduce demand for civilian goods and services. To conduct a major war without such an austerity program risks inflation.

If inflation is a risk during a war, recession is another risk at the end of it. The massive expansion in production to provide resources for the war effort, if suddenly contracted by the cancellation of all defence contracts, throws large numbers of people out of work. The unemployed reduce their consumer spending, causing further cuts in aggregate demand, which throws yet more people out of work. World War I was followed by recession. Because much of the war damage along the Western Front was confined to the vast, static battlefields across France, where the destruction was mainly human and the cost was mainly in war materials, there was no need for a massive reconstruction program. Also, the damage on the Eastern Front was swept behind the newly formed Soviet state, which for ideological reasons eschewed capitalist reconstruction. After the war factories closed down, removing a flow of wages and profits into the economy, the demobilization of troops put surplus labour into an economy that was already in recession.

Recession was averted at the end of World War II by reconstruction of the cities and economies of western Europe and Japan. Reconstruction rapidly transformed the war economies into mass consumer economies supported by the pent-up demand that had been frustrated by the lack of civilian goods and by high taxes during the war. In Europe's case there was a transfer of capital from the United States through the Marshall Plan.

As the war economies were dismantled, economic growth surged, and those countries that did best economically were those that dismantled their highly regulated, government-controlled war economies quickest (West Germany, for example). Those countries that were least successful in dismantling their regulated economies were the slowest to recover. Among these were Britain, which increased state intervention from 1946 to 1951, and the Soviet-controlled economies of eastern Europe, which went even further down the road of government-managed economies.

NEW CRITICISM IN DEFENCE ECONOMICS

There is a developing field in the economics of conflict: an area traditionally the preserve of political scientists. Here, one contribution by economists is to focus on the costs of conflict. Wars are costly. However, there is a lack of empirical work on the costs and benefits of conflict (Sandler and Hartley,

2003). For example, a cost-benefit framework for considering a possible conflict with Iraq.

Problems of Estimating Costs

For the participants, estimates of military costs involve the following:

- The *additional costs* of the conflict
- The need to include the costs of replacing equipment
- The need to value the human capital losses (ie. based on the discounted value of future earnings)
- Recognition that estimates will differ from out-turns
- Possible long-term costs such as the need for peacekeeping forces and a greater threat from terrorism
- Possible financial contributions from nations not participating in the conflict.

There are costs for the civilian economy. These include impacts on oil prices; on airline and tourist markets; on share prices and the state of general confidence in various economies; possible recession effects; and on public spending plans (e.g. greater spending on defence at the expense of social welfare programmes). In undertaking such analysis, the counterfactual cannot be ignored, namely, what would have happened without any conflict? For example, would the airlines have experienced a recession in their markets? Nor can the costs incurred by and imposed upon Iraq be ignored: these involve physical and human capital losses.

Estimating Profits

A cost-benefit approach to conflict requires estimation of both costs and benefits. For the participants, what are the likely benefits from a war with Iraq and how highly are such benefits valued ? Here, one possible approach is to use costs to indicate the *minimum valuation* which must be placed on the benefits. For example, the Gulf War cost the UK some £2.5 billion with contributions to the UK from other nations of over £2 billion (1991 prices). Today's costs to the UK of a Gulf-type war with Iraq would be over £3 billion.

Scope and Definitions

Consider how economists might analyse the events of September 11th 2001. These attacks on the USA involved macro-and micro-economic impacts, the economics of military alliances and the challenge of modelling terrorist behaviour. Throughout, there is also the need to recognise the counterfactual: what would have happened in the absence of September 11th?

The end of the Cold War has led to the growth of non-conventional conflict in such forms as revolutions, civil wars, guerilla warfare and terrorism. These result in new threats to national security. Terrorism is defined as "... the premeditated use of, or the threat to use, extra-normal violence or brutality to gain a political objective through intimidation or fear". Terrorism is not new. There are examples from World War II and the German occupation of Europe.

More recently, there is the example of Northern Ireland which demonstrated the costs of terrorism in the form of deaths and injuries to military and civilian personnel, adverse effects on trade and exchange and the loss of foreign investment and tourists. Peace resulting from the Good Friday Agreement provided a range of economic and other benefits, with peace representing a public good. The features of recent terrorism involve individuals or groups attacking civilian targets: these are asymmetric attacks (not the traditional armies versus armies). The attacks are also transnational and some are state-supported.

Macroeconomic Impacts

The immediate cost to the US economy from the September 11th attacks were lives lost, property destroyed or damaged and lost output. Initial estimates of lost output were $100 billion, with a present value of economic damage to the USA estimated at $2 trillion. Lloyds of London reported losses of almost £2 billion on the World Trade Centre and the Pentagon buildings. Other macroeconomic impacts included:

- A loss of confidence affecting firms and their investment plans and households shifting from consumer spending to savings.
- The role of government reflected in counter-cyclical policies. Monetary policy favoured lower interest rates and fiscal policy resulted in increased government spending (e.g. increased US defence spending). Micro-economic impacts on US markets

There were direct impacts on four markets:

The property and building industry. There was an increased demand for replacement office accommodation in New York and Washington possibly leading to higher rents. There was also an increased demand for demolition and rebuilding work, all of which affected the construction industry.

The insurance market. There were losses to insurers, higher premiums following the attacks, a restructuring of the insurance industry to meet greater and new risks and insurers offering lower premia for increased security measures in buildings.

The defence market. New security threats have emerged (e.g. terrorism; weapons of mass destruction in 'rogue states'). New threats require new structures and equipment for the Armed Forces (e.g. forces with a worldwide capability; rapidly-deployable forces and equipment). Armed Forces have also acquired new roles in deterring terrorism and in emergency response to terrorist attacks (e.g. responding to chemical-biological attacks on civilians). The result is pressure to raise defence budgets to meet the new threats.

The airline market. This market and the associated travel market was directly affected by the September 11th attacks. There was a reduced demand for air travel resulting in job losses, capacity reductions (e.g. aircraft stored or scrapped) and exits from the airline industry (e.g Sabena and Swissair in Europe). Airlines incurred substantial losses.

For example, the major US airlines reported losses of £2.4 billion in the first quarter of 2002: but how large would the losses have been in the absence of September 11th? The US government responded by providing cash assistance to US airlines (are such losses a case for subsidy?). Interestingly, the low-cost European airlines were reporting increased business and major orders for new aircraft! There was also an increased demand for substitutes such as rail travel, telecommunications (fax; e-mail), private corporate jets and low-cost airlines. Increased airport security has meant higher costs for passengers (including waiting time). Nor have aircraft manufacturers been immune (e.g. Boeing; Airbus). Cancellations of orders for new aircraft have meant job losses, including supply chain impacts, and lower prices for new airliners.

The Economics of Military Alliances

Following September 11th, a US-led coalition conducted military operations in Afghanistan. This raises the general question of whether a nation benefits from being a member of a military alliance (e.g. NATO). There is a considerable defence economics literature on military alliances (Hartley and Sandler, 2001). This literature models alliances as 'clubs' providing a public good in the form of collective defence-security (e.g. US strategic nuclear umbrella which is non-rival and non-excludable for members of the alliance). One prediction of this model is free riding whereby the more defence a nation's allies provide, the less the nation will spend on defence. As a result, there is exploitation with small nations exploiting the willingness of large nations to provide alliance defence.

Are there economic models explaining terrorist behaviour? Whilst there is a complex literature in this area, the topic can be approached by considering the economics of crime and punishment (ie. illegal activities). Consider the example of theft. Criminals considering theft will evaluate its likely benefits and costs. The benefits of theft include the value of the goods which are stolen (in present value terms) as well as the possibility that some criminals might be risk-seekers and enjoy the 'thrills of robbery. Benefits have to be compared with costs to assess whether the robbery is 'worthwhile.' The costs of crime include the 'set-up' costs which might be for an individual or group (e.g. planning; search; observation; bribery of insiders). Then there are the costs of implementation (the robbery and escape) and the probability of capture and a penalty (fine or imprisonment).

The possible policy solutions to crime include changes in the distribution of income and wealth in society, private insurance, private security systems, more police and social penalties providing greater deterrents such as longer imprisonment for criminals. Economic models of terrorist behaviour use the standard consumer choice models with individuals and groups facing an allocation and choice problem. Terrorists aim to maximise their individual or group utility. But they are subject to limited resources (income, wealth, labour, time) which have to be allocated between various terrorist and non-terrorist activities. Further allocation decisions are needed between alternative terrorist attack options, such as skyjackings, kidnappings, bombings, assassinations and the use of chemical, biological and nuclear weapons. These economic models of terrorism offer various predictions:

Substitution effects. If a government increases the price of one form of attack, terrorists will seek lower-cost alternatives. For example, increased airport security might mean more bombings of other civilian targets (e.g. city centres).

Income effects. Governments can try to reduce terrorist activity by denying access to funds (budget constraints).

Increase the costs of terrorism. Deterrence is one option (tit for tat policies). Or, costs might be imposed on nations supporting terrorist groups (e.g. Afghanistan).

Free riding. Nations have incentives to free ride on any nation (e.g. USA) which actively pursues international terrorist groups.

Future EU Defence Policy

The EU aims to create a Common European Security and Defence Policy (CESDP). Already, there have been a number of developments towards this objective:

The creation of an EU Rapid Reaction Force (60,000 troops) by 2003. This Force is designed for the Petersberg tasks of conflict prevention and crisis management including humanitarian aid, rescue missions and peacekeeping.

The Six Nation Framework Agreement (1998: France, Germany, Italy, Spain, Sweden, UK). This aims to facilitate European defence industry restructuring and maintain competitiveness.

OCCAR (France, Germany, Italy. UK). This is the four nation armaments agency for European collaborative projects.

Industrial restructuring amongst European nations has resulted in the creation of EADS, Airbus Military Company, MBDA, Eurocopter and Agusta-Westland.

European collaborative projects including Eurofighter Typhoon, the A400M airlifter, the Meteor missile and European involvement in the US Joint Strike Fighter.

EU Defence Markets

The EUs defence markets are inefficient in providing both Armed Forces and defence equipment. Here, the comparison is with the US model. Compared with the USA, the EU lacks a single EU Army, Navy and Air Force and a large Single EU Market for defence equipment. The EUs Armed Forces are characterised by massive duplication of national defence ministries, national armies, navies and air forces together with national training, support and basing arrangements. As a result, EU states are failing to obtain the economies of scale and scope from large-scale operations in the provision of Armed Forces. National Armed Forces in separate EU states are 'too small' reflecting the costs of non-Europe in defence (nationalism). However, there is a lack of published data for assessing the possible cost savings and efficiency gains from a single EU Army, Navy and Air Force.

There are similar inefficiencies in EU defence industries. Typically, Europe is characterised by the duplication of costly R&D programmes (ie. aircraft, helicopters, missiles, tanks, warships).

Also, production is for small national markets so that EU states are failing to obtain the economies of scale and learning which are available in the large US defence market (hence, the importance of exports to EU firms). Combat aircraft are a good example of inefficiencies in the EUs defence industries. Currently, the EU is developing three different types of combat aircraft, namely the Gripen (Sweden), Rafale (France) and Eurofighter Typhoon (four nations: Germany, Italy, Spain and the UK). The result is three R&D bills and small-scale production for national orders.

Alternatively, if all six EU nations had agreed to buy one type of aircraft, there would have been savings in R&D costs and the economies of scale and learning from an order for over 1000 units, which would be much closer to US scales of output.

There are gains from creating a Single EU Market for defence equipment. This would require the abolition of Article 296 (formerly Article 223) so enabling the existing Single Market for civil goods and services and civil public procurement to be extended to defence procurement. Economic studies estimate the cost savings from a Single Market for defence equipment in the range of 10% to 20% (lower bound estimates).

Three scenarios for a Single Market in defence procurement have been costed. Each scenario is based on assuming that the Market is restricted to firms from EU member states only or open to firms from the rest of the world. Scenario 1 is for a liberalised competitive market. If such a Market were restricted to the EU only, then firms from other EU member states would be allowed to bid for national defence contracts (e.g. BAE Systems bidding for a French defence contract). Scenario 2 assumes the creation of an EU Procurement Agency which would buy common, standardised equipment for a single EU Army, Navy and Air Force with the Agency replacing national defence ministries.

This scenario is the most attractive economically but politically the most difficult to achieve. Scenario 3 is the twin track approach involving competition for small to medium size projects (e.g. ammunition, artillery, guns, small missiles) and collaboration for large-scale air, land and sea projects. Under this scenario, work on collaborative projects was assumed to be based either on *juste retour* or competition. 2.18. EU defence policy is topical and dominated by politics. It has been shown that defence economists can make sensible contributions to the debate and to knowledge.

The existing EU defence arrangements are highly inefficient. There is scope for efficiency improvements in the EUs Armed Forces and its defence industries. Efficiently organised military alliances offer benefits to their members. Efficiency improvements mean benefits to the Armed Forces and taxpayers, but costs for some of the EUs defence industries. The long-term future might be a Trans-Atlantic Market for defence equipment (USA and the EU).

THEORETIC UNDERPINNINGS OF DEFENCE ECONOMICS

The relationship between defence and economics has had a long and rich theoretical tradition. Furthermore, the articulation of the distinct field of 'defence economics', and the development of various research agendas and approaches, has been fraught with difficulties simply because of these highly contested traditions. In terms of methodology, this paper adopts an essentially neoclassical approach, but also suggests that in understanding the dynamics of defence industrialisation, as well as the role of the state in that process, it would be fruitful to temper the economistic approach with a 'political economy' dimension. Indeed, as will be shown in subsequent sections, the emergence of Singapore's defence industrial base can best be explained by a combination of political and economic factors, rather than solely economic ones.

The first theoretical tradition discussed in this section is mercantilism, which is the economic doctrine that deals most directly and explicitly with the question of defence and national security. There are two main reasons for this. First, mercantilism as an economic doctrine can be seen as a corollary to realism in international relations theory in that they both proceed from the premise that 'states must seek both security [for the realists] and prosperity [for the mercantilists] in an anarchic international environment' (Kapstein 1992: 1, additional comments mine).

Hence, the state played an important interventionist role, domestically and internationally, to secure and expand on its objectives of political, military and economic security. Mercantilism therefore consisted in 'the pursuit of wealth and power...that would be needed, among other things, to finance warfare (Kapstein 1992: 2). This resonates strongly with the realist view of international relations in which a powerful state is underpinned by, among other things, a strong economy. The mercantilist economic doctrine also led to the 'infant industries' argument often made in favour of protecting industries that are deemed important to the state, including the industries that constitute the defence industrial base. The argument is essentially that 'not only the wealth but the independence and security of a county appear materially connected with the prosperity of manufactures'.

The second theoretical tradition, liberalism, is no less concerned with issues of defence and national security. According to Kapstein:

> The liberal would agree that the provision of national security is the foremost goal of the state, and that in order to fulfil this goal the state may have to intervene in certain instances in order to mobilize capital, labour, and natural resources (1992: 10).

Indeed, classical liberal economists such as Adam Smith and David Ricardo identified on one hand a fundamental tension between the laissez faire doctrine of market forces and the limited role of the state, and on the other hand the unique feature of defence as a public good.

Because defence as a non-rival and non-excludable public good is prone to market failure, it was incumbent on the state to correct that market failure by being the monopoly supplier of defence and national security. Hence, as Kapstein puts it, 'national defence...fell outside Smith's laissez faire framework' (1992: 5).

The mercantilist and liberal approaches to the questions of defence and national security share common ground in that national defence and economic well-being are intertwined: economic gains and access to materiel fuel a country's ability to defend itself, while a country secure from conflict and strife provide a stable platform on which prosperity can be created. The two schools of thought diverge on the question of the trade-off between defence and growth, and the methods in which countries undertake defence production. The mercantilists believe that in matters of defence, countries should be autarkic or self-sufficient. Furthermore, this stance is maintained even in the face of comparative disadvantage in defence sectors.

Compared to the liberals, mercantilism pay little attention to the explicit and opportunity costs that are incurred when productive resources are allocated away from the civilian sectors towards defence production. However, the liberal tradition is concerned about the economic cost extracted by military spending. Furthermore, given the dictates of comparative advantage, defined broadly to mean that countries should produce and trade the goods in which they have an inherent advantage in specialising, maintaining a domestic defence industrial base would be for many countries a highly inefficient exercise and tolerated only because of the peculiar 'public good' nature of defence. In an overly simplistic fashion, therefore, it would seem that the liberals are apologists for the role of the state in providing national security, whereas the mercantilists unabashedly celebrate state interventionism in the defence sector.

Given the theoretical framework articulated above, how might one explain the Singapore government's approach to questions of defence economics? Roughly speaking, one could argue that Singapore has evolved from a broadly mercantilist perspective in the 1960s, and has since the late 1980s and early 1990s graduated towards a liberal approach, especially in the areas of procurement, exports of its own defence products and the civilianisation of the defence firm. This change has also coincided with the globalization of the defence industry and the revolution in military affairs (RMA). The evolution of Singapore's defence industrial base is examined in the following section. The development of Singapore's defence industrial base and the implications for the broader economy, it is necessary to study the the 'defence industrial base' in greater detail. Dunne adopts a fairly basic definition of the defence industrial base as one that is '[constituted by] those companies which provide defence and defence related equipment to the defence ministry' (1995: 402). He justifies this definition by pointing to its 'rather ephemeral character'. A report by the Center for Strategic and International Studies defines the defence industrial base in functional terms:

[The] defence industrial base is defined as the aggregate ability to provide the manufacturing, production, technology, research, development, and resources necessary to produce the materiel for the common defence (1989: 11).

The defence industrial base lies at the heart of the defence-growth nexus simply because its emergence is due to decisions (economic and non-economic ones) made on the allocation of a country's resources between 'guns' and 'butter'.

As mentioned before, the uniqueness of the defence sector and the imperatives of national security are such that many countries maintain a defence industrial base even though it may not be efficient for them to do so.

The mercantilist and liberal paradigms offer contrasting justifications for this. For the mercantilists, the maintenance of the defence sector results from the desire to 'pick winners' and nurture 'infant industries' even in the face of comparative disadvantage. The liberals, however, recognise the intrinsic market failure in the provision of the defence public good, and hence a role for the state to play in correcting that market failure. Given the necessity of the state's role, the object of the exercise is to maximise efficiency given such exogenously determined constraints.

There are also extra-economic reasons for building and maintaining a defence industrial base. As Nicole Ball puts it in her analysis of defence industrialisation in the developing world,

> Third World countries seek to produce their own weapons for a combination of political, military and economic reasons. A domestic weapons production capacity can be seen as an expression of national sovereignty, tangible evidence that a country intends to defend its independence (1991: 175).

In a nutshell, a national defence industrial base is regarded as a vital aspect of national pride and sovereignty. There are other reasons that are often cited for defence industrialisation. One major reason is that a national defence industrial base affords security of supply and eliminates the risk of potentially unreliable foreign suppliers of vital defence equipment, especially in times of crisis or conflict. Hence, the strong desire to avoid dependence on foreigners for critical defence hardware. The second reason with implications for broader economic growth is the potential impact of defence industrialisation on overall economic growth, particularly for the developing world. Developing an indigenous defence industry that can satisfy most of the defence establishment's needs might be a way to save scarce foreign exchange; it might facilitate the mastering of new technologies; and it might kick-start a broader socio-economic process of industrialisation (Bitencourt 1995: 171).

The point of departure for this debate is typically Benoit's studies on the effect of defence spending on economic growth in developing countries from 1950-1965, roughly the period corresponding to the wave of decolonisation in the Third World (1973, 1978).

Benoit's studies found that developing countries with heavy defence spending generally had the highest growth rates, while those that spent least on defence had the lowest growth rates. Several explanations have been offered to account for how defence spending could stimulate growth in the developing world. The first is the fiscal stimulus effect that occurs in countries experiencing periods of unemployment (or under-employment), which could be caused by under-consumption.

There are also extra-economic reasons for building and maintaining a defence industrial base. As Nicole Ball puts it in her analysis of defence industrialisation in the developing world, Third World countries seek to produce their own weapons for a combination of political, military and economic reasons.

A domestic weapons production capacity can be seen as an expression of national sovereignty, tangible evidence that a country intends to defend its independence (1991: 175).

In a nutshell, a national defence industrial base is regarded as a vital aspect of national pride and sovereignty. There are other reasons that are often cited for defence industrialisation. One major reason is that a national defence industrial base affords security of supply and eliminates the risk of potentially unreliable foreign suppliers of vital defence equipment, especially in times of crisis or conflict. Hence, the strong desire to avoid dependence on foreigners for critical defence hardware. The second reason with implications for broader economic growth is the potential impact of defence industrialisation on overall economic growth, particularly for the developing world. Developing an indigenous defence industry that can satisfy most of the defence establishment's needs might be a way to save scarce foreign exchange; it might facilitate the mastering of new technologies; and it might kick-start a broader socio-economic process of industrialisation (Bitencourt 1995: 171).

The point of departure for this debate is typically Benoit's studies on the effect of defence spending on economic growth in developing countries from 1950-1965, roughly the period corresponding to the wave of decolonisation in the Third World (1973, 1978). Benoit's studies found that developing countries with heavy defence spending generally had the highest growth rates, while those that spent least on defence had the lowest growth rates. Several explanations have been offered to account for how defence spending could stimulate growth in the developing world. The first is the fiscal stimulus effect that occurs in countries experiencing periods of unemployment (or under-employment), which could be caused by under-consumption or under-investment. Put simply, a heavier defence burden would result in an increase in the level of resource utilization, thereby generating growth. Furthermore, as is often the case in developing countries, civilian uses of resources might not be optimal to begin with, and hence the defence-growth trade-off does not apply. The stimulus effect that defence spending has on the economy would also tend to be short-lived, and would cease as soon as the economy is at or near full employment.

The second positive externality is the longer-term structural effect of technological and infrastructure modernization that is brought about by defence industrialisation. According to Hartley and Sandler, 'nations can experience direct technological effects and spin-offs from the defence sector' (1995: 201). Advances made in the defence sector are transmitted to the civilian sector through a process of technology and knowledge transfer, thereby improving a country's long term growth prospects. In addition, Ball cites the instances where defence industrialisation and modernization resulted in job creation and manpower training or human capital formation (1991: 182). Again, these benefits apply more to the case of less developed countries, where the initial starting conditions for technology and manpower infrastructure is a low base, and where such benefits would experience a diminishing rate of return as the country becomes more developed.

Despite the number of studies, neither economic theory nor analyses of the data provide any conclusive support for the growth promoting or growth inhibiting effects of defence spending. Chan sums up the unsatisfactory state of the field in the following manner: [...] even though we understand the processes through which military spending can affect economic performance much better now than [before], there remains much that we do not know or that we disagree about (1987: 35).

While broad generalisations on the defence-growth dynamic remain problematic, the studies by Benoit et al. have proven to be extremely useful insofar as they offer alternatives to the conventional thinking about defence. These studies point out that military spending 'crowd out' private investment and current consumption, and divert resources from other public goods such as health and education. Defence spending also siphons R&D resources away from the civilian sector, which is viewed to be more efficient and of greater socio-economic utility. Finally, military spending usually results in budget deficits, which reduce the national savings rate, and hence impinges on the long-term rate of investment. For example, if military spending is financed through increased taxation, this could in turn reduce consumption (which would impact short-term growth) and/or investment (which would affect the longer-term structural growth dynamics). Finally, there is little concrete evidence of positive spin-offs from defence industries to the civilian economy (Bitencourt 1995: 171-2).

Arms exports. This is the most obvious and straightforward means by which second-tier firms have attempted to respond to inadequate domestic demand. However, given the global trend towards reduced defence budgets (the US notwithstanding) and consequently decreased demand, second-tier firms exports of 'mid-tech' defence goods may not prove viable in the long term, especially in the face of the unfolding IT-based RMA. Still, Singapore Technologies' land systems division, ST Kinetics, has managed to strengthen its position in the traditional defence core business by shifting its emphasis to 'smarter, network-centric solutions' such as multi-role land systems and guided weapons and munitions (Singapore Technologies Engineering Limited Annual Report 2003: 95). At the same time, ST Kinetics retains its core competency in delivering on battlefield engineering systems on the domestic front, with the Primus howitzer, and external front, with its Bronco All Terrain Tracked undergoing rigorous trials by potential customers in Europe and Turkey.

Globalization and international collaboration. The globalization/internationalization is a key strategy for Singapore Technologies: [ST Engineering] is a company that wants to grow. Globalization will enable us to do that. It opens new opportunities and untapped markets beyond our shores. It gives us access to new capabilities to enhance our existing expertise. We have made the internationalisation of our business a core objective in recent years...[and believe] that an increased global presence and network is absolutely critical to sustain long term growth....

However, ST Engineering's globalization strategy is predicated on a mix of acquisitions, alliances and joint ventures with companies in the US and China, just to name a few. However, there is a critical difference between tying up with first-tier defence firms and non-first-tier firms: the variant of defence globalization in which second-tier firms are junior partners to first-tier companies results in. As Bitzinger puts it: [S]econd tier firms] formally subordinat[e] themselves to first-tier companies...[with] plans for self-sufficient arms production...[and] supplanted by a return to greater degrees of dependence upon foreign armaments and technologies...(2003: 75).

Clearly, Singapore Technologies has employed a multi-pronged approach to respond to the challenges and constraints of defence globalization and escalating economic and technology costs. In terms of the civilianisation, dual-use technologies and exports strategies, the central question is to what extent these measures continue to be viable in a shrinking defence market place. The more critical issue, however, is globalization strategy. It can be argued that Singapore Technologies' partnerships with first-tier defence firms (especially in the US) pose serious obstacles to defence autarky. Furthermore, combined with the ever-increasing rate of technology adoption within the SAF, the globalization strategy is paradoxically making Singapore more and more beholden to foreign suppliers. Ironically, defence globalization, while diffusing technology from the first-tier countries to the periphery, has at the same time allowed the leading-edge defence companies to concentrate and consolidate its hold over the second-tier countries through its monopoly on advanced technologies and R&D.

Given the above, the unveiling of the Singapore Self-Propelled Howitzer 1 - called the Primus - by the Singapore Armed Forces (SAF) in November 2003 was particularly noteworthy, even anomalous. The development and launch of the Primus was noteworthy for being an in-house enterprise by the Defence Science and Technology Agency, ST Kinetics and the SAF, and essentially going against the current trend of second-tier countries outsourcing, buying 'off-the-shelf' and customising to local requirements. The Primus emphasised the limits to which the outsourcing of defence production could occur and that the decision to develop and produce locally was rarely based purely on economic criteria. (Kuah 2004: passim).

Singapore's defence industrial base has taken measures to ameliorate against the rising costs of domestic design and production and the small domestic market, as can be seen in some of ST Engineering's latest moves both locally and abroad.

Furthermore, with global tensions (to the extent that such tensions affect conventional arms spending) receding, the economic rationale for the defence industrial base has begun to supersede the political one. In the case of Singapore's defence industrial base, the transition from mercantilistic origins in the 1960s (with the announced intention of autarky) to liberal approaches in the 1990s (with the tacit acceptance that true autarky was not viable) has been borne out in some of the strategies adopted by Singapore Technologies.

ECONOMIC DEVELOPMENT AND THE GROWTH OF THE SAF

Several explanations have been forwarded to explain the relationship between defence and economic growth in Singapore. One of the key elements has been the development of human capital that stemmed from the expansion of the SAF and the concomitant need for greater 'professionalisation'. The shifting emphasis towards high technology weapons systems and capabilities to counterbalance the lack of geostrategic depth and its geopolitical weaknesses (e.g. small population size) generated a need for highly trained and educated professionals, particularly in the naval and air services (Chin 1987: 212-5). Furthermore, during economic recessions, the SAF has proved useful in soaking up excess unemployed manpower (Chin 1987: 217), especially in the case of less qualified Singaporeans. Between 1984 and 1985 (the year of recession), SAF enlistments of other ranks up to Warrant Officer increased from 1,851 to 2,304. In the same period, contract service personnel in these ranks who decided to stay on increased from 539 to 711.

An alternative reading of the defence-growth nexus can be understood in terms of the dichotomy between the developmental and democratic models. The Singapore experience is a variant of the democratic model of the relationship between defence and economic growth. The emphasis is on a minimal military involvement, such as providing security as the basis for economic development. If the military is any more involved in economic growth, it is likely to be in security-oriented development projects (such as construction of infrastructure), civic action, or disaster relief operations. In this framework, a stable and secure polity (as a result of strong defence capabilities) is able to attract foreign direct investments (FDI) that provides for economic growth and development. In other words, there is a positive, linear progression between establishing a strong defence capability on the one hand, and experiencing economic growth and development on the other. More recently, Alagappa has argued that the closing of the differential in military and civilian-economic skills has allowed the SAF to play a more direct developmental role (1988: 33).

It is also possible to argue that at least in a few industries, defence spending had a positive effect on it. Chin argues that this is especially the case with the aerospace industry, which has benefited from its linkages with the SAF (1987: 214-5). The point made is that although Singapore lacks the heavy industrial infrastructure to get into aircraft manufacturing, the aerospace industry has developed the potential to compete in smaller-scale aerospace enterprises, such as avionics, engine and airframe maintenance for small aircraft. This is also the case for other maintenance and upgrading services – tapping into the Singapore experience in upgrading its various combat platforms at air, land and sea dimensions – which can be marketed at least to the immediate region.

THE FUTURE DEFENCE COMPACT

During the 1990s, defence firms had to adjust to the end of the Cold War. The result was job losses, plant closures, exits from the industry and major mergers creating larger defence firms. This raises the question of what will the defence firm of 2050 look like? The general answer is that the firm of 2050 is likely to be as different from today's defence firm as today's defence firms are from those of 1950 and 1915.

The characteristics of the future defence firm are likely to be:

i) It will be radically different.

ii) It will focus on more profitable defence activities, such as systems integration.

iii) There will be new forms of industrial organisation. Firms will buy rather than make and they will be global with international supplier networks and international alliances (the Joint Strike Fighter consortium).

iv) There will be greater military outsourcing with defence firms involved in support activities for the Armed Forces.

v) Electronics and IT companies are likely new entrants to form the next generation of prime contractors.

vi) Some major suppliers will become 'mini-primes' responsible for whole subsystems (including R&D) and absorbing greater risks.

vii) Firms will have a 'mix' of defence and civil business.

Civil work will provide insurance against defence downturns; it will allow the transferability of human and physical capital; and it will facilitate dual-use of technology, products, management and production expertise (eg. lean manufacturing; Just-In-Time Inventory; partnership sourcing; e-commerce used in the civil sector will be transferred to defence work).

2

Indian Defence Industry in the 21st Century

India's defence industry entered a new phase of self-reliance on the eve of the 21st century. Since the mid-1990s, several initiatives have been undertaken by the government to effect changes in the defence industry. Soon after the liberalisation of the economy was announced in 1990/91, the defence industry started realising the importance of civil-military interaction in the industrial sector. The private industries in India, which were thus far debarred from entering into defence production and whose role in the defence sector was limited to supplying spare parts and other minor contributions, started demanding a share in defence production.

In 1994, the then Defence Minister founded six Task Forces on major areas of defence modernisation, of which reforms in defence industry was an important part. This was carried out by the government in consultation with institutions like the Confederation of Indian Industries (CII). The CII, on its part was instrumental in bringing out a series of proposals in the broad field of private participation in the defence sector and armed forces–industry cooperation. Soon after this, the government initiated a programme called 'Army-Industry Partnership', under the auspices of CII which highlighted the importance of cooperative arrangements between the armed forces, defence industry and the government. After India's nuclear tests, various sanctions were imposed on India, of which sanctions related to the import of military and dual-use goods and technologies were considered the most important.

Sanctions were imposed on more than 150 items, which affected the progress of many defence products. However, the impact of sanctions on military technology was taken up as a another phase of challenge for the defence scientists as they had faced similar sanctions after the test in 1974. At that time they had faced more difficulties as the defence industry was not in a position to withstand such severe cuts which had resulted in delays in many major programmes. This time around, the defence industry had made significant progress to be able to withstand sanctions. After the Kargil conflict in mid-1999, the government started looking into security gaps and founded a committee under Mr K. Subrahmanyam. He brought out a major report on this conflict, which is known as the 'Kargil Committee Report'. This report, among other recommendations, highlighted the importance of reforms in higher defence management and reforms in institutional processes in the security sector.

The Government also founded a Group of Ministers' committee to look into major aspects of the overall security management of the country. The committee submitted its report to the government, which is known as GoM Report on 'Reforming the National Security System. This report highlighted the importance of self-reliance in India's defence industry and recommended several steps to introduce institutional changes into the system. Coupled with changes at institutional and organisational levels, India's defence industry entered an entirely new era after the Government announced a major change in policy by outlining codes of conduct for and inviting private participation in the defence industry. This is seen as by far the most important policy shift in the defence-industrial sector in the last fifty years.

By doing so, the Government, through an official notification No. 5(37)/2001-FCI, allowed private sector participation up to 100 percent and permitted foreign direct investment (FDI) up to 26 percent. This decision has been hailed by both the private industry and the government-owned defence industry. Institutions like CII and FICCI, which represent interests and views of the private sector, have been instrumental in influencing such a marked change in policies. According to Mr Sushanto Sen, the Director General of CII, such a policy change is certainly going to benefit both the defence industry and the private sector.

In tune with the stated objectives of India's defence industry to achieve a higher degree of self-reliance and a desire to make its flagship units globally competitive, thus entering into competitive defence markets, the Government has also introduced some institutional changes that are expected to smoothen operations both at structural and organisational levels. Earlier, procurement procedures were considered cumbersome, and there were overlaps in organisational responsibilities of respective organs responsible for procurement. Under the new system, the Services Headquarters were integrated into the Ministry of Defence to provide closer interaction.

The procurement structure is now a three-tier structure with the recent establishment of the Defence Acquisition Council (DAC) at the apex. Its primary role will be to accord in-principle-approval of long-term perspective plans (15-20 years), acceptance of necessity for the capital acquisition plan (5 years), identify 'Make', 'Buy' and 'Make and Buy' projects and monitor progress of the three Boards under it – the Defence Procurement Board, Defence Production Board and the Defence R&D Board. The Defence Procurement Board under the Defence Secretary will have the primary role of capital procurements and coordination. The Defence Production Board will be headed by the Secretary Defence

Production and Supplies and will oversee all activities related to indigenous manufacture, progress in 'make' projects and will provide support to DAC. The Defence R&D Board will be headed by the Secretary Defence R&D and will oversee progress, monitor and report on all R&D proposals in consultation with the user service and production board. Other measures at institutional level include direct linkages between the armed forces and the Ministry of Defence through integrated headquarters, which include respective perspective planning branches. In sum, organisational and institutional changes brought about recently seem to complement policy changes.

RROUBLES AND PROSPECTS: AN JUDGEMENT

India's quest for self-reliance has produced mixed results. Some of the lessons that India has learnt in the past fifty years are worth noting here. First, a combination of factors have led to the indigenous design and development component of self-reliance slowing down to almost zero for over a quarter of a century after 1962.

This has led not only to a huge technology gap but also contributed to severe difficulties in technology assimilation in the industrial sector. However, since the mid-1980s, activities toward achieving a greater degree of self-reliance have taken up momentum. The technology gap also widened the scope for acquisition of production technology rather than design technology from foreign sources. This in turn has created a license production regime at the cost of indigenous production. During the 1990s, the activities to encourage joint ventures and co-production in the defence-industrial sector is largely seen as a step to reduce license regime and boost indigenous industrial capabilities. How far this will achieve desired results are yet to be seen as such activities are only of recent origin and they need lead time to prove themselves. For example, the market for Brahmos missiles is estimated to be large, but it depends on how much is it likely to penetrate the cruise missile market at a global level. Success of this kind will not only validate India's defence-industrial capabilities to meet domestic demands but also increase its confidence in many ways.

Second, private participation in the defence-industrial sector has started after a long delay. This is attributable to several factors, ranging from the socialist and protective nature of the defence sector to fears of what is called 'security diffusion'. The latter especially relates to a fear of below-expectation performance by the private sector as it is hardly specialised to meet strict high military standards, hence compromising security standards. This kind of fear has been criticised by many who argue that private participation is essential in the defence sector which is primarily technology driven and capital intensive.

The recent opening up of the defence sector for private participation has generated a lot of interest in the country. Institutions like CII caution that while such initiatives are always welcome, the government should come out with a clear 'road-map' for the private sector participants in defence so as to enable them to prepare themselves for the new reality.

Fears regarding the ability of the private sector to match expectations of the country in the highly demanding and technology-dominated industrial sector are countered by industrialists like Atul Kirloskar (Chairman of Committee on National Defence, CII), who claim to have absolute faith in their abilities. Many also claim that given a chance, the secondary role of the private sector can be turned into a primary one in a short period of time. Some of the leading industrialists even claim that they have or intend to possess capabilities to produce complete weapons systems.

Several companies like Mahindras and Mahindras (M&M), the Tata Group, Kirloskar Brothers, Larsen and Toubro (L&T), and many others have already jumped into the fray to obtain orders from the defence industry. Since 2002, the Government has received more than ten applications from the private sector to manufacture weapons systems. It has recently awarded five licenses to L&T and M&M to produce military vehicles and some weapons systems.

Third, the government has emphasised measures to enhance the defence industry to cope with future challenges. Such measures are carried out by both OFs and DPSUs, apart from respective branches of the Government and the armed forces. Digitalisation, strict quality control, performance-related benefits, professional management systems, allowing the private sector to carry out R&D activities in the government-owned laboratories, are some of the measures which have come up in recent years and are likely to impinge the defence-industrial landscape.

A simplification of production and procurement rules promise better buyer-seller relations. There were some protests coming from employees' unions of OFs and DPSUs against privatisation. The Government has assured these unions that employees' interests will be borne in mind but that it will give priority to performance.

In one instance, the Defence Minister is reported to have appealed to the workers in one DPSU to not to worry about possible relocations due to privatisation and assured them to take effective steps to safeguard their interests. It seems that rationalisation of the defence industry is on the cards which might bring some unrest in the form of reduction of employment in the defence-industrial sector.

There are even rumours that some of the units, especially from the ordnance sector might be closed down. The private sector participants are, however, optimistic. They argue that their factories can effectively be converted into profit making civilian units. In several rounds of interviews with senior officers and industry analysts by the author, it seems that some of the industrial units may come under close scrutiny.

Conversion to civilian production in their cases is not ruled out. In brief, significant rationalisation, diversification and closer private participation are coming and are likely to influence India's defence industry in many ways.

DEFENCE INDUSTRY AND THE ECONOMIC CHARACTER

The transformation of China's defence establishment into a system capable of independently sustaining modern armed forces was one of the major goals of the military modernization program. In the late 1970s and 1980s, defence spending remained relatively constant despite the shift in resources in favour of overall economic development. Reforms focused on reorganizing the defence research-and-development and industrial base, more closely integrating civilian and military science and industry, and selectively utilizing foreign technology. China sold arms for hard currency to provide additional funds for defence industries. The PLA continued to play its role in economic development by participating in selective construction projects, providing dual-use training, and producing most of its food needs.

Military Expenditures

In the 1980s Chinese statistics indicated that defence spending represented a decreasing percentage of government expenditures, falling from 16 percent in 1980 to 8.3 percent of the state budget in 1987. However, United States Department of Defence studies suggested that the published budget figures understated defence spending by about one-half. With the growth of the Chinese economy under the modernization program, defence spending also represented a smaller percentage of the gross domestic product (GDP) than previously. United States Central Intelligence Agency analysts estimated that defence expenditures in 1978 absorbed 8 to 10 percent of GDP; in 1986 United States Department of Defence analysts estimated that China's military expenses fell within the range of 6 to 8 percent of GDP. Comparison of indices of defence procurement spending and industrial production from 1971 to 1983 revealed that the former increased by 15 percent, whereas the latter rose by 170 percent. These studies indicated that Chinese leaders have indeed subordinated military modernization to economic development. United States Department of Defence officials in 1986 estimated Chinese defence spending by resources and force categories for the 1967 to 1983 period. Roughly 50 percent of defence expenditures were for weapons, equipment, and new facilities; 35 percent for operating costs; and 15 percent for research, development, and testing and evaluation.

By service, these costs broke down to 25 percent for the ground forces; 15 percent for the Navy; 15 percent for strategic air defenses; 5 percent for ballistic missile forces; 5 percent for tactical air forces; and about 35 percent for command, logistics, personnel, intelligence, medical care, administration, research, development, testing and evaluation, and other support. Beginning in the late 1970s, China devoted more resources to its Strategic Missile Force, indicating an effort to increase its strategic security while modernizing the economy, and to national command and support activities, reflecting an emphasis on modernization of the defence structure.

MILITARY R&D AND NDSTIC

The National Defence Science, Technology, and Industry Commission was the coordinating body for military research and development and industrial production. The NDSTIC reported to the party Central Military Commission's National Defence Industries Committee and the State Council's Leading Group for Science and Technology. The NDSTIC supervised weapons research and development, coordinated military production of defence industries, and controlled funding for weapons procurement. The establishment of the NDSTIC was a reform measure designed to break down the barriers between civilian and military research and development and industry. Military science and industry previously had been secretive, segregated, and privileged sectors, having material, financial, and personnel resources superior to those available to the civilian sector. The creation of the NDSTIC was one measure by which Chinese leaders hoped to facilitate the transfer of technology between the military and civilian sectors. The NDSTIC, in particular through its trading arm, China Xinshidai Corporation, coordinated procurement of foreign technology for military purposes.

Defence Industry

Beginning in 1978, Chinese leaders set out to transform the defence industries, which had a huge excess capacity and were criticized for having a "golden rice bowl" (rich but always begging for more). To utilize this excess capacity better and to break down the barriers between military and civilian industry, the machine-building ministries were reorganized, and civilians were appointed to manage them.

The civilianized, renamed ministries and their responsibilities consisted of the Ministry of Nuclear Industry—nuclear weapons; Ministry of Aeronautics—aircraft; Ministry of Electronics Industry—electronics; Ministry of Ordnance Industry— munitions and armaments; Ministry of Astronautics—ballistic missiles and space systems; and China State Shipbuilding Corporation—naval construction. In 1986 the Ministry of Machine Building, which produced civilian heavy machinery and industrial equipment, and the Ministry of Ordnance Industry were consolidated into the new State Machine-Building Industry Commission as a way to strengthen the unified management of the national machine-building and weapons enterprises. In 1987 little information was available about this new commission or its relationship to the NDSTIC or to the State Economic Commission, whose Defence Bureau coordinated the civilian production of the defence industry. Further changes in defence industry structure occurred in 1986 and 1987, when inland defence enterprises were either relocated closer to transportation links or cities, closed down, or transferred to local civilian control and production.

Weapons Production

In 1987 China adopted a new contractual system for weapons research, development, and production. It was not clear from available information how this contract system would affect the role of the NDSTIC as the coordinating body for defence science and industry. Previously, the NDSTIC controlled procurement funding, reviewed proposals for weapons requirements funneled through the General Staff Department's Equipment Subdepartment, and coordinated with defence industries to produce the needed equipment.

Under the new system, the state divided defence research and development funds into three categories: military equipment research, basic and applied sciences research, and unidentified technological services. The first type of appropriation went to military arms and services, which signed contracts with research institutes or enterprises to develop and manufacture the required weapons.

The contract system involved the PLA, which had been removed to a large extent from such activities, in the development and manufacture of the weapons it would use. The second category of funds was devoted to basic research and applied science to help modernize the defence industry. The third category went to technological services necessary for research programs. This reform was another measure designed to integrate military and civilian industry by placing the military production of defence industries within the framework of the planned-commodity economy. The new system further sought to provide the military with better equipment at a minimum cost, to force the defence industry to upgrade weapons designs and improve production, to improve the management of weapons research and development through state application of economic levers, to promote cooperation between research institutes and factories, and to increase the decision-making powers of the enterprises.

Procurement of weapons and equipment represented 45 percent of the defence budget during the 1967 to 1983 period. This figure included 25 percent for aircraft, 15 percent for ground forces weapons, and about 10 percent each for naval and missile systems. China's military-industrial complex, the third largest in the world, produced a wide variety of weapons, including light arms and ammunition, armor, artillery, combat aircraft, fast-attack craft, frigates, destroyers, conventional and nuclear submarines, electronic equipment, tactical missiles, and ballistic missiles.

With the notable exception of China's indigenously produced nuclear submarines, nuclear missiles, and satellites, most Chinese weaponry was based on Soviet designs of the 1950s and 1960s. Much of this equipment was obsolete or obsolescent, and beginning in the late 1970s China made great efforts to upgrade the equipment by changing indigenous design or by incorporating Western technology. The greatest weaknesses were in conventional arms, precision-guided munitions, electronic warfare, and command, control, communications, and intelligence. China attempted to address these weaknesses by focusing military research on electronics—essential to progress in the previously mentioned areas—and by selectively importing key systems or technologies.

INDIAN DEFENCE MANUFACTURE

A nation's military strength is determined by its economic might. Industry provides the military with the wherewithal to fight the nation's wars. Since independence the policy relating to Strategic Defence Production has been evolving. For too long, India depended on foreign industries for its military hardware. The desire to achieve self-reliance has always been there. Constraints of technology and resources prevented the process from fructifying to the extent desired.

The first phase, was characterized by the State led industrialization. Since the era of liberalization, which began in 1991, the role of private sector and also that of competition, both domestic and international is playing a much greater role in the national economy. Naturally, this also meant changes in policy for Defence production.

Production of defence equipment has been under the purview of Government right from its inception. The Industrial Policy of the country had kept defence production in the public sector since First Industrial Policy outlined in the Industry Policy Resolution of 1948. The Industries (Development & Regulation) Act, 1951 gave statutory base to the Industrial Policy. Under this policy, the Defence Industry, which required heavy investments, strong R&D backing and on which there could be total reliance because of its criticality, remained under Government Control at all times. The control over defence industry was exercised under the Industries (Development & Regulation) Act, 1951, which made licensing compulsory. As a consequence of the then industrial policy, a large infrastructure for Defence production consisting of 39 Ordnance Factories, 8 Defence PSUs and 50 Research & Development laboratories was created in the country.

However, contrary to the common perception, the Private Sector has been playing significant role in the Defence industry sector as sub contractors and ancillary industry. The private sector mainly has been involved in supply of raw materials, semi-finished products, parts and components to Defence PSUs and Ordnance Factories to a great extent and also to Base Workshops of Army and Base Repair Depots of Air Force and the Dockyards of the Navy. Defence PSUs and Ordnance Factories are outsourcing their requirements from private sector (mainly SMEs) in the range of 20-25%. Out of this outsourcing, about 25% requirement is met through small-scale sector.

Several hi-tech equipments have also been successfully produced by the private sector. In the quest for self-reliance in the crucial sector of defence, the Government has been continuing its efforts to indigenize defence equipment wherever technologically feasible and economically viable. It has been a part of indigenization efforts to locate and develop broad-based indigenous supply source – both in the public sector and in the civil trade for many complicated and intricate equipments. The economic liberalization in 1991 resulted in the high degree of deregulation and allowed the private industry to progress more rapidly. With the initial difficulties encountered by the Indian Industry today one has witnessed positive impact of this liberalization. There has been tremendous growth in the private sector and today many Indian companies are global players.

After considering the capital intensive nature of defence industry sector as also the need to infuse foreign technology and additional capital including FDI, Govt. decided in May, 2001 to open Defence industry for private sector participation up to 100% with FDI permissible up to 26% - both subject to licensing. Now with this policy change all defence related items have been removed from Reserved Category and transferred to the licensed category, as a result of which private sector can manufacture all types of defence equipment after getting a licence. Consequent to the Government's announcement about the policy change, Department of Industrial Policy & Promotion (DIPP) in consultation with Ministry of Defence, issued detailed guidelines regarding the modalities for consideration of applications for grant of Industrial Licence. After the announcement of policy changes, there has been a paradigm shift in the role of private sector in the field of indigenisation, i.e., from the role of supplier of raw materials, components, sub-systems, they have now become partners in the manufacture of complete advanced equipment/system. The basic objective of allowing private sector participation is to harness available expertise in the private sector towards the total defence efforts and search for self-reliance. In-built advantages of the private sector are its reservoir of management, scientific and technological skills coupled with its ability to raise resources. The involvement of private sector with its world-class expertise and high technology would not only augment India's indigenous defence production capability but also lead to creation of employment and infrastructure in the country, giving a strong impetus to the economy. It must be acknowledged that the policy change of May 2001 for allowing private industry to produce any defence item under licence was a logical outcome of liberalization initiated in India in 1991. The private sector industry in India is now just beginning to become significant partner in production and development of Defence items.

After opening up of defence production for the private sector, the industry has shown keen interest in this field. Many large industries have shown definite inclination to invest both in R&D and infrastructure to develop capabilities in defence production to assume the role of system integrators.

TENDENCIES IN THE GLOBAL DEFENCE INDUSTRY

The global defence industry has undergone profound changes in recent years. Changes in demand for military weapons and equipment, the allocation of resources for national security, national and international security priorities especially by major states, among others, have affected the defence industry in many ways. While the Cold War era witnessed a massive military build-up by many countries, thus fuelling demand for this lucrative sector, the immediate post-Cold War period witnessed just an opposite scenario. Demand for military equipment went down during the late 1980s and early 1990s. Budgetary allocations for security sectors fell. Military downsizing occurred. In just a period of half-a-decade, roughly from 1987 to the early 1990s, the defence industry witnessed a different scenario and shrank considerably. It had to shift priorities to adjust to the new environment. In brief, since the end of the Cold War, the defence industry has faced numerous challenges from all quarters. Most of the decline in the volume of arms production took place during the early and mid-1990s. During this time, significant down-sizing, rationalisation and diversification (primarily into dual-use and civilian production) were witnessed in the defence-industrial sector.

Mergers and acquisitions during the 1990s resulted in the creation of a few giant companies like Boeing, Lockheed Martin, British Aerospace, Northrop Grumman, EADS, and others. This also resulted in many smaller companies either having to merge with big ones or having to shift their priorities toward civilian production, thus leaving the defence sector. Defence industries of major countries like the United States and of Western Europe were affected most during this period although countries like Russia, Israel, South Africa, Brazil, India, and others were also affected. Arms reductions during the 1990s were extensive and fetched a sizeable 'peace dividend'.

It was desirable that such a decade of disarmament should have been extended. However, as evidence suggests, indicators of disarmament and conversion now show stagnation; in many cases even a reverse trend toward a strengthening of military postures are witnessed. A decade of cuts in military expenditure ended in 1998/99 when it went up again. The upward trend in military expenditure is likely to continue in future. The 11 September 2001 terrorist attacks in the United States are likely to result in a major shift in defence-industrial developments because of their impact on security requirements at national and international levels. But this is not to suggest that the upward trend in military expenditure was a product of such an unfortunate event.

This trend had already started in the late 1990s, primarily because of increased military spending by countries like the United States and regions like the Middle East and South and East Asia. In this changed scenario, the defence industry seems to gear up to meet new challenges. As procurement budgets have started to swell again and are likely to stay that way, new opportunities are expected for the defence industry. In fighting terrorism, additional defence programmes initiated by countries like the United States will most likely change the structure of the defence industry. While it is expected that giant weapons producers, especially in the United States, are likely to benefit most from the on-going 'War on Terror', national defence industries elsewhere are also likely to reorient themselves to meet future challenges. In brief, the global defence industry, after a period of significant downsizing and rationalisation, is likely to enter into a phase of renewed attention. Demand for smart weapons, increased emphasis on military technology including investment in R&D, growing demand for aerospace and cutting-edge technology products, are all likely to boost defence-industrial activities in many parts of the world.

Trends of India's Defence Industry

Trends in global defence industry have impinged India in many ways. India's defence industry has witnessed significant changes since the end of the Cold War. In the 1990s, changes in both institutional and policy spheres became more prominent. The most far reaching change that has occurred in recent years in India's defence-industrial sector is related to its opening up to the market. Long protected as a closed sector, India's defence industry has now opened up for private participation. As if this was not enough, it is also showing enough willingness to become an exporter and dares to venture into the competitive global arms market. How far it will succeed in its objectives is examined elsewhere, but changes are certainly a product of and response to the contemporary changes in the global industrial defence scenario. At the same time, it is also showing willingness to diversify its range of products, which not only include modern weapons systems but also technologies for wide and popular civilian uses. The Indian defence-industrial sector targets the national, and even global, civilian market to sell its products, especially in the fields of civilian space, medical, and electronics. Thus conversion through diversification has been witnessed in many areas of defence production in India.

India's defence industry has come a long way from being at the lowest end of the production spectrum, catering to the maintenance and repair and overhaul of imported weapons, to a stage where it can boast of designing and developing a range of state-of-the-art weapons systems. Half a decade of defence-industrial experience in India shows that while it started from scratch, it has been able not only to learn and absorb various stages of production intricacies but also produce complex systems that are primarily an indigenous activities. Another important factor is that the Indian defence industry has produced various weapons systems under licenses acquired from various foreign sources.

Although the first Prime Minister of India, Jawaharlal Nehru, believed in 'self sufficiency' in arms production, which became a policy mantra for subsequent years, it had to be supplemented by what is roughly called 'self-reliance in defence'. Self-reliance does not preclude accessing external sources for technology and systems, or external help in any stage of the production cycle. It is the degree of dependency on external sources that is tested in the case of India's quest for self-reliance.

India opted to choose an incremental path, in which it was necessary to continue to meet urgent requirements through imports while striving hard on achieving indigenous capabilities in defence production. Both policies continued till the late 1980s and many of the components of both still continue till today. The 1990s witnessed a series of far-reaching initiatives in the field of national security, of which defence industry was a critical component.

The creation of six Special Task Forces to reform major aspects of national defence coordination and management, under the Chairmanship of the then Defence Minister in 1994 may effectively be considered as the first major step after a long time to initiate and implement much-desired reforms in the defence-industrial sector. This was followed by a series of intensive interactions between various organs of the armed forces, government departments and institutions like the Confederation of Indian Industries (CII). The 'Army-Industry Partnership', a partnership between CII and the Indian Army to get acquainted with each other's needs and to facilitate channels of communication between the armed forces and the private industry, was a result of this process and, in turn, led to other cooperative initiatives. Events like India's nuclear tests in mid-1998 and the Kargil conflict in mid-1999 provided grounds for an intense debate on various aspects of India's national security. Also, as a by-product of the current disinvestment programme, which is primarily aimed toward lessening or wiping out government control and responsibilities in state-owned public enterprises in India, the debate on a reform of the defence industry got a major boost as demands for a privatisation of and private participation in this hitherto closed sector grew more in tune with the changing times.

In January 2001, the Government of India initiated a series of major initiatives that, among others, included Foreign Direct Investment (FDI) up to about 26 percent and full private participation in certain sectors in the defence industry. This policy indeed marks a critical departure from the past. Followed by this, the Group of Ministers (GoM) Report on 'Reforming the National Security System' was made public in early 2001. This laid stress on reforms in all-encompassing aspects of national security, of which changes sought in higher defence management emphasised the need to create specific institutions like the Defence Acquisitions Board to adapt and facilitate changing needs of the defence industry.

While these far-reaching institutional and policy-oriented changes have been underway for quite some time especially since the early 1990s, the demand for private participation has assumed significance in recent years. In such a scenario, analyses of India's defence-industrial sector and policies have become critically important to understand the complex web of linkages that determine national policies in the defence-industrial sector. This, in turn, needs a closer look into the past performance of the defence industry, lessons learnt and a peep into the likely future course.

Research Objectives

The objectives are primarily four-fold. First, we will examine critical aspects of defence-industrial policies adopted by India in the past and link those to performance. It will examine the factors that have influenced India's defence production and their co-relationship with policies and decision-making in this sector. Second, we will examine the main trends during the 1990s, during which major policy changes occurred.

It will critically examine the impact of such policy changes. Third, we will examine the contemporary scenario. Fourth and last, it will look into future problems and prospects. The last two are essential in understanding the intricacies involved in India's defence-industrial strategies and are expected to give some clues related to the future course of action in this sector.

Some of the major queries that will be examined here are: Why a quest for self-reliance in the past? Has the policy of self-reliance paid off? If not, what are the options for the future? Why the changes in defence-industrial policies during the 1990s? Are the objectives achievable? What are likely options for the future? Does it have scope for more diversion, thus leading to conversion through the increase in civilian production, in future? We will invariably try to find answers to these queries, although not necessarily in the same order.

Methods and Sources

We will follow a general descriptive-analytical approach. The scope is limited somewhat to policy analyses due to constraints in the availability of information. This is because India's defence industry has long been a 'closed' sector and thus been under exclusive government control. It is only in recent times that it has opened up, thus leading to an availability of information in a low to medium scale. We will also follow a historical method whereby it will emphasise linkages at policy-and decision-making levels to performance, and this is important in understanding the nature of development that this sector has undergone for the past half-a-century. Available data on specifics will be evaluated. Emphasis will be on an evaluation and interpretation of data from primary (especially government) sources. In brief, the overall approach will be descriptive and analytical.

Literature on the subject is scarce. At international level, the study of India's defence industry has attracted very little attention. The same is true at national level. Barring a few books, written by scholars like K. Subrahmanyam, Air Marshal Samir Sen, Major General Pratap Narain, Chris Smith, WPS Sidhu, and others, substantial work is not evident on this subject. Occasional research papers by G. Balachandran, Rahul Roy-Choudhury, Ajay Singh and others have also focused on limited themes. Secondary and tertiary sources are scarce. Primary sources, however, constitute the most important component of this study. Annual Reports (published by the Ministry of Defence, Government of India), Annual Reports of major Defence Public Sector Units (published by respective organisations), periodic reports published by the Comptroller and Auditor General of India, Parliament Secretariat and similar other reports constitute primary sources for this endeavour. Select interviews with senior government officers, analysts and industry-watchers have been taken into account.

STUDY POLICY ISSUES AND CHALLENGES

The end of the Cold War brought the defence sector into a world of uncertainty, a world where there is no longer a powerful and well-defined enemy, but a world that is, nevertheless, a dangerous place. Since the early years of the 1990s, the global military economy has been transformed by trends in military expenditure and technology that have reinforced US dominance. Unlike most other countries, the US is forecast to increase its military spending rapidly. The fixed costs of research and development (R&D) for major systems continue to grow, both for platforms and for the infrastructure (such as satellites, strategic air assets) and information systems needed to support network-centred warfare. Developments in the defence industry sector include the increasing internationalisation of production, growing importance of information technology (IT) companies and the privatisation of services that were once provided by the military.

In Europe, the defence industry is an important user of skilled labour and resources and has faced a period of change and uncertainty since the end of the Cold War. It is also an industry where national governments have had considerable control. The recent EU Code of Conduct for defence procurement is intended to bring more openness to the market and the European Defence Agency (EDA) is meant to strengthen cohesion. The changes in demand and the nature of production, and the dominance of the US, are all factors likely to shape the sector's future.

Strategy and Security

The changes in the nature of security threats and in the roles of the defence forces have immediate short-term and medium-term effects. Four effects stand out in the short term:

1. The US and Europe (in the form of the North Atlantic Treaty Organisation, NATO) are unlikely to face an

enemy that is as well armed, they will thus have to deal with asymmetric conflict.

2. The lack of a clearly identifiable enemy, the nature of the war on terror and national security concerns are changing the nature of demand for defence resources; they are also making communications and surveillance technologies more central to defence activities.
3. The armed forces are being called upon to assume more peacekeeping responsibilities around the world. This role necessitates changes in training and composition of the forces, as well as in the equipment required.
4. These changes in the role and nature of the armed forces are happening at the same time as the existing structures of NATO and the EU feel the pressures of enlargement.

Over the medium to long term, there are two broad areas where the range of possibilities makes it difficult to forecast what will happen:

1. The extent and nature of links between the EU and the US will need to be determined. One current example in this area concerns the presence of European defence companies in the US market. European companies are increasingly buying US companies in order to gain a presence in the US market, and so far the US is satisfied with this.
2. It is likely that the US will continue to take a capability approach to defence production and be willing to use foreign suppliers in order to gain access to their technology; but this policy could change.

As for strategy and security issues, while it is highly unlikely that a confrontation of the nature of the Cold War will exist again, many factors will shape the future geopolitical and security environment, including:

- the future role and nature of China and its relationship with the West;
- competition from emerging markets;
- the future of the war on terror and the relations of the West with the Muslim world;
- the success or failure of the peace process in Palestine;
- US foreign policy in the Middle East and oil;
- the success and role of the United Nations (UN) in future security structures.

The range and interrelationships of such issues make the future a very uncertain one. They also make it extremely difficult to predict the ways that these issues will affect the defence industry, whether by geographical location within Europe, or in relation to other industries, or even in relation to the gender distribution of those who work in the industry. It is clear, however, that these geopolitical and strategic factors-in conjunction with the other trends in technology and governance that relate more immediately to defence activities-will make the environment in which the defence industry functions one of continual change.

Geographical and Sectoral

The effects of changes in strategy and security are likely to be felt in defence industries across the EU, but change will obviously be felt most in the major arms producing countries. Two different kinds of change are possible and neither excludes the other:

- a widening of the range of industries whose products and services are sought by defence organisations;
- consolidation of the sector.

The first kind of change will come about if changes in the nature of defence activities increase the use of what are at present civilian products and, thus, expand the types of goods and services procured by defence ministries. Such a development could on Europe's industry, by increasing demand for goods in IT and communications, and security services. The demand for a wider range of goods and services for use in defence would involve new entrants to this field, who will almost certainly be smaller than the leading defence contractors. It is also possible that the main contractors will take over such new entrants, thus bringing about further consolidation in the industry. The benefits of such changes in the industrial base of the defence industry may not be limited to Europe. The internationalisation of supply chains allows for increased competition from emerging markets.

Gender

As arms manufacture is a male-dominated industry, any changes are likely to have greater impact on men than on women, at least within the traditional defence companies. Insofar as changes in defence activities lead to more civilian companies becoming involved, female employment would be affected. However, the women involved would continue working as before and would not necessarily enjoy the traditionally higher than average wages of long established defence workers. Their companies would simply be supplying a new market, which, of course, could lead to the creation of more jobs. These remarks about the implications for gender apply to all three policy issues; and so will not be repeated under the following two policy headings.

GOVERNANCE

At present, two major initiatives are under way within the EU. They will alter the nature of the defence industry, but it is too early to tell how much of a difference they will make or when their effects will be seen. Their impact, if they are successful, is likely to be felt more in the medium and the long term. The European Defence Agency was created to help EU Member States to develop their defence capabilities for crisis management operations under the European Security and Defence Policy. The EDA's aim is to encourage EU governments to spend defence budgets on meeting future challenges, rather than past (Cold War) threats, and to help them identify common needs and promote cooperation.

The Code of Conduct for the defence sector should open up the EU national markets to competition from other EU countries. Where exemptions are invoked, which is the case today for more than 50% of defence equipment purchases, the EDA Code of Conduct is intended to ensure that there is transparent and fair competition. How well this will work in practice is unclear, but, given the other pressures that have been discussed, it is likely to increase competition and hence lead to a consolidation of the industry.

Apart from the effects of these two initiatives, there is also the question of corporate governance. In the US and the UK, financiers have played an increasing role in the restructuring of the defence industry, but this has not happened in mainland Europe, because of the different ownership and corporate governance structures there. In the medium term, the privatisation of arms producers and their involvement with the US market may bring about changes in the role of finance. If capital plays the role it has played in the US, this could well lead to considerable consolidation in the medium term. However, it is difficult to assess the implications of changes in governance structures, because any implications will be shaped by the other policy issues. It is not yet clear whether the two EU initiatives will succeed in creating an EU-wide governance structure for the defence sector in the medium term. If there is the political will and if the EU governance structure can manage the formation of an EU defence force, this will have a major impact on restructuring of the industry. However, several forces complicate the development of an EU-wide governance structure:

1. There is the role that NATO has managed to gain for itself. NATO has taken many of the roles that an EU defence force would have had, but it also maintains transatlantic ties.

2. There is EU enlargement and its effects over the medium and long term. EU enlargement could remove potential areas of conflict and, thus, make the development of a governance structure easier; but it could also increase the threats to which the EU is exposed, making it more difficult to develop a governance structure.
3. The way in which links between the EU and the US develop will be important, whether or not an EU defence force is created. These links are likely to determine the involvement of EU companies in the US market and of US companies in the EU. Such involvement will have an important influence on the size and composition of the industry.

Moreover, any such changes will be taking place at a time when competition from emerging markets could be making life more difficult for European producers.

Geographical and Sectoral

As in the case of strategic and security issues, changes in governance will be felt mainly by the major arms producing countries. However, companies in these countries have links with the smaller producers in the second rank of EU countries so that the effects will certainly be felt across Europe. Although much of the restructuring that would result from changes in governance would affect the larger contractors, larger companies may also take over smaller companies to maintain or develop expertise. They may relocate to particular areas. Furthermore, they may make increasing use of overseas companies in their supply chains which would weaken the position of smaller companies that are dependent on larger contractors.

TECHNOLOGY AND INDUSTRIAL STRUCTURING

Many of the technology issues are already apparent; but, by their nature and the nature of the defence industry, they will work themselves out over the medium to long term rather than have their effect in the short term. One major issue is the afterlife of previous Cold War weapons systems. Some of these are still in production despite the loss of their direct justification, e.g. Eurofighter/Typhoon. At the very time when these weapons systems are coming into production, different future systems are being planned, but the long lead times and the expense of the semi-redundant systems ensure that they will be around for a while yet.

Another-arguably the major-technology issue is the change that has replaced the spin-off from defence to civilian technology, with the latter now taking a leading position of influence. Contractors are increasing their use of civilian technologies in weapons systems because of their superior technological development. This is changing the nature of contractors: it has already made them systems integrators rather than producers and, in time, they may become designers, project managers and providers of R&D services.

The increasing use of commercial off-the-shelf products (COTS) has reduced barriers to entry at all but the highest level of defence contactor, while joint ventures and other forms of collaboration are undermining the comprehensive control that major contractors and subcontractors used to exercise over systems. Not least among the technological forces for change is the increasing importance of communications and control in the field of operations. Network-centred warfare is changing the nature of demand and creating the so-called Revolution in Military Affairs. Closely allied to this change is the noticeable growth in the use of unmanned vehicles (drones), which could lead to new types of systems and technologies.

All of these changes influence the nature and composition of the industry and move it further away from its Cold War form as time passes. In the short to medium term, there is likely to be consolidation in Europe, stimulated partly by cooperation between countries and companies, and by the continued internationalisation of supply chains.

There will also be an increase in the use of civilian technologies, bringing more civil firms into the industry through product sales or company takeovers. Another trend likely to remain important is the privatisation of defence services and support, as the security services industry expands as a periphery around the core arms industry. This expansion is creating a new sub-sector, important as a supplier to governments and defence ministries. Indeed, the former defence industrial base is becoming a security industrial base. This could have implications for the influence, visibility and accountability of the industry.

In summary, it is likely that there will be further important changes in the nature, structure and location of the defence industry over the longer term; however, the uncertainties of strategic and governance factors make it difficult to judge exactly what they will be. It is clear that R&D policy will need to change because the old Cold War specificity of military technology has become far less appropriate. Some technologies have only military applications, such as stealth, but the increasing dominance of civilian technologies suggests that the types of resources needed are changing.

Geographical and Sectoral

Changes in technology could mean that defence production is not necessarily going to remain in the long-established locations. Systems integrators may need to be closer to clusters of high-technology civilian production than to other defence contractors. Furthermore, many weapons factories were sited in particular areas for security purposes; however, this rationale for their location has disappeared. If there is the expected consolidation across the EU, there are likely to be important geographical changes. For example, it is likely that there will be one major area for producing warships (probably in Germany or German-dominated production in the Baltic region), and it is also possible that other major types of systems production will be sited in particular areas of Europe. On the other hand, it is also possible that the Airbus model of polycentric production will be adopted which seems rather unlikely.

The geographical changes will affect all companies. Major contractors are already changing their nature; the composition of the defence sector is also changing, as outlined in the three articles of this series. The EU will play an important role in managing the regional changes taking place as a result.

3

The Economics of Defence Industry

In addition to the role of government, defence industries have a number of economic characteristics which are essential to understanding their performance and problems:

Cost levels and trends. Defence equipment is costly and the trend is towards rising costs. For example, the UK is purchasing three Astute Class nuclear-powered submarines at an estimated total cost of £2.01 billion, whilst the 4-nation Eurofighter combat aircraft is estimated to cost £13.8 billion for development and a unit production cost of £41.7 million per copy. And the trend is towards rising costs. Since 1945, the real unit costs of combat aircraft designed for the RAF (excluding strategic bombers and adjusting for different production runs) has risen at a compound annual growth rate of 11.5% (Kirkpatrick, 1995). As a result, the real unit cost of tactical combat aircraft has increased by a factor of 2.5 per decade. These cost trends reflect the technical arms race (technical leapfrogging) leading to higher development costs and higher unit production costs so resulting in fewer aircraft being purchased from a limited defence budget; but with each new generation of aircraft being "more productive" (ie. effective).

Technical progress has affected markets and the structure of defence industries. Technical advance has resulted in new products such as the jet engine, missiles, electronics, radar, helicopters and space systems with a greater emphasis on R&D. Since 1945, the long run structural trend has been towards a smaller number of larger firms, reflected in mergers and exits from the industry and this trend has been especially evident since the end of the Cold War in 1990.

Entry is costly. Entry requires technology and R&D expenditures, with the associated requirements for qualified scientists, engineers and other skilled labour. R&D costs will vary with the type of equipment being developed (e.g. simple trainer to advanced combat aircraft). Learning costs are also significant in aerospace industries.

Learning economies and costs. Quantity is a major determinant of unit costs and hence of competitiveness. Long production runs enable fixed R&D costs to be spread over a larger volume; and in addition, there are learning economies in production. Learning reflects the fact that productivity improves with experience and through learning-by-doing. An 80% learning curve-which is often used in aircraft manufacture-suggests that man hours and labour costs will decline by about 20% for each doubling in the cumulative output of a given aircraft type. Learning economies mean that the US aircraft industry benefits from its much larger scale of output compared with the Europeans. The US industry also benefits from steeper learning curves with typical slopes of 75% in the USA compared with 80% in Europe. Also, US learning curves show continuous learning with European learning curves tending to "flatten out" after 100+ units.

The incentives to collaborate. Ideally, collaboration between two or more nations can lead to the sharing of high R&D costs and to scale and learning economies from longer production runs as nations combine their orders. On this basis, collaboration results in cost savings to each nation.

Industrial restructuring: adjusting to disarmament. Disarmament following the end of the Cold War has resulted in some cancellations, fewer new projects, smaller orders, shorter production runs, delays in ordering and the stretching-out of programmes. The result has been job losses, plant closures, mergers and exits from the defence business. Some firms have moved from prime contractor to sub-contractor status, whilst others have merged either with other aerospace firms or with other defence companies. Some of the largest mergers have occurred in the US aerospace industry enabling American aerospace companies to obtain the economies of both scale and scope, although the price of efficient scale has been reduced competition. In aerospace, the US examples have included the creation of the Boeing Group and Lockheed Martin (General Dynamics (combat aircraft business) and Loral), whilst in the UK British Aerospace acquired much of Royal Ordnance (land systems) and GKN (armoured fighting vehicles) acquired Westland (helicopters). In late 1999, there was further restructuring and mergers in Europe (BAE Systems, EADS; Thomson-Racal).

The complexity of supply chains. Typically, studies of defence industries focus on the major prime contractors to the neglect of their suppliers at the first, second and third tier. Little is known about supply chains: for example the technical capabilities of subcontractors, their location, their dependence on defence business and their importance in local labour markets.

ADJUSTMENT STRATEGIES AND GRANTS

Throughout their history, defence industries have been the focal point of technical change and external shocks, all of which have required appropriate adjustment strategies. For example, revolutionary technical change resulted from the shift from piston engines to jet engines, from manned aircraft to missiles and manned space flight. External shocks resulted from wars, with major increases in the demand for defence equipment, which also led to further technical change (e.g. radar). Some of these "military-induced" technical changes were subsequently applied to the civil economy (e.g civil aircraft). Inevitably, wartime industrial expansion was followed by contraction associated with a return to peacetime conditions.

To survive, defence industries have had to adjust to the uncertainties resulting from technical change and external shocks. Firms required R&D resources to be innovative in military and civil markets. Some firms diversified to "insulate" themselves from the uncertainties of the defence business; others merged or were taken-over to become part of a larger group; whilst others exited the industry for alternative activities which appeared to be potentially more profitable. Of course, adjustment strategies differed between state-owned and privately-owned enterprises. Privately-owned aerospace firms had to earn at least normal profits to induce them to remain in the defence business (and to satisfy their shareholders). Not surprisingly, both private and state-owned defence firms often survived through receiving government subsidies. Inevitably, following the end of the Cold War, national defence industries have been lobbying their governments for support (e.g. to maintain the national defence industrial base and/or to assist the industry to adjust from defence to civil markets).

Some of the typical arguments used for state support of the defence industries are as follows:-

- Defence benefits in the form of independence, security of supply during a conflict, and the ability to design equipment for the needs of national forces.
- The infant industry argument whereby government support is needed to meet the high costs of entry into this industry. The belief is that eventually the new industry will be able to compete with established suppliers (cf. Airbus).
- Strategic trade policy where international trade is characterised by strategic rivalry between a small

number of giant firms or 'national champions' of different countries (or indirectly between governments acting on their behalf). In such markets, an established firm might try to create strategic entry barriers to maintain and enhance its market power. The market for large civil aircraft is an example. Without Airbus, Boeing would be a monopolist; and it may be worth using subsidies (e.g. launch aid) to prevent such an outcome. Subsidies by European governments for Airbus might also have induced other US civil aircraft firms to exit, so increasing Airbus market share; and furthermore, such European government support might send a clear signal to Boeing not to attempt a price war to try to force Airbus out of the market. Economically strategic industries are characterised by imperfect competition, decreasing costs, high technology and spin-offs. Governments might subsidise entry into such industries to obtain a share of monopoly profits. But, here, care is needed since subsidies do not guarantee market success (cf Concorde).

- Market failure in R&D as a result of which private firms might undertake less R&D than society regards as desirable: hence the need for government intervention to 'correct' this market failure.
- Externalities: external economic benefits in the form of jobs, technology, spin-offs, and the balance of payments (ie. exports and import-saving) contributions of defence industries: this is a further aspect of market failure.
- Foreign governments are subsidising their defence industries.
- The Exchequer contribution in the form of tax receipts from home and overseas sales (e.g. income taxes; corporation taxes) as well as avoiding unemployment pay when projects are cancelled. Such arguments need to be assessed far more critically. The arguments for

state support of a national defence industry (as outlined above) are often dominated by myths, emotion and special pleading from groups with an (income) interest in continued state support and in avoiding the costs of change (which would make them worse-off). Such arguments need to be specified carefully and subjected to both empirical testing and critical evaluation. In particular, questions need to be asked about the alternative-use value of scarce resources. For example, consider the "foreign rivals are subsidising" argument. The obvious reply is that if foreigners wish to offer free gifts, a nation could respond by willingly accepting them and specialising elsewhere (doing something else)!

Economic theory suggests that subsidies are required to correct for certain types of 'market failure' (ie marginal cost pricing in decreasing cost activities; and where there are substantial social benefits such that private markets provide 'too little' of a socially-desirable output). However, the markets which are failing have to be identified (e.g. R&D; capital market; labour market), and it has to be shown that subsidies are the appropriate solution.

Moreover, it is by no means a simple matter to operationalise the broad guidelines for subsidy policy. "It is all too easy to think up plausible arguments based on externalities, merit wants and the like for subsidisation of this, that and every industry. Thus, an infant industry can be said to need a subsidy because it is growing; and an elderly industry can be said to need a subsidy because it is declining".

And once introduced, subsidies attract interest groups of producers, consumers and administrators opposed to their abolition and hostile to any attempts to evaluate the results of subsidy policy! In such circumstances, subsidies are likely to depart from the economists market efficiency model and to be based on *ad hoc* interventionism reflecting various interest groups in the economy (Mueller, 1989).

GLOBALIZATION AND MERCANTILISM

Defence markets and defence industries are changing. They have been adjusting to disarmament, to 'revolutions' in both military and financial affairs and to further technical change affecting defence industries. New forms of industrial organisation have emerged as defence companies have developed their prime contracting and systems integration capabilities and have changed from national to international (global) companies. The major defence companies have both military and civil businesses, whilst some are specialist defence companies (e.g. embracing air, land and sea systems).

Globalization has already affected civil industries such as computers, electronics, information technology, jet airliners, motor cars, pharmaceuticals, telecommunications, drinks, food products and restaurants. To be competitive, defence companies are following the example of the civil global corporations, seeking markets throughout the world and suppliers from overseas countries able to provide skills and components at least-cost. Global companies can achieve economies of scale and scope from supplying world markets rather than a small national market and they locate their various research and production activities in nations where costs are lowest. Defence industries have the economic characteristics of global industries, but traditionally, they have relied on their home market and sales to their national armed forces. The major civil aircraft companies have developed into global companies (e.g. Airbus; Boeing); but globalization is now affecting the major military aerospace and defence companies.

The US Competitive Threat

A long-run trend towards higher unit costs of equipment and smaller numbers creates pressures to reduce unit costs through importing and collaborative purchasing rather than buying small numbers from a national defence industry. Faced with falling defence budgets, governments will be more willing to 'shop around' to provide their armed forces with modern equipment at affordable prices: they will no longer be willing to pay the price of supporting a small-scale national defence industry. Here, US aerospace and defence companies form a major competitive threat to small-scale arms industries throughout the world. They offer proven high technology equipment at competitive prices and delivery dates, all of which are attractive to Armed Forces demanding modern equipment from falling defence budgets. Work-sharing arrangements (offsets) provide 'compensation' to the national defence industry likely to 'lose' from importing US equipment. The US competitive threat will be seen in the national markets of European countries and in overseas markets throughout the world.

Mergers in the USA have created large arms companies able to obtain economies from the scale of their output and the scope of their activities. In 1997, four companies, namely, Lockheed Martin, Boeing, Northrop Grumman and Raytheon accounted for about 30% of all US Department of Defence purchases. Of course, large size does not guarantee success and mergers incur transaction and adjustment cost and take time to create a new competitive and profitable enterprise. Conflicts also arise since the price of efficient scale from mergers is the loss of domestic competition and the question of whether the benefits from mergers will be reflected in lower prices to the armed forces or higher profits for shareholders. The US competitive threat also provides a challenge to European aerospace and defence firms.

DEFENCE INDUSTRIES ADJUSTING TO CONVERT

Disarmament since the end of the Cold War has led to major changes in the size and structure of defence industries. Change has been characterised by 'downsizing,' mergers and exits associated with job losses, plant closures and the search for new markets, including arms export markets. Technical change has also impacted on defence industries through creating requirements for new weapons (e.g. unmanned combat air vehicles and the revolution in military affairs) and new forms of industrial organisation (e.g. E-commerce and globalization).

Defence economics focuses on the need for difficult choices in a world of uncertainty. The defence economics problem arises from two pressures. First, declining defence budgets; and second, rising equipment costs. Both pressures mean that defence policy-makers cannot avoid the need for some difficult choices. Economists can contribute to the policy debate by identifying the range of choices and the implications of various policy options. For example, with further reductions in defence budgets, a nation might have to abandon a worldwide role for its Armed Forces; or it might have to choose between a modern air force and a smaller navy and army; or it might have to rely more on reserve forces; or it might have to abandon support for its national defence industrial base. This article examines the economics of defence industries. It shows the importance of government, the economics of defence industries, the case for state support, the range of alternative industrial policies and possible future market developments. A starting point is a description of the major defence industries.

The Major Defence Industries

The world's major defence industries over the period since the end of the Cold War in 1990. Employment has fallen at the world level and especially in the industrialized nations (e.g Europe; former Soviet Union). Nonetheless, total world employment in arms industries was 8.7 million in 1997 with 55% of this employment in industrialized countries and 45% in developing nations. China, the USA and Russia accounted for some 70% of world arms industry employment.

Countries have differed in the magnitude of the decline in their defence industry employment. Europe and Russia experienced major employment reductions over the period

1990 to 1997. Within Europe, employment reductions were especially severe in central and eastern Europe (e.g in 1990, Hungary with an index of 600 and Bulgaria with an index of 400).

In contrast, compared with the world average, employment reductions were below average in the USA, the UK, France and China. Even so, output reductions in nations such as the United States have been substantial. For example, the annual output of military aircraft for US Armed Forces declined from 3,085 units in 1970 to 664 units in 1990 and 150 units in 1998.

THE GRANDNESS OF GOVERNMENT

Governments are central to understanding defence industries. Governments are major buyers and sometimes, the only buyers of defence equipment (monopsony). A government can use its buying power to determine the size and ownership of its national defence industry, its structure, entry and exit, prices, efficiency and profitability (structure, conduct and performance). Governments can support their defence industries by preferential purchasing and/or through direct subsidy payments.

They can also regulate the industry by controlling profits on government contracts (e.g. preventing excessive profits and excessive losses); they can determine prices and profits on non-competitive contracts; they can affect the conduct of firms (e.g. favouring non-price competition such as R&D); and they can control arms exports (e.g. via licences).

Procurement of defence equipment involves government in a set of complex choices in a world of uncertainty. Typically, procurement decisions involve the following choices:

a. *What to buy*? Choices are required about the type of equipment to be purchased and its performance characteristics which, in turn, determines technical progress and the possibilities of technical spin-offs for the defence industry (e.g. civil aircraft) and the rest of the economy.

b. *Who to buy from?* A contractor has to be chosen either by competition or by direct negotiation with a preferred supplier, with the market either restricted to domestic firms or open to foreign suppliers.

c. *When to buy?* Choices have to be made as to which point in a project's life cycle selection will occur. Broadly, projects can be chosen at the drawing board stage, or during development, or at the prototype stage, or when the project is in full production. Risks are reduced the more project selection is delayed to the point at which production takes place and the equipment has entered operational service with a foreign air force. Similarly, competition can take place at various stages in the life cycle-ie. at initial development, or there could be competing prototypes, or competition for production work and/or for midlife up-dates.

d. *How to buy?* Choices have to be made between alternative industrial policies ranging between the two extremes of independent development or imports, or the intermediate options of collaboration involving both development and production, or licensed or coproduction, or an offset programme (each option involving different work sharing arrangements for a national defence industry).

e. *Contracting.* A contract has to be selected between the extremes of cost-plus and firm or fixed price or some form of target cost-incentive contract.

f. *Choice criteria. Policy objectives: military v wider policy objectives.* In making procurement choices, governments have to decide whether to focus on narrow defence criteria or to embrace wider economic and industrial objectives (e.g. employment; technology, etc.).

ECONOMIC EFFECTS OF DEFENCE INDUSTRIAL BASES

Generally, economic theory has no distinctive role for military spending; it is just another form of government spending. Briefly (and superficially), for neoclassical theory, security may be necessary for trade, but there is a trade-off between 'guns and butter.' For Keynesians, security – as government spending – can have a positive demand effect. For Marxists, the story is mixed (Dunne, 1990). The Underconsumptionists, however, do have a clear and positive role for military spending, though it is not backed up empirically.

There are a number of channels through which the DIB can affect the economy. It can support jobs, but can also divert resources from other uses. It can create negative externalities through its influence on other areas of the economy and can crowd out investment from the civil sector. A positive impact may be that it spins off technology to the civil sector, but while this may have been the case a few decades ago, increasingly there is what is termed 'spin in,' with civil technology being increasingly used in weapons systems. A positive impact could be achieved through the creation of demand, but this might create bottlenecks in the economy and impact negatively on the civil economy. Military spending has sociopolitical effects, such as militaristic nationalism, or helping control labour, which may impact on the economy. It can, however, lead to the creation of a coherent set of vested interests, the 'military industrial complex,' which acts in its own interests and invents threats to bargain for increased resources. Whether the overall impact is positive or negative is clearly an empirical question (Dunne, 1996).

A number of forms of empirical analysis have been undertaken. These include institutional and historical studies, econometric analyses and model simulations. Overall, the results suggest: a negative effect of military spending on economic growth for advanced economies, at the expense of investment rather than consumption; and that reductions in military spending can improve economic performance, particularly when the savings are reallocated.

To this can be added the fact that the threats facing countries are different than during the Cold War period and are likely to require non-traditional responses. In the post-Cold War period, the focus was on pariah states, terrorism, crime and peacekeeping. The activities of the armed forces – as well as what they do, where they do it and how – are likely to be very different. They are likely to require different equipment and force structures. Strategic mobility and global information and communications systems are likely to be increasingly important and there is considerable dependence on the US for these. With changes in technology, it is becoming impossible for countries to maintain the capability to independently produce a comprehensive range of weapons. The UK defence industry has moved from strategic justification to economic justification for its existence. It is, however, a declining employer and is heavily subsidised. It is also now stuck with programmes and industries that are a legacy of the Cold War. The economics of maintaining this capability have meant a push for arms exports, but there is excess capacity in the market, with weapon systems selling at near marginal cost and the extensive use of offsets and other measures.

Clearly, the South African defence industry has undergone considerable restructuring in the last few years in response to internal and external changes. This has manifested in the breaking off of state arms production to form Denel, although until recently, the government had adopted a 'hands off' approach. The massive reductions in procurement have led to downsizing, increased concentration and a push for exports. The changing international scene, both on the supply and demand sides, has also influenced the industry and continues to do so. The declining demand for exports has exacerbated local cuts in procurement and the changing nature of international arms producers has made maintenance of a national DIB impossible. This has heightened the spread of the major players into other countries to expand their network of component and sub-product suppliers and their search for markets. The changes in procurement relations in major arms-producing companies has been reflected in South Africa to some degree, with marketing and lobbying becoming an increasingly important tool of the public and private industries. There is still a strong set of interests around arms production that has influenced and is influencing government policy and these interests have been strengthened by the involvement of a number of major international players.

THE UK DEFENCE INDUSTRIAL BASE

The DIS contains a substantial amount of data about the UK DIB and the key features are summarise. Some data are newly-available in the public domain, especially on specific defence markets. The Table shows annual MoD spending and its allocation between R&D, equipment and support services. Support services accounted for over 50% of MoD spending. Indeed, the DIS forecasts a significant growth in future support business.

For example, on the new UK aircraft carriers, initial acquisition will account for about one-third of total life-cycle costs. More emphasis on support business provides further opportunities for military outsourcing. The UK has already achieved significant outsourcing under its Private Finance Initiatives and Public Private Partnerships (e.g. outsourcing of aircrew training; plans for outsourcing military flying training and the UK's air-to-air refuelling capability).

The broad planned spending figures also show the aerospace industry (aircraft, helicopters and missiles) accounting for almost 50% of indicative spending, followed by the maritime and C4ISTAR sectors. Interestingly, a comparison of the *actual* MoD equipment spending in 2006/07 with the *indicative planned* equipment expenditure (at some £5.8 billion in 2006/07) shows the pressures on the equipment budget and the difficult management problem facing MoD.

However, indicative planning assumptions are not firm spending commitments with only about 40% of planned spending being contractually committed in 2006/07, and this share declining to under 20% in 2014/15.4 As a result, budget pressures can always be handled by 'shifting the new equipment programme to the right', reflected in delays in major programmes.

The DIS confirms the relative openness of the UK defence market, where 32% of MoD industrial spending was with foreign-owned companies, collaborative programmes and imports. In contrast, 81% of US defence industrial outlays were with US-owned companies and 9% with foreignowned companies.

There is also extensive foreign inward and outward investment involving the UK DIB, the USA and Europe. UK defence companies (e.g. BAE Systems; Rolls-Royce; VT; QinetiQ) have acquired US firms; similarly, US and European firms have made acquisitions in the UK (e.g. GEC; Raytheon; Finmeccanica; Thales). Overall, about 25% of the UK DIB is foreign-owned.

This feature is recognised in the DIS definition of the UK DIB to comprise all defence suppliers that create value, employment, technology or intellectual assets in the UK, including UK and foreign-owned firms. Employment in the UK DIB has declined substantially from 740,000 employees in 1980/81 to 550,000 in 1990/91 at the end of the Cold War and the current level of 310,000 personnel.

The UK defence industry has experienced major mergers and is dominated by domestic monopolies in air, land and sea systems (BAE Systems; Rolls-Royce; AgustaWestland helicopters). BAE Systems is the dominant UK defence contractor with domestic monopolies in armoured fighting vehicles (reduced from five prime contractors in 1995), ammunition, fixed wing aircraft and nuclear-powered submarines.

The UK industry is mostly privatelyowned, with the Defence Science and Technology Laboratory being the exception as a state-owned enterprise (an agency of MoD). The Government also retains special shares in BAE Systems and Rolls-Royce. In assessing the performance of the UK DIB, its labour productivity compares favourably with the average for UK industry, with defence productivity almost 15% greater than the UK average. This suggests that UK defence industries are more productive than the average alternative uses of the resources (i.e. the UK DIB makes a net contribution to UK national output).

Defence R&D spending is recognised as critical to the delivery of battlewinning capability. The DIS presents evidence of the relationship between equipment capability and R&D investment over the past 10 to 25 years. The relationship shows that 'you get what you pay for' with a time and equipment capability advantage from R&D spending, although the relationship is subject to diminishing returns. The high levels of US R&D spending has bought it a time advantage of about 5 years over the UK, but at a cost of some ten times the level of UK R&D spending. However, the UK's current position in relation to the USA is due to its R&D spending in the 1980s. If UK defence R&D spending continues to decline, the technology gap with the USA will increase, and this will lead to a decline in the UK's export performance. In 2001, the UK's defence R&D spending gave it a time advantage over France, Germany and Sweden. The DTS aims to identify those areas of defence science and technology essential to maintain national sovereignty, provide maximum leverage in strategic terms and provide the maximum technology benefits to the UK.

THE SANDF PROCUREMENT PACKAGE

The decision to procure weapons systems for the SANDF from foreign suppliers made clear an already implicit government view that the maintenance of a general capability in military production was not feasible. As we have seen, developments in international markets suggest that the future might entail a small industry operating in niche markets, possibly in collaboration with a major international player. This recognition of the new reality, where even second-level producers are unable to sustain a comprehensive arms industry, led to the decision to procure externally. Once this decision was made, a considerable amount of effort was put into attempts to wring as much from the potential suppliers as possible, both in the form of defence-related industrial participation, and in order to maintain the competitive parts of the industry and of non-defence products. A major justification for the packages was the economic benefits through these offset deals.

The proposals included: direct contracts with South African defence firms; investment in Denel; and diverse non-defence investments ranging from automotive components, manufacturing, telecommunications, stainless steel and specialty steel plants, gold jewellery, plastics and high-quality textiles. Credits were given for technology transfers and for economic empowerment. Under guidelines that took effect from September 1996, all government and parastatal contracts with an import content exceeding US $10 million must include an industrial participation component. The value of the offsets was to comprise a minimum 30% of a bid's imported component for civilian contracts. For defence contracts, the offsets should comprise 50% of a bid's imported components.

The industrial participation portion of the bid was assessed according to 'credits' awarded for each type of benefit. To illustrate, the number of credits for job creation should equal the estimated value of salaries and wages. New investments, research and development, and links with previously disadvantaged persons (either as shareholders or contractors) earned double credits. Bidders must fulfil their obligations within seven years, and must provide a performance guarantee equal to 5% of the offset component. Once the contract is awarded, the supplier must file bi-annual progress reports.

Ministry of Finance and the Department of Trade and Industry personnel – who assisted in the final stages of negotiation once the structure of the deal was essentially in place – are convinced that they achieved a particularly good deal. The anticipated export percentages of the projects well exceed the stipulated 50% level, and returns on investment on the overall cost of the procurement package are estimated to be approximately 94.5%. Furthermore, throughout the duration of the deal, exports are expected to be in the region of 280% of the original purchase price. Many of the projects under the DIP scheme are still to be finalised, and others are in the exploratory and negotiation phases.

The defence offsets, especially the DIP components, have certainly provided a substantial lifeline to the South African defence industry, while at same time undercutting any remaining aspirations for South Africa to maintain its own DIB. While the industry response in general has been favourable, there are some dissenting voices, especially from the aviation sector. The impact of the deal has been more on defence and related industries, as more progress has been made on the DIP side of the offsets than with the non-defence industrial participation scheme. Batchelor and Dunne (2000) raised concerns about the capability of the local industry to benefit from the deals. They suggested that while the aerospace sector seemed best placed to benefit and to prove themselves attractive to foreign companies, the electronics sector might have a harder time, and the maritime sector was likely to struggle. This would seem to have been borne out by recent developments.

The impact has been to provide orders to domestic companies and opportunities for companies to develop niches in the international market through links with the foreign companies. Private companies and Denel have been drawn into international circuits of defence production, both in terms of indirect and direct DIP.

For instance, Denel has been contracted to build the tail section of the RAF's fleet of Hawk fighter trainers. It is also building landing gear fuselage sections for the Gripen jet fighter, and rudders and ailerons for other BAE Systems aeroplanes. These are not overly high-tech manufacturing operations and may reflect some watering down of the technological path/expertise of Denel. Other DIP contracts are of a nature that is obliging contractors to rethink their niche business, e.g. Tellumat/Eloptro and their form.

There is increasing participation of European defence groupings and investors in the South African industry, at prime contractor and sub-contractor levels. This participation is part of ongoing restructuring and expansion of international defence groups such as EADS and Thales. Local divisions can influence government-to-government dealings to the benefit of the parent company and local subsidiary.

There have been some concerns raised over the value of the offset deal to the South African economy. The limited but growing international literature on defence offsets and their economic effects does not instill confidence. The impact of offsets is often found to be problematic in terms of job creation, the strengthening of backward and forward linkages, and technology enhancement (Struys, 2001). Nor do offsets constitute a 'third way' for the economic development of least developed countries. A recent study of Saudi Arabia's defence offset programmes reveals that instead of a proclaimed 75 000 local jobs, the various programmes had generated approximately 2 000 jobs. Few countries appear to have been successful in using defence offsets to sufficiently utilise, embed and extend technology transfers. Those domestic defence industries that are expected to benefit from offset deals are often characterised by a 'technologically sophisticated conservatism' (BAEC 1998: 33; Batchelor and Dunne 2000), which does not lend itself to the densification of intellectual and social capital. What is required is a 'high degree of local technological absorptive capacity' to be achieved through a state-sponsored 'civil-military, science and technology strategy'. In addition, new modes of structuring technology-intensive production appropriate for the 'new economy' are needed.

While still in their formative stages, the policies have come under public criticism on a number of fronts. The prices of the systems have been condemned as being inflated by the offset arrangements, while reports have identified beneficiary companies that are linked to the head of the weapons procurement committee. Hidden costs have been highlighted, including unanticipated capital expenditure to activate imported equipment and the research and development expenditure required to benefit from technology transfers. Furthermore, as is acknowledged by Denel staff, there will be a variety of possibilities arising from defence offsets for technology transfer and other opportunities that the economy is not in a position to exploit. The government claimed that the impact on the budget would be 'relatively attenuated and is entirely manageable.' In addition, it claims that the 'net effect on the total procurement on the South African economy is broadly neutral'. By contrast, the Institute for Democracy in South Africa (IDASA) Budgetary Group, anticipates that the R30-43 billion procurement package, despite being spread out over several years, will increase defence's share of the budget and somewhat reduce the percentage allocated to infrastructure and public works programmes. This will, in turn, undercut the provision of more funds for poverty relief and affect the more peripheral provinces such as the Eastern Cape. Moreover, Batchelor and Dunne (1999) suggest that the arms acquisition programme could lead to more imports and place pressure on South Africa's balance of payments.

As regards regional development, there are promises of important contributions, but these are not tied into a clear policy framework. The initiative is project-driven, but there is little in the way of public awareness of the investment possibilities on offer. There is no doubt that the procurement programme will impact on the economy, but its spatial effects are more difficult to estimate. The initial estimate of 65 000 jobs and earnings of R110 billion for the original R31 billion investment have been downscaled, and even these figures have been questioned. The DIP may have a positive effect on the defence industry, but it is at a cost to the economy and there is a clear opportunity cost for the use of these resources.

These concerns raise important questions as to the value of this particular deal, but also the use of offset deals in arms procurement generally. The move to justify procurement of weapons systems by economic rather than security benefits is problematic and obscuring the true price of weapons systems by offsets creates problems. It provides scope for corruption and policy confusion, as well as compromising debates over alternative paths to security and development. The impact of companies – used to operating in the world of arms trading with its commissions, bribes and murky deals – in a new democracy is unlikely to be a positive one. The restructuring of the South African defence industry still has some way to go and there are many lessons to be learned, both for future policy and for other countries facing similar policy choices.

The analysis in this paper suggests that there have been significant shifts in the nature, scope and workings of the South African defence industry in recent years, and that these have to be understood within the context of: changes in the international arms market; restructuring of the international defence industry; and the discourses accompanying these processes. The changes cannot be understood in terms of globalization, but rather are a complicated process of internationalisation, where companies remain wedded to their home countries but increasingly have international joint ventures and other links. With the concentration and growth of major defence companies, brokered and networked production has become pervasive.

Another discernible trend is that new generation defence conglomerates are becoming more like non-defence companies and are increasingly influenced by financial capital. In both developed and developing countries, the 'military industrial complex' is reconstituting itself in more informal and less visible forms.

As part of this process, the larger companies have found new ways to influence governments. This has clear implications for any country with a defence industry, as it implies that a comprehensive DIB is impossible to maintain. For relatively small economies, the only possible future lies in becoming a niche producer. A standard argument is that defence industries are vital to national economies; however, a growing body of research suggests that military spending has essentially adverse macroeconomic effects. Increasingly too, defence companies are more reliant upon exports and use economic arguments to justify them. Nevertheless, arms exports are subsidised heavily by the government and the economic benefits are not clear.

There has been a marked restructuring of the South African defence industry, with downsizing coming to an end due to the termination of military spending cuts and the offsets from the procurement package. The industry still maintains a state producer that, prior to privatisation, is restructuring with foreign strategic partners. Compared with similar countries, it could be argued that there is still potential for further reductions in military spending, although the defence actions of the concerned vested interests seem to have stopped reductions. This reflects similar developments in other countries of a renewed but less visible 'military industrial complex,' which is enhanced by the involvement of powerful international arms companies. Future government policymaking will need to recognise this important feature of the political terrain. Given the evidence of the economic costs of defence industries, a large opportunity cost is likely to be attached to any strengthening of their importance in the economy. It would seem better that the government aim to retain intelligent customer status – allotting a recognisable subsidy where needed – rather than develop policies that require a potentially costly resource, where subsidies and costs may be hidden from view through the brokering of procurement deals with offsets. At present, these proposals are based upon concerns and warnings emanating from recent developments. It is important that research is conducted for the life of the projects to inform future policymaking and to provide important lessons to other countries considering similar policies.

INDIAN DEFENCE INDUSTRY SNAPSHOT

The Indian defence industrial base and production capacity is now one of the largest in the world. This has painstakingly been built both pre-independence (1947) and also made rapid strides during the decades after independence. India now has 40 Defence Ordnance Factories and 8 Defence Public Sector Undertakings. These produce a large range of armaments, ammunition, vehicles, helicopters, fighter aircrafts, sophisticated electronics equipment, missiles and naval crafts. The defence sector is fully government controlled with the ultimate aim to reduce dependence on imports and become self reliant in this critical sector at the earliest.

Notwithstanding the large industrial base and advancement in various technologies, research and development in defence has not kept pace with the requirement of modern and high technology weapon systems. This has resulted in import of major armaments and other systems involving critical technologies. Till the 80's India was largely dependent on Soviet Russia and other East Bloc countries for its defence requirements. As a matter of fact the entire tank fleet, mechanized infantry BMP/ICV fleet, Air Defence systems, bridges, and a large portion of field Artillery presently in front line service in the army is of Soviet/Eastern bloc origin. Despite the economic upheaval in India in 1991 coinciding with the end of the cold war, the two countries continued their defence relationship. The Indo-Russian defence programme is currently set to continue until 2010, but the future is not certain. India in the last 6-7 years has bought the SU30 aircrafts, 310 T-90 battle tanks (347 more are on order), the air craft carrier, Smerch rocket launchers etc. The view on further major purchases is divided due to a number of problems being faced on maintenance support of current and past equipment.

The era of liberalization which commenced in 1991, coincided with the enhanced role of the private sector in defence. Up to the late 90's the private sectors' role was mainly limited to providing large quantities of raw material, sub assemblies and limited quantities of high technology items to the Ordnance Factories, Defence PSU's and the Army's repair agencies.

In May 2001, the government decided to open up defence to private participation up to 100%, with FDI permissible up to 26%. With this change in policy a larger role for the private sector has emerged. Initially, the private sector was slow to absorb this change primarily due to the large requirement of funds, uncertainties of sustained defence requirements and long lead times for trials and eventual introduction of equipment. However, over the last 4-5 years with the active participation of various chambers of commerce a number of large private sector companies have successfully entered the defence sector with tie ups both with large foreign defence conglomerates and defence PSU's/Ordnance Factories.

As per SIPRI Book of 2008, US military spent $547 billion in 2007 which corresponds to 4%of its GDP. UK ranked second with a spend of $60 billion, India ranked 10th in global spending with an expenditure of $ 24 billion of which approximately $10 billion was on capital expenditure, 80% of this was towards buying new equipment. ABOUT $11 BILLION ARE FOR CAPITAL PURCHASES during 2008-2009.

With the entry of the private sector, large resources in terms of latest technologies, management and scientific skills, and its ability to raise large sums of money have brought defence production to center stage. This will not only enhance best practices but will assist in increasing indigenous production, employment and move faster towards the aim of self reliance. It is in this stage of transition that India needs large scale infusion of the latest technologies which is critical to self reliance. This can be best provided by collaboration with foreign companies excelling in a range of diverse equipments. Both the private sector and defence establishments are moving in this direction, albeit a little slow.

India is likely to reach an annual budget of $40 billion by the end of the 11th defence plan (2011-2012). Of this, about $16-17 billion would be available for capital expenditure. An analysis of major purchases during the last 5-6 years shows that major contracts have been signed for the Air Force and Navy. Defence observers feel that this trend is likely to continue. Big ticket contracts like 126 jets to replace the ageing MIG-21 worth about $10 billion, 6-C-130 aircraft, six refuellers, long range maritime patrol air craft for the Navy, utility helicopters for the Army and Air Force are on the anvil.

Indigenous defence industry and foreign manufacturers need to closely observe the Armys requirement. Large induction of four types of 155mm guns, the TCS, BMS, dry and wet bridges, fuzes, bi modular charge systems, specialist vehicles, Air Defence gun and missile system, night vision devices are among a host of requirements the Army wants urgently. Conceptually the Army works on an equipment profile of 30: 40: 30, this implies that 30% of the equipment of a type is approaching obsolescence, 40% is current and 30% is state of the art.

The best example to illustrate this is the tank profile, while the T-55 is approaching obsolescence, the T-72 is current and the T-90 is state of art. If this concept is interpolated to others, the requirement of hardware over the next 5 to 10 years can be assessed broadly. Collaboration and transfer of technology will be the mantra in all these requirements.

Defence Procurement Procedure-2008 is in place wef 01 September 08. Very clearly India has entered free market economy in defence requirements.

The Indian defence industry is in transition with increased participation from the private sector. In all fairness Indian industry is nascent and catering for the huge demand of defence equipment by themselves is extremely difficult, thus the window of opportunity for foreign manufactures to partner with Indian industry and provide Indian Defence Forces the state of art equipment is for real.

RISING DEFENCE EXPENDITURE IN INDIA

The Government of India has been investing heavily into its Defence industry due to strained relations with its neighboring countries and growth in international terrorism. The Defence budget for the year 2005 was $17.80 billion, a growth of 7.6 percent from the budget allocation of 2000. Typically 5.0 percent to 10.0 percent of the Defence budget is allocated for modernization and weapon induction. The larger share is allocated for payment, allowances, and for maintenance of aging military equipment. The Government of India expects its Defence expenditure to exceed $20.00 billion by 2008.

Private Investments on the Rise in the Indian Defence Industry

The Defence industry in the past has been dominated by the government-run public sector undertakings (PSU). This scenario has changed significantly with the Ministry of Defence providing license to private companies to manufacture select aerospace and Defence products.

In 2001, the country opened for up to 100 percent Indian private sector investments in the Defence industry and allowed foreign direct investment (FDI) of up to 26.0 percent in select areas of the Defence industry. Some of the key non-PSU industry participants supplying Defence equipment and services include Mahindra & Mahindra, Tata Group, Kirloskar Brothers, Larsen & Toubro, Ashok Leyland, Jindal, Max Aerospace & Aviation, and Ramoss India.

Increasing Public-Private Collaborations

The Defence industry is gradually liberalizing and the public sector is facilitating greater private sector participation in the area of Defence goods production. There are about 5,100 companies supplying around 20.0 percent to 25.0 percent of components and subassemblies to state-owned contractors and the market size is expected to be around $6.20 billion in 2005. Of India's current Defence procurement of capital items, more than 30 percent is imported, however, this is expected to change with the creation of more public-private partnerships.

The Indian Space Research Organization (ISRO) has a strong partnership with the Indian industrial sector for space programs execution. Over 500 small, medium, and large-scale enterprises work with ISRO, supplying hardware, undertaking fabrication jobs, and establishing fabrication and test facilities. The Indian industrial sector provides all raw materials and high-tech electronic items required by ISRO and has also contributed toward developing systems for launch vehicle spacecraft, remote sensing, and ground equipment. Around 231 technologies developed by ISRO were transferred to the Indian industrial sector for commercial use. ISRO also undertakes technical consultancy projects for industries.

INDIA'S OFFSET POLICY TO ENCOURAGE DOMESTIC PRODUCTION

India's offset policy for Defence goods has been designed to leverage the country's position as a large buyer and exporter. India's offset policy for the Defence industry states that any purchase from a foreign supplier in excess of $70.0 million will require a reinvestment of 30.0 percent of the total purchase amount in terms of components and services from India. The offset policy applies to imports by Defence PSU's, ordinance factories, and private participants of the industry.

The offset policy is also expected to act as a driver to create market-entry opportunities for mid-rung companies, which are looking at investing in research and development and manufacturing of Defence goods. The proposed offset policy is conducive for the private companies to have a larger presence.

Growth Opportunities in the Indian Defence Industry

The domestic capability of the Indian Defence industry is largely concentrated around the production of the PSUs and ordinance factories. This trend is expected to change with the recent selective liberalization of the Defence industry and a sound offset policy, which are expected to create greater private sector participation and facilitate bigger FDI inflows into the Indian Defence industry.

The Government of India has shown keenness in allowing international collaboration for the production of weapon systems, which are purely used for non-lethal purposes. The production of the following weapon systems are expected to be promoted in the future:

- Technologies/equipment for counter terrorism

- Surveillance, communication equipment, and sensors for border management
- Cyber security-synergies in the field of information technology
- Devices to neutralize improvised explosive devices (IEDs).

Suppliers and manufacturers of the above-mentioned weapon systems are expected to be some of the chief beneficiaries of the increased indigenization of the production process in the Indian Defence industry. Key areas of growth identified within the industry are expected to arise from the up gradation of the production capacity expansion, technology transfer, and modernization of Defence infrastructure.

DEPARTMENT OF DEFENCE PRODUCTION

The Department of Defence Production was set up in 1962, in the aftermath of the war with China, to create an indigenous defence production base which is self-reliant and self-sufficient. Indigenisation, particularly of armaments, proceeded apace in 1963. In November, 1965, Department of Defence Supplies was created to forge linkages between the civil industries and defence production units. The two departments were merged in December, 1984 to form the Department of Defence Production and Supplies.

Since 1962, 16 new ordnance factories have been set up and their capacities have been augmented and modernised selectively keeping in mind the emerging requirements of the Armed Forces. Presently, 39 Ordnance Factories and 8 Defence Public Sector Undertakings (DPSUs) are engaged in the task of manufacture of equipment and stores for Defence Services. In addition, capacities of civil sectors are also utilised for the purpose.

India maintains an extensive Defence industrial base principally owned by the government. At independence, industrialization was viewed to be the engine of growth and jobs for the rest of the economy, and since then the government has owned a large fraction of the industries and also tightly regulated the private sector. India believed that public ownership was necessary to insure developments that would benefit the entire country. India decided early that the Defence industries would be owned by the public sector, and the Indian penchant to establish a "socialist pattern of society" still dominates the Defence industrial base.

India's Defence industrial capacity lies in three main classes of enterprises: the Ordnance Factories (OF), the Defence Public Sector Undertakings (DPSU), and, to a much lesser extent, selected civilian public and private sector manufacturing establishments. The OFs, founded in 1801, are departmentally run government units. There are 39 OFs, grouped into five areas based on the type of armaments they produce: Ammunition and Explosives, Weapons, Vehicles and Equipment, Armoured Vehicles, and Ordnance Equipment. There are eight publicy-owned DPSUs: Hindustan Aeronautics Limited; Bharat Electronics; Bharat Earth Movers; Mazagon Dock Ltd; Garden Reach Shipbuilders and Engineers Ltd; Boa Shipyard Ltd; Bharat Dynamics Ltd; and Mishra Dhatu Nigam Ltd. Both the OFs and the DPSU's are trying to move toward greater self-reliance. The government is also trying to promote greater civil sector participation in the armament process.

The indigenisation of defence equipment is an ongoing process and is achieved by transfer of technology and indigenous research. Indigenisation of spares of defence equipment has been undertaken in aircraft, warships, armament, tanks, vehicles and electronic as well as engineering equipment.

While the Ordnance Factories and Defence Public Sector Units (DPSUs) are manufacturing a wide range of products for the defence forces, the private sector has been involved in the supply of raw material, semi-finished products, parts and components of defence equipment. The combined value of the products of Ordnance Factories and Defence PSUs during 2000-2001 has been approximately Rs. 14000 crore as against approximately Rs. 1800 crore on import of stores (which excludes capital equipment) comprising components, spares, overhaul etc.

The Government has recently allowed private sector participation in the defence industry upto 100 per cent and with foreign direct investment permissible upto 26 per cent both subject to licensing, for manufacture of all types of defence equipment within the country. This is expected to add to the investment already made in the public sector.

The Defence industry sector has been opened for participation by Indian Private Sector upto 100 % of equity, with Foreign Direct Investment (FDI), component of it being permissible upto 26 %, both being subject to licensing permissions. This includes all types of defence equipment. Guidelines have been issued by the Department of Industrial Policy & Promotion (DIPP) in consultation with the Ministry of Defence regarding the modalities for consideration of applications for grant of licences. The private companies are allowed to apply either individually or by a partnership firm amongst themselves. The Chief Executive of the company/ partnership will be a resident Indian. The company/ partnership firm can have Foreign Direct Investment upto 26 % of the equity. Preference would be given to original equipment manufacturers or design establishments and those having a good track record of supplies. However, there would be a three years lock-in period for transfer of equity from one foreign investor to another foreign investor and such transfer would be subject to prior approval of Foreign Investment Promotion Board (FIPB) and the Government.

All applications from the private entrepreneurs will be considered by the Department of Industrial Policy & Promotion in consultation with the Ministry of Defence and the licenses would be granted by the DIPP. The licensees are required to put in place adequate safety and security procedures, which would be subject to verification by authorized Government agencies. The quality of the product will be assured by the Quality Assurance Agencies of the Ministry of Defence. The exports of manufactured items would be subject to policy and guidelines as applicable to Ordnance Factories and Defence Public Sector Undertakings.

The objective of the policy is to attract more investment in the Defence Sector and not to change the ownership of the Ordnance Factory Board and the Defence Public Sector Undertakings. These represent the core strength of Defence Industry in India and their continued growth and full utilisation of capacities would be encouraged by the Government.

4

Defence Economics Policy in Major Transition

Recently the US journal Defence News reported that the Indian government is working on a program whereby Israel would replace Russia as India's largest supplier of weapons and defence equipment by 2008. Since Russia now supplies some 70 percent of India's weapons imports, this report, if true, would mark a major transformation in Indian defence policy. Under the terms of the program, India would identify the products it wants and ask the Israeli government to negotiate with domestic firms on its behalf as Jerusalem does with regard to its own weapons. Israel is already the second-largest supplier of military systems to India, so this program could affect a major transformation in India's security relationships.

The potential repercussions of this project, which would clearly show a serious break with Moscow's arms salesmen, are immense. Given the deep ties between the US and Israeli defence industries, if this program does materialize it will also probably enhance the United States' competitive position in the Indian defence market and result in further substantial increases in the already rising amount of US arms sales and security cooperation with India. Those sales could either be bilateral or brokered through Israel, such as weapons made jointly by Israel and the United States, including missile defence systems that India reportedly is interested in acquiring.

This program would then also strengthen the developing tripartite relationship among Israel, India, and the US in regard to defence sales. We can see this already occurring, because the United States has brushed aside Pakistan's objections to India's receiving the Israeli Phalcon radar, made with US technology and thus subject to US veto on its transfer to a third party.

Realization of the projected Indo-Israeli project would also simultaneously symbolize and express India's rising continental Asian status as a great power with interests and capabilities across the continent, allowing it to break free of its confining chains as merely a major South Asian power if not the regional leader, something that both Indian and foreign observers have labelled as a prerequisite for a full partnership with the United States. Not only would those trends strengthen Indo-Israeli ties, they would provide fuel to the oft-reported desire on the part of at least some US elites to create a tripartite alliance with India and Israel against terrorism (if not for other, broader objectives that would emerge later).

Joint Indo-Israeli defence collaboration on a scale envisaged above would also, or so these advocates hope, tie into the US alliance and Israeli partnership with Turkey, creating a kind of pan-Asian bloc. The new program grows out of India's difficulty in negotiating a US$10 billion multi-year defence acquisition program with Russia. Three areas in particular seem to have caused some anxiety in New Delhi.

In March 2002, The Times of India reported that the Parliamentary Standing Committee had urged the government to avoid overdependence on Russia for armaments and spare parts. The committee reportedly acknowledged Russia's previous contributions and reliability as a provider of defence equipment to India but cautioned that the current dependence on Moscow for almost 80 percent of its arms imports is unhealthy.

It also observed that Russia was not providing military hardware on the same beneficial financial terms that it had during the Soviet era. Therefore the committee also urged the Indian government to cease making advance payments for weapons acquisitions from Russia, and that in the future it seek to put more defence contracts up for competitive tender. Russia also has come under criticism because of India's difficulty in obtaining and negotiating speedy delivery of spare parts for these weapons systems. At the same time it became clear that given its worsening relations with Pakistan, India is seeking to diversify its foreign purchases and use foreign partners to develop its own defence industrial capability, e.g by conditioning purchases on obtaining offsets from the sellers to develop its own indigenous capability.

The alliance, if it were to materialize, would build on the already greatly improved Indo-Israeli relationship that has led to large-scale military sales from Israel and to India's rapprochement with the United States as well. As the Phalcon deal suggests, it could become possible to envisage tripartite collaboration among these states on missile defence, especially if India's great goal of securing the end to all US sanctions on the transfer of both civil and military technology is realized.

Moreover, the broadening of India's ties and reach in political-military terms through the acquisition of top-quality defence systems would enable it to play the kind of role that analysts in both India and the US postulate as being essential to any serious strategic partnership with the United States. And that role also accords very much with some of the deepest aspirations of India's foreign and defence policy elites, thus highlighting a congruence of visions concerning India's future international position.

In effect India's aspiration to play a major role "from Socotra to Sumatra" would have been both realized and blessed by the United States, as Secretary of State Colin Powell implicitly suggested in 2001. India would then become not just a South or even Central Asian power but a major player in the Persian Gulf, the Middle East, and Southeast Asia.

At the same time, India's search for new vistas in defence acquisition and production relates very much to its rising economic, technological, and military-industrial capabilities as well as to its desire to strengthen existing long-standing partnerships, e.g with Russia. For example, beyond the existing $10 billion weapons sales from Russia to India, India is collaborating with Russia on joint production of a fifth-generation fighter that Russia feels vital to its military future. Both are also collaborating on research that is probably tied to missile defence and nuclear systems as well. More broadly, India is the only country with whom Russia is collaborating on joint production of sophisticated and futuristic weapons systems. Likewise India, not China, gets the best weapons currently being produced in Russia, systems that not even Russia's armed forces can obtain. Moscow offers offsets in the form of technology transfer of production skills and know-how to India, one of its largest customers. Although India obviously seeks to diversify its sources of foreign procurement, Russian producers have until now been confident of their ability to obtain the bulk of Indian defence contracts.

Whether or not this confidence is misplaced, time will tell, but diversification and strengthening of India's own capabilities surely would increase India's scientific-technological and manufacturing capabilities for weapons production. This objective also appears to be a major goal of the deals now being made with Russia, Israel, and presumably the United States. We see similar deals with Italian and French firms for joint manufacture of weapons systems.

India's leading defence firm, Hindustan Aeronautics Ltd (HAL), is also pressing an outsourcing program whereby it would help private Indian companies find and choose foreign partners to undertake such high-tech projects as avionics integration, weapons-system integration, and other related efforts to "lay the foundation for a credible domestic aerospace industry base that could meet the majority of India's military aerospace requirements in the next 10 years".

And it is no less logical to assume that India would be thrilled to duplicate this particular kind of relationship with Washington, especially as India already has a large space program with military applications and very much wants US conventional-weapons systems and technology transfer.

Indeed, a Pentagon-commissioned study of Indo-American perceptions reported that on the basis of many interviews, a uniform conclusion was reached that "for Indians, technology transfer from the United States is military cooperation's touchstone". Other Indian assessments confirm the great importance that India attaches to transfer of both civil and defence technology as a critical and essential element in any partnership with the US. While India's aspirations in the defence industry are common to other countries that seek the capability for indigenous production of most, if not all of their weapons, it is nevertheless clear that this deal, if it materializes, would utterly transform defence relationships among major players in the defence business: India, the US, Israel, and Russia. The major transformations in Asian security that accelerated after September 11, 2001, have clearly not yet run their course. Nor is it clear when the overall Asian situation will stabilize or when also the rising tide of weapons sales will abate.

But there can be no doubt that major changes are in the offing and that the future holds many more surprises and jolts for all of those who seek to play a key role in the security and defence of Asia.

INDIA'S DEFENCE COMMENCEMENT POLICY

India inherited some defence industries from Great Britain. They included Hindustan Aeronautics Limited (HAL), which is today India's largest defence public sector undertaking (DPSU), Mazagon Docks Limited (MDL), the largest shipyard in the nation, and more than half a dozen ordnance factories. The growth of the domestic defence industry has, however, been sporadic since Independence. It did not follow any definite plan though emphasis was placed on enhancing indigenous defence production capability.

Some analysts have also traced certain vigorousness in the Indian effort at developing an indigenous defence capability to the early 1960s spawned by the 1962 India-China war. The war is seen as having underscored the urgency of building a domestic defence industry through foreign assistance. It was also in consonance with Nehru's policy of building a strong industrial base patterned on the Soviet model. But while the war with China has been identified as the catalyst in the effort at developing a domestic defence base, there was no concerted, systematic and well-orchestrated effort towards the achievement of this goal.

There were many factors that stood in the way of India building a strong military-industrial base. India's comparatively easy access to various types of defence equipment from the former Soviet Union (FSU) and their purchase against deferred rupee payments and on "friendship" price were some of them. Sophisticated defence equipment was transferred to India under the favourable rupee-rouble arrangements from FSU. Some license production facilities were also established in India, for instance for the Mig-21 aircraft. The Cold War also ensured that India continued to have a favourable and preferred source of defence systems and equipment from FSU. It did not find the superpower wanting in any critical manner in fulfilling India's defence requirements. However, this had the unintended consequences of dampening any sense of urgency in India to develop an indigenous defence industry. Coupled with this was the reluctance of the US to help in India's effort to develop a domestic defence production base. Nevertheless, trudging along, India was able to develop the largest defence industry among developing nations.

However, with the collapse of the FSU, India lost easy access to sophisticated defence equipment at cheap prices. The problem was compounded by the absence of an alternate source of modern defence equipment. The situation became worse with the almost complete disruption in the supply of services and spare parts necessary to maintain the predominantly Soviet-equipped Indian armed forces. The navy was particularly affected, as it was dependent on Soviet designs and equipment for some of the ships that were under construction in India. This led to huge cost and time overruns in the indigenous construction programme of naval vessels.

Ironically, the need to service and maintain various kinds of equipment imported from FSU compelled India to seek ways and means to develop some level of indigenous capability. Towards this goal, certain technologies and know-how were obtained, both for the repairs and for the local production of some critical spare parts. These efforts were, however, largely case-specific and were not components of any systematic strategy for the comprehensive development of an indigenous defence industry. They were also service-driven in the absence of any coherent strategy to achieve self-reliance. However, the liberalisation of the Indian economy that almost coincided with the collapse of FSU and promised to unlock India's productive capabilities gave impetus to the goal of developing a domestic military-industrial complex.

It was, however, not until 2005 that India formulated a defence offset policy to contribute to the nation's goal of developing its domestic defence industry. This policy was incorporated in the Defence Procurement Procedure (DPP) 2005. The policy introduced a 30 per cent offset in contracts valued above Rs 3 billion under "buy" and 'buy and make" categories.

Under the policy, foreign vendors had the liberty to discharge their obligations either through the execution of defence exports of Indian items and services or through investments in India's defence infrastructure. They also had the option of selecting Indian firms in consultation with an industry associate of their choice to implement their offset obligations. The hallmark of this policy was its non-obligatory nature, or in other words, these offsets were non-mandatory. It was left to the Services Capital Acquisition Plan Categorisation Committee (SCAPCC) to recommend the incorporation of offset obligation in acquisition proposals.

The offset policy was, however, in the nascent stage and it lacked clarity in many areas. It also suffered from the absence of any designated agency in the Ministry of Defence (MoD) for guiding, overseeing, executing and monitoring the implementation of the policy. In reality, confusion reigned in equal measure in the corridors of South Block as in the minds of the vendors on how to implement the offset obligations. Consequently, the offset policy did not yield any dividend.

The absence of any offset benefit to the Indian defence industry led the Government of India (GoI) to make significant changes in DPP 2006 and they included the following:

- offset was made mandatory in defence contracts of the size and nature as prescribed in the 2005 policy;
- foreign firms were allowed the flexibility of forming joint ventures (JVs) with Indian firms, and;
- a new organisation called the Defence Offset Facilitation Agency (DOFA) was established comprising of representatives of all stakeholders; the Services, DPSUs, Defence and Research Organisation (DRDO), etc.

Offset Policy in DPP 2008

The limited success of the offset policy of 2006 led to its elaborate revision in 2008. India had by now become one of the largest importers of defence equipment, with nearly 70 per cent of its requirements being met by foreign suppliers. The demand of the armed forces also resulted in the high growth of India's defence budget. During the period 2003-07, it registered the fourth highest growth in real terms amongst the 10 largest military spenders in the world. Therefore, the 2008 policy aimed at the creation of conditions for assisting in the development of a domestic military-industrial complex. The salient changes introduced in DPP 2008 include:

- the introduction of a list of products which would qualify for the discharge of offset obligations (Annexure-VI of the DPP);
- the removal of the requirement for private industry to obtain industrial license to participate in offset programme unless stipulated by the regulations of the Departmental of Industrial Policy and Promotion (DIPP);
- offset credit banking;
- banking of surplus offset credit with a validity period of two years after the conclusion of the relevant contract, and;
- exemption of acquisitions under fast track from offset obligations.

Will the 2008 offset policy facilitate the creation of a military-industrial base in India?

With the defence outlay steadily increasing and with only around 30 per cent of the requirement being met indigenously, emphasis has been laid on utilising the growing sophistication of the domestic industrial base to achieve self-reliance in the defence sector. It is now seen as both a necessity and an increasingly achievable goal. But the introduction of the 2008 policy in itself is no guarantee that it will contribute significantly to this goal. Offsets though beneficial, come with certain inherent risks. The offset policy, therefore, has to be carefully calibrated to reduce its negative impact and maximise its yield. There is almost complete unanimity among defence economists, who have analysed the impact of defence offsets on the development of the defence industry in various countries, that the process is highly complex and therefore defies easy conclusion.

Their efforts have been stymied primarily by the absence of data relating to offset implementation and the notorious level of secrecy with which defence firms guard such details. Offsets have been termed as "smoke and mirrors", with nobody being sure as to "who benefits". Also, almost all of them have questioned the economic efficiency of offset transactions. Offsets are no free lunches. They are neither freebies. There is an economic cost to offsets. For instance, in a survey conducted in the UK, it was concluded that "evidence suggests that offsets do cost more than off-the shelf purchase and, not surprisingly, that vendors seek to include most of this premium in the selling price." In a study of defence offset implementation in Belgium, it was estimated that the nation had to pay between 20-30 per cent in increased costs in connection with "offsets tied to its military procurement." Depending on the economic conditions prevalent in the offset applying nation, its industrial base or its capacity to absorb technology, vendors hike the cost of their goods/services to compensate for the inefficiency inherent in the nation seeking offsets. Therefore, an offset implementing nation pays more for the import of defence items than it would otherwise have to do if it did not impose mandatory offset obligations.

Among offsets, mandatory offsets have been further estimated to yield less economic dividends. In view of this, it has been concluded that "there is no good reason for a mandatory offsets scheme" to be introduced, as such schemes "merely shift the initiative away from the purchaser and give suppliers scope for opportunism at the expense of the buyer."

From the above, it is seen that India has opted for the use of an economically inefficient vehicle to promote its domestic defence industry. By opting for the mandatory offset scheme, it has further bartered the leverage buyers have in sale and purchase of competitive goods. Given the overwhelming evidence that offsets are generally not welfare enhancing, implicit in the Indian offset policy is the assumption that it is willing to forsake economy in the acquisition of weapons for the long-term goal of creating a defence-industrial base (which according to existing studies is difficult to achieve) through the induction of technology, co-production, license production, etc., that the policy may compel. Therefore, the moot question is whether India has carefully calibrated its regulations and put in place a system that can optimise the benefits of an offset policy that in the first place comes at a cost. An analysis of the situation in India, however, reveals that the mandatory offset obligations will yield greater dividends if necessary changes are made in all relevant rules and guidelines that have a bearing on the success of the policy. Some of the extant rules are archaic and were not, in the first place, formulated to encourage the absorption of the benefits that offsets offer. Such rules and procedures that were formulated prior to the incorporation of the policy of offsets (licensing policy requirement for private firms to produce defence items, for instance), it is argued, cannot but reduce the benefits the policy can yield. Some of the areas that are glaringly deficient and where new initiatives may be needed are the following:

FOREIGN DIRECT INVESTMENT (FDI) IN DEFENCE SPHERE

"Direct foreign investment in Indian defence industries for industrial infrastructure for services, co-development, joint and a production of defence products and components" have been identified by DPP 2008 as a method to discharge defence offset obligations. But in order to encourage investment and transfer of technology to India, it will be important to give foreign defence firms the confidence that they will have greater share in the profits and larger say in the management of the entities they create. Larger stakes should be allowed to foreign firms in such entities whose creation would not have been possible but for these foreign companies. Ironically, Foreign Investment Promotion Board (FIPB) guidelines do not encourage this.

According to the FIPB guidelines, foreign firms that may tie up with Indian entities are allowed only 26 per cent equity in such ventures. The remaining equity has to be owned by Indian entities. The ceiling of 26 per cent is a major impediment to the success of the offset policy. First, foreign firms are reluctant collaborators in any mandatory offset arrangement. Otherwise, these firms would have tied up with Indian entities for the production of defence equipment without any compulsion. But as offsets have been made mandatory in cases involving acquisition over Rs 300 crore, foreign firms can nevertheless be expected to collaborate with Indian firms, as otherwise they will lose the opportunity to profit from the contract that can only be signed with the offset obligation. But, if the created entity has to survive on a long-term basis, the collaborating foreign firm should have a stake in it. This can only come through the creation of attractive prospects for the foreign firms to make greater profit than investments made elsewhere. Therefore, there is a need to make them, not reluctant parties, but willing and enthusiastic partners in JVs by increasing their stake in such collaborations. An example of how higher stakes in companies can help add value to the offset policy is the Boeing purchase of 34 per cent of Aero Vodochody, a Czech firm, as an offset deal. Boeing's subsidiary Ayers bought LET Kunovice, a Czech plane manufacturing firm, with plans to move part of the production line for its own planes to LET.

Second, if the balance of the 26 per cent that a foreign company brings has to be raised by Indian partners, it can lead to many difficulties. Since 26 per cent equity is the upper ceiling that a foreign vendor can invest in India, it has to find an Indian firm that is willing to raise the balance 74 per cent.

This raises two difficulties. First, it has to find an Indian partner willing to find resources for this high level of investment. Second, if the foreign firm decides to use a JV as the sole means of fulfilling its 30 per cent obligation under offset, then it will have to find an Indian partner or partners willing to invest more in terms of equity. To illustrate, if a company X enters into a contract for Rs 1,000 crore, it will have to invest Rs 300 crore to discharge its offset obligations. But since a foreign vendor is only allowed 26 per cent equity, to invest Rs 300 crore, it will have to form a JV that involves a total investment of Rs 1,153.8 crore (Rs 300 crore by the foreign vendor and Rs 853.8 crore by the Indian entity or entities). Both the choices are difficult, as is would not be easy to find Indian entities that can make such high investments.

Conversely, increasing the equity may benefit the nation in several ways. Given the above dampeners (arising from the upper ceiling of 26 per cent), it may encourage greater participation by foreign firms in JVs if they have larger share of the equity. Also, foreign vendors will be reluctant to invest 26 per cent in equity and transfer proprietary technology that may have been developed at high research and development (R&D) cost. There is always a stubborn resistance to transferring technical capability and it can only come at a price as "the transferring country does not simply stand still while its 'beautiful princess' (Williamson, 1983) is shipped abroad and effective competition is created." Therefore, a foreign firm will be less reluctant to grudge competition from an entity established in India in which it has substantial stakes and from whose sales it stands to profit.

Given that comparatively cheap factors of production exist in India, the foreign parent company may even chose to outsource components/items from their Indian JV. Though not in the defence sector, the export performance of Hyundai Motors in India should give India reasons to allow more liberal FDI in the defence sector also. Second, a foreign firm that invests higher equity will have a stake in the success of the project. It will be more willing to outsource items from India to its other holdings to make the project a success. Otherwise, there is a danger of the interest of the foreign vendor dissipating once the contract is completed, as without a reason to retain their interests, they will shut shop and return. This point can be illustrated with the instance of armoured personnel carriers purchased by the Philippines Army from the UK. After eight of these were imported from the UK and the remaining 142 were assembled in Philippines, the assembly line was closed, with only minimal offset benefits to the nation. Third, as offset banking has now been allowed, it will give such vendors incentive to accumulate credits for discharging their obligations in future contracts by making value additions and introducing new products.

There should be further transparency in dealing with prospective foreign vendors. At present, GoI does consider higher investments on a case-to-case basis. This concept of case-to-case approach is indeed intriguing to a foreign vendor who in any case finds Indian procedures, bureaucratic control and the penchant for secrecy rather perplexing. The recent reports that the GoI turned down a joint venture proposal of Mahindra and Mahindra with the British defence giant BAE Systems has not helped convey the right message, coming as these did only weeks after the revised offset procedure was announced. This rejection has even raised doubts on the seriousness with which India is pursuing its policy to attract foreign investment in the defence sector. Perhaps, GoI may have had strong reasons to reject the proposal. But explaining the reasons to the firms may have limited the damage. There should be more transparency in expressing our views and this will result in increased vendor confidence in the nation.

It may also be difficult to argue that increasing the limits of equity participation for foreign firms will impinge on national security. The only danger perhaps is that such foreign firms may end up buying Indian entities (a view expressed by one of the large Indian entities in response to the questionnaire sent by the author). If this is a serious concern, the problem can be addressed by making it a requirement to obtain the approval of GoI before the takeover of any defence establishment by a joint venture.

DOMESTIC INDUSTRY IN DEFENCE PLANNING

Private entities are answerable to their shareholders and are in the business to make profits, whether in defence or any other sector. Attractive return on investment, more than what can be expected in non-defence sectors, is the only mantra that can make them divert their finite resources to the defence sector. Gestation period is also quite high in defence sector as establishing a defence venture can take more time than other commercial ventures. Therefore, advance information of the acquisition plans of the government can give potential domestic investors the lead time and the opportunity to study the prospects of raising funds and also seek foreign collaborations. This is a necessary precondition for creating the right atmosphere for developing an indigenous defence industry.

At present, private players do not have prior knowledge of the defence plans of the country. Though we have 15-year long-term integrated perspective plan (LTIPP) that flows into the 5-year Services Capital Acquisition Plan (SCAP), which in turn flows into the 2-year roll-on plan for Capital Acquisitions, the acquisition proposals are most often than not guarded as secrets. The Indian domestic industry is not privy to these plans. As a consequence, information is sent to them only when requests for proposals (RFPs) are issued. Potential Indian investors, therefore, lose the lead time that is required to plan and prepare for such large investments.

The solution may lie in sharing with a select group of Indian industries the LTIPP and the SCAPs to the extent they relate to items proposed for acquisition. The argument that revealing in advance what the nation seeks to acquire will be detrimental to national security also does not hold much water. Private companies have been involved in the development of closely guarded defence projects in India. Even those relating to some of the most sensitive projects, find their way into leading arms publications sooner than later. Again, there is no reason to believe that private sector can be less trusted in keeping state secrets than the public sector. In any case, we lose some of our eminent public sector personnel to private sector. Like in the US, we should involve the private sector at the planning stage itself. To ensure secrecy of information, suitable regulations may be put in place, like in the US. If necessary, in very sensitive projects, the information need not be shared.

Defence Items

As argued above, private entities will not embark on any manufacturing venture, defence or otherwise, unless they are confident of reaping dividends from it. Therefore, prudence lies in opening up this sector. Let the market forces regulate the industry.

Defence contractors are most often not large. Even large entities source components and subcomponents that make up complex systems from countless small enterprises. In India too, there are thousands of small and medium producers. Several of them do not have licenses as many of the items used in defence equipment also have civilian application. Therefore, the requirement of licenses for the manufacture of defence-related items not only complicates the existing situation but also destroys individual and entrepreneurial initiatives.

Introduce Offset Credit Trading

The 2008 procedure has introduced offset banking. According to the guidelines, offset banking is permissible for a maximum of two-and-a-half years. Given the lead time available from the time RFPs are issued, this time-frame may be around 5 years or even 10 depending on the completion schedule of the project. This is a very positive step and has been very widely welcomed. But the bankable years should not end with the end of the project as "rather than linked to the life of a specific offset project, the technology strategy needs to embrace productive opportunities across the broader economy. Offset policy thus needs to be framed accordingly." It has been estimated that credit transfers account for around 7.5 per cent of all offset transactions and that the banking of offsets has resulted in a trend to permit offset commitments over longer periods of time covering several projects rather than limited to specific projects. This will undoubtedly give confidence to foreign firms hoping to bag Indian contracts get a return for their investment. But this alone is not enough. The most encouraging step will be to introduce offset trading.

Offset trading is the sale of credits accumulated by firms over a defined period. The introduction of this provision will make it possible to sell offset credits to any firm that bags a contract in India and has certain offset obligations to fulfil. It will yield several benefits. First, every prospective firm that is hopeful of bagging any defence contract in India will be assured return on their investment even if they are unsuccessful in securing the contract they may have targeted. It may at least ensure that they may have no losses and also obtain profit in many cases.

This may motivate firms to shed their fears of investing in the military sector in India. Second, India has attractive factors of production. The prospect of offset trading will only increase the willingness of foreign firms to capitalise on these advantages and invest in the defence sector in India. While allowing offset trading, government can also consider prescribing diminishing value to credits over a period of time unless there is value addition to the product. This will encourage firms to sustain their investments in India over a longer time horizon. Third, a firm that is already discharging its offset obligations can continue producing defence equipment over a longer period of time, hoping to accumulate credits for future contracts. Even if it does not bag the contract it may have hoped to, it will be able to trade the offsets. This policy can lead to a win-win situation for both foreign firms and India. The key to success is the prosperity of all the key stakeholders and hope of future profits for investors. Nothing else will succeed. Success will come from giving foreign firms the incentive to sustain their interests in India by encouraging innovativeness and hope of profits through it.

Directing Offsets

The 2008 procedure (Annexure-VI) lists the defence products that qualify for the discharge of offset obligations. This list is generic in nature and ranges from small arms to directed energy weapon systems. In effect, there is no precise direction in which offsets are channelised. Any vendor will be well within his right to produce any item related to the aforementioned list to fulfil its offset obligations. But this will not yield optimum results.

For instance, it has been concluded that the Netherlands and Switzerland have been able to displace jobs in the US through offset arrangements by transferring production facilities to themselves. To achieve this, the two nations exercised careful control to ensure the "precise direction in which offset-resources are steered. Almost never are they aimed at increasing indigenous military production capacity." In the study by Brauer, he has cited Molas-Gallart to argue that Spain had to abandon its dream of an "integrated, comprehensive, indigenous industry to be generated via arms trade offsets." It was also argued that when offsets are bureaucratically mandated and applied to some vaguely specified national interests, net benefits may not exist. Therefore, prescribing a generic list from which offset obligations are to be chosen for implementation may not be the best strategy to serve India's defence needs. This issue deserves further examination.

India is a nation that has a reasonable defence industrial capability. It is more advanced in some areas than in others. For instance, in the field of naval shipbuilding, India has been able to achieve a fair degree of indigenisation and in some cases around 76 per cent. India today is designing stealth frigates and constructing them in Indian yards. But almost all the weapon systems are imported though India has developed and is using many indigenous sensors. Therefore, for instance, the navy should be able to identify areas of high priority such as the weapon systems that it will prefer to produce indigenously and incorporate them in the list.

Through this process, the benefits of offset can be channelised into identified areas. For instance, given the plan of the navy for a 160-plus ship force by 2022 from the 145 that it has at present, a prospective vendor will be inclined to invest in identified areas included in the list to: 1) fulfil its offset obligations; 2) accumulate offset credits knowing that orders for the weapons or other naval items will be assured for a known period, given the navy's maritime plan; and 3) be reasonably assured of future orders.

Assured of continuing orders, firms will also be inclined to provide value addition over time. To give further impetus to foreign vendors to endeavour towards this goal, a system of procurement through repeat orders, say for 10 years or so, from the same source that had produced indigenously such critical items should be seriously considered. Provision of value addition, etc., can also be made mandatory for such repeat orders. Similarly, critical items for the three services can be compiled and included in the list eligible for discharging offset obligations.

INDIA'S ECONOMIC POLICIES

Many early post-independence leaders, such as Nehru, were influenced by socialist ideas and advocated government intervention to guide the economy, including state ownership of key industries. The objective was to achieve high and balanced economic development in India in the general interest while particular programs and measures helped the poor. India's leaders also believed that industrialization was the key to economic development.

This belief was all the more convincing in India because of the country's large size, substantial natural resources, and desire to develop its own defence industries. The Industrial Policy Resolution of 1948 gave government a monopoly in armaments, atomic energy, and railroads, and exclusive rights to develop minerals, the iron and steel industries, aircraft manufacturing, shipbuilding, and manufacturing of telephone and telegraph equipment. Private companies operating in those fields were guaranteed at least ten years more of ownership before the government could take them over. Some still operate as private companies in India.

The Industrial Policy Resolution of 1956 greatly extended the preserve of government. There were seventeen industries exclusively in the public sector. The Indian government took the lead in another twelve industries, but private companies could also engage in production.

This resolution covered industries producing capital and intermediate goods. As a result, the private sector was relegated primarily to production of consumer goods. The public sector also expanded into more services. In 1956 the life insurance business was nationalized, and in 1973 the general insurance business was also acquired by the public sector. Most large commercial banks in India were nationalized in 1969. Over the years, the central and state governments formed agencies, and companies engaged in finance, trading, mineral exploitation, manufacturing, utilities, and transportation. The public sector was extensive and influential throughout the economy, although the value of its assets was small relative to the private sector.

Controls over prices, production, and the use of foreign exchange, which were imposed by the British during World

War II, were reinstated soon after independence. The Industries (Development and Regulation) Act of 1951 and the Essential Commodities Act of 1955 (with subsequent additions) provided the legal framework for the government to extend price controls that eventually included steel, cement, drugs, nonferrous metals, chemicals, fertilizer, coal, automobiles, tires and tubes, cotton textiles, food grains, bread, butter, vegetable oils, and other commodities. By the late 1950s, controls were pervasive, regulating investment in industry, prices of many commodities, imports and exports, and the flow of foreign exchange.

Export growth in India was long ignored. The government's extensive controls and pervasive licensing requirements created imbalances and structural problems in many parts of the economy. Controls were usually imposed to correct specific problems but often without adequate consideration of their effect on other parts of the economy.

For example, government of India set low prices for basic foods, transportation, and other commodities and services, a policy designed to protect the living standards of the poor. However, the policy proved counterproductive when the government also limited the output of needed goods and services. Price ceilings were implemented during shortages, but the ceiling frequently contributed to black markets in those commodities and to tax evasion by black-market participants. Import controls and tariff policy stimulated local manufacturers toward production of import-substitution goods, but under conditions devoid of sufficient competition or pressure to be efficient.

Private trading and industrial conglomerates (the so-called large houses) existed under the British and continued after independence. The government viewed the conglomerates with suspicion, believing that they often manipulated markets and prices for their own profit. After independence the government instituted licensing controls on new businesses, especially in manufacturing, and on expanding capacity in existing businesses. In the 1960s, when shortages of goods were extensive, considerable criticism was levelled at traders for manipulating markets and prices.

The result was the 1970 Monopolies and Restrictive Practices Act, which was designed to provide the government with additional information on the structure and investments of all firms that had assets of more than Rs200 million, to strengthen the licensing system in order to decrease the concentration of private economic power, and to place restraints on certain business practices considered contrary to the public interest. The act emphasized the government's aversion to large companies in the private sector, but critics contended that the act resulted from political motives and not from a strong case against big firms. The act and subsequent enforcement restrained private investment.

The extensive controls, the large public sector, and the many government programs contributed to a substantial growth in the administrative structure of government. Indian government also sought to take on many of the unemployed. The result was a swollen, inefficient bureaucracy that took inordinate amounts of time to process applications and forms. Business leaders complained that they spent more time getting government approval than running their companies. Many observers also reported extensive corruption in the huge bureaucracy. One consequence was the development of a large underground economy in small-scale enterprises and the services sector.

India's current economic reforms began in 1985 when the government abolished some of its licensing regulations and other competition-inhibiting controls. Since 1991 more "new economic policies" or reforms have been introduced. Reforms include currency devaluations and making currency partially convertible, reduced quantitative restrictions on imports, reduced import duties on capital goods, decreases in subsidies, liberalized interest rates, abolition of licenses for most industries, the sale of shares in selected public enterprises, and tax reforms.

Although many observers welcomed these changes and attributed the faster growth rate of the economy in the late 1980s to them, others feared that these changes would create more problems than they solved. The growing dependence of the economy on imports, greater vulnerability of its balance of payments, reliance on debt, and the consequent susceptibility to outside pressures on economic policy directions caused concern. The increase in consumerism and the display of conspicuous wealth by the elite exacerbated these fears.

The pace of liberalization increased after 1991. By the mid-1990s, the number of sectors reserved for public ownership was slashed, and private-sector investment was encouraged in areas such as energy, steel, oil refining and exploration, road building, air transportation, and telecommunications. An area still closed to the private sector in the mid-1990s was defence industry. Foreign-exchange regulations in India were liberalized, foreign investment was encouraged, and import regulations were simplified. The average import-weighted tariff was reduced from 87 percent in FY 1991 to 33 percent in FY 1994. Despite these changes, the economy remained highly regulated by international standards. The import of many consumer goods was banned, and the production of 838 items, mostly consumer goods, was reserved for companies with total investment of less than Rs6 million. Although the government had sold off minority stakes in public-sector companies, it had not in 1995 given up control of any enterprises, nor had any of the loss-making public companies been closed down. Moreover, although import duties had been lowered substantially, they were still high compared to most other countries.

Political successes in the mid-1990s by nationalist-oriented political parties led to some backlash against foreign investment in some parts of India. In early 1995, official charges of serving adulterated products were made against a KFC outlet in Bangalore, and Pepsi-Cola products were smashed and advertisements defaced in New Delhi. The most serious backlash occurred in Maharashtra in August 1995 when the Bharatiya Janata Party (BJP—Indian People's Party)-led state government halted construction of a US$2.8 million 2,015-megawatt gas-fired electric-power plant being built near Bombay (Mumbai in the Marathi language) by another United States company, Enron Corporation.

5

Defence Production and Supply

The Department of Defence Production and Department of Supply set up in 1965 were merged in 1984 to constitute the Department of Defence Production and Supplies. Presently, 39 Ordnance factories and eight Defence Public Sector Undertakings (DPSUs) come under this department. The Directorate of Quality Assurance, Air Technical Development and Production (Air), Standardisation, and Exhibition Organisation also form part of this Department. The Ordnance Factories produce more than 1,500 items of arms, ammunition, equipment and components. Most of these products constitute relatively low to medium technology items. Twenty per cent of the output goes to non-defence customers. Due to the very high cost of production, delivery delays and suspect quality, it has not been possible to meet export targets and, sometimes, even orders given by the Services. Ordnance factories as well as DPSUs need to shed the manufacture of low technology items to the private sector and focus on hi-tech products. They should also be in a position to take up substantial product improvement themselves and not be dependent on DRDO.

DEFENCE PLANNING INSTRUMENTS

In recent years, defence economics and management techniques have made an important contribution to defence planning. A number of techniques such as Operational Research and Systems Analysis (ORSA), Planning

Programming and Budgeting System have been developed to make the planning process more systematic and to maximise the benefits obtained from the given amount of resources. Systems Analysis can assist in developing rational procedures for procurement of new weapons systems. Systems performance at design stage can be evaluated through computer simulation. Planners all over the world are using computerised war-gaming techniques and structure analysis. Prospects exist for a more enlightened approach that can bring together military officers, historians, technologists and quantitative analysts. In many countries, there is a growing interest in analytical realism, operational relevance and integrated defence planning. In India the Services are far behind in introducing these aids in our defence planning system. The planning directorates in Service Headquarters do not even have data banks which can provide relevant information on a specified subject. Most of the planners have high combat and command qualifications but little clue of the modern techniques. There is an urgent need to introduce modern planning aids into our planning system. Defence planners should also learn the basic principles and techniques of economic analysis and not leave it to their 'Finance' colleagues.

MANAGEMENT OF DEFENCE BUDGET

A major lacuna in defence planning and implementation has been lack of financial commitment for the Plan period. Financially, the defence plans are treated more as annual plans rather than composite five years plan. There is a rush to spend the annual capital budget by the end of the financial year since the amount not spent has to be surrendered. In FY 2004-05, the previous government had proposed to institute a non-lapsable Defence Modernisation Fund of Rs 25,000 crore. This was a long awaited reform in the defence-finance mechanism as budgeted capital expenditure worth thousands of crores was surrendered year after year. However, the new government, being of the view that there are no provisions in the budgetary rules and regulations to carry forward unspent funds for three years, has done away with this reform. It needs to be pointed out that a similar procedure was being followed in the 1930s and 1940s. The provisions invoked at that time need to be studied carefully and could be used as a precedent. Action should be taken expeditiously to revive the Defence Modernization Fund.

Otherwise, funds earmarked for capital expenditure on an annual basis will continue to lapse, leading to lack of systematic defence preparedness. In the Revenue Budget, there is a need to include incentives to save and reduce annual maintenance expenditure without adversely affecting operational efficiency. It is also necessary to exploit the increasing domestic industrial capability to support the existing infrastructure and thus reduce maintenance costs and enhance the quality of maintenance.

Human Resources Management

The development of human resources must keep pace with the modernisation of the armed forces so that new, state-of-the-art equipment can be optimally exploited by well trained and motivated soldiers, sailors and airmen. The age profile of military personnel, particularly in the Army, and the age of commanders at battalion and brigade levels needs to be looked into. Currently, a soldier has to serve for 15 to 17 years to earn his pension. When he retires, besides the lifelong pension that has to be paid, a trained individual is lost to the nation. Similarly, while there is a shortage of approximately 14,000 officers, most officers retire in rank of Lieutenant Colonel or Colonel at the age of 52-54 years when they still have years of productive life ahead though they are no longer fit for active combat.

Innovative measures need to be adopted to reduce the effects of the current national loss on this account. The best method would be to institute a procedure of 'lateral induction" under which both officers and personnel below officer rank can be transferred to central police and paramilitary forces (CPMFs). The colour (active) service of jawans should be reduced to 7-10 years with no pension liability after which the volunteers are transferred to the BSF, CRPF, ITBP, CISF and other such forces.

Similarly, the Shipping Corporation of India, National Port Trust and other such maritime organisations can fruitfully employ Naval personnel. Ex-servicemen will be expected to serve in these organisations till superannuation, after which they would be entitled to pension. This will improve the age profile of the Services, provide trained manpower to the CPMFs, ensure productive long-term employment for a large number of trained men till superannuation, and also reduce the pension bill of the Central Government. The Army should increase the recruitment of Short Service Officers to make up its shortfall. Induction of these officers to the CPMFs after five years of service will improve junior leadership and effectiveness of these forces in internal security and counter insurgency operations.

Recommendations

- Given the fluid strategic environment and the rapid advances in defence technology, there is a need for judicious allocation of the limited budgetary resources. Long lead times are required for creating futuristic Forces, hence the need to make long-term defence planning mandatory. Greater synergy between defence and development plans is required.
- The lack of a cohesive national security strategy and defence policy has resulted in inadequate political direction regarding politico-military objectives. The Government should prepare a clear national security strategy, defence policy, and review it every 4-5 years.
- In view of the time taken to create the capabilities necessary for facing future threats and challenges, it

is essential for the Defence Services to evolve 10 to 15-year perspective plans with the required budgetary support.

- The Chiefs of Staff Committee has not been successful in preparing comprehensive 'integrated defence plans' due to emphasis on single Service planning and constant competition among the Services for a bigger share of resources. The civilian bureaucrats in the MoD do not have the professional expertise to decide on inter-Service priorities. Hence, the early appointment of Chief of Defence Staff (CDS) is essential as he will be the cornerstone for integrated defence and operational planning.
- A non-lapsable Defence Modernisation Fund must be expeditiously created to ensure that allocations are optimally utilised and funds earmarked for capital acquisitions are not allowed to lapse.
- The Revenue Budget of the Services needs to be better managed. Annual maintenance expenditure can be curtailed by greater exploitation of the available public and private sector industrial infrastructure capability and offering incentives to the Services to save.
- To ensure smooth progress towards self-reliance in defence technology, the Government must undertake a periodic performance audit of the DRDO plans and projects. The review should reinforce efforts in areas of success and weed out unproductive projects.
- Ordnance Factories should produce only hi-tech products and shed the production of low-tech items to the private sector.
- Integrated Defence Staff and the Services' perspective planners should acquire expertise in operational research and systems analysis, as also financial planning, for evolving complex integrated defence plans.

- In order to improve the age profile of the Services and simultaneously reduce the pension bill of the Central Government, personnel below officer rank should be transferred to central police and paramilitary forces (CPMFs) after active service of 7-10 years.
- The Army should increase recruitment of Short Service Officers to make up its shortfall. Induction of these officers to the CPMFs after five years of service will improve junior leadership and effectiveness of these forces in internal security and counter insurgency operations.

Defence planning has been neglected for long in India. This has led to ad-hocism in decision-making and adversely affected the modernisation plans of the Services. The key issues needing immediate attention include the need for formal prior approval for five-year defence Plans, better management of the defence revenue and capital acquisition budgets, streamlining of the defence procurement process and better human resources management. The Government of India should appoint a group of eminent experts to study the present defence planning process, identify the lacunae and grey areas in the process and recommend structural and procedural changes. The aim should be to streamline defence planning, harmonize it with national development plans, and make the process more responsive in order to deal effectively with the rapidly changing geo-strategic and regional security environment.

THE STATE DEFENCE CONCEPT

The goal of the State Defence Concept is to define the guidelines for strengthening and improving the defence system in accordance with Latvia's geopolitical situation and Latvia's obligations to the collective security of the North Atlantic Treaty Organisation (hereinafter – NATO), of which Latvia is preparing to become a full member in the middle of 2004. The Concept determines the basic strategic principles that will guide the implementation of the tasks associated with state defence and is the basis for planning the development of the National Armed Forces (hereinafter – NAF). The State Defence Concept is formulated on the basis of Analysis of Endangerment to the State, the Military Risk Analysis and forecasted trends in the development of international security. The state's defence policy and strategy have been formulated to avert possible threats. The Constitution of the Republic of Latvia [Satversme], the National Security Concept and Foreign Policy Concept and other regulations adopted by the Republic of Latvia determine principles, goals, tasks and legal mechanisms of state defence.

Latvia's regulations and action plans related to state defence are updated in accordance with the basic principles of the State Defence Concept. The goal of the State Defence Concept is to define the guidelines for strengthening and improving the defence system in accordance with Latvia's geopolitical situation and Latvia's obligations to the collective security of the North Atlantic Treaty Organisation (hereinafter – NATO), of which Latvia is preparing to become a full member in the middle of 2004. The Concept determines the basic strategic principles that will guide the implementation of the tasks associated with state defence and is the basis for planning the development of the National Armed Forces (hereinafter – NAF).

The State Defence Concept is formulated on the basis of Analysis of Endangerment to the State, the Military Risk Analysis and forecasted trends in the development of international security. The state's defence policy and strategy have been formulated to avert possible threats. The Constitution of the Republic of Latvia [Satversme], the National Security Concept and Foreign Policy Concept and other regulations adopted by the Republic of Latvia determine principles, goals, tasks and legal mechanisms of state defence. Latvia's regulations and action plans related to state defence are updated in accordance with the basic principles of the State Defence Concept.

SECRET SECTOR IN DEFENCE PRODUCTION

The Government of India has been reiterating its commitment to achieve the much-publicised target of procuring 70 per cent of its defence requirements from indigenous sources by 2010. Despite its best efforts over the last two decades, India is nowhere near that figure as yet. The Government is well aware of the emergence of private sector as a vibrant and dynamic force, especially in information technology, service sector and manufacturing fields. It has come to realise that self reliance would remain a pipe dream if it continued to bank on public sector alone. One of the objectives mentioned in the new defence procurement procedure is to achieve self-reliance in defence equipment. But the whole procedure is silent about the role of the private sector and no worthwhile initiatives have been proposed to integrate its potential in India's quest for self reliance.

In addition to economic factors, defence industry is generally considered to be an instrument of national sovereignty and pride. Defence industry comprises of all industrial undertakings engaged in the production of hardware and services for use by the defence forces. The origin of the Indian defence industry can be traced to the establishment of Gun and Shell Factory at Cossipore in 1801. At the time of the Independence, India had 16 Ordnance Factories, established by the British to produce low tech items. Bharat Electronics Ltd was the first Defence Public Sector Undertaking (DPSU) established in 1954 to manufacture electronic equipment for the forces. Today, India has 39 Ordnance Factories and eight DPSU.

The Industrial Policy Resolution of 1956 divided industry into three parts:-

- Schedule A: Basic industries which are the preserve of the state, including defence and heavy engineering.

- Schedule B: Industries in which private industry was allowed to operate.
- Schedule C: All other industries.

Manufacture of components, assemblies and sub-assemblies was thrown open to the private sector in 1991. With a view to promote defence-industry partnership, the Ministry of Defence (MoD) constituted six Joint Task Forces in collaboration with Confederation of Indian Industry in 1998. Consequent to their recommendations, the Government opened defence production to the private sector in January 2002. It allowed 100 percent private equity with 26 percent Foreign Direct Investment (FDI). It was a major policy change. Subsequently, the Department of Industrial Policy and Promotion issued detailed guidelines for the issuance of licence for the production of arms and ammunition.

The Kelkar Committee, constituted in 2004, made many radical recommendations. The Government has accepted a majority of them but their implementation has lacked earnestness and focus. The Department of Industrial Policy & Promotion (DIPP), in consultation with Ministry of Defence, has so far issued 37 letters of intent for the manufacture of various types of defence hardware which include armoured and combat vehicles, radars, electronic warfare equipment, warships, submarines, avionics, military aircraft, safety and ballistic products, armaments and ammunition.

Despite the above measures, there has been no discernible change in the ground situation. Only a handful of India's top companies are involved in small value defence contracts. The private sector has to remain content with the supply of some low-tech items to the public sector. Its supplies to DPSU and Ordnance Factories grossed over Rs. 1200 crores and Rs. 1900 crores respectively last year. Whereas these figures signify the contribution made by the private sector, they also highlight the fact that the private sector continues to be merely an outsourcing base for the public sector.

CONTINUED NON-PARTICIPATION OF THE PRIVATE SECTOR

A number of defence-industry seminars, conferences and exhibitions have been held in the recent years. Given decades of insulation and prejudices, this was no small achievement. But old mindsets, complexity of procurement procedures and clout wielded by the public sector have been acting as major deterrents to any meaningful participation of the private sector. New aspirants, in particular, find the whole regime to be highly forbidding.

Policy and Procedural Issues

Decisions are taken by the Defence Acquisition Council to categorise a proposal as 'Buy' or 'Buy and Make' or 'Make' based on the advice given by Defence Research and Development Organisation and the public sector. No inputs are sought from the private sector. Its competence and potential are given no consideration. In all deals where transfer of technology is negotiated, the nominated recipient is always a DPSU, even if a private sector company is better placed in terms of infrastructure and know-how to absorb the technology. A DPSU may have to establish complete facilities ab initio, whereas a private sector company may need only incremental technology.

Requirements of the armed forces are not made known to the private sector sufficiently in advance, with the result that it does not get adequate time, either to scout for foreign tie-ups or to establish the necessary facilities. The time given for the submission of technical and commercial proposals is grossly inadequate for a new entrant in the field. Parameters for the equipment to be procured are formulated with foreign equipment in mind, after reading manufacturers' brochures. Private sector is not consulted in this process, whereas minor acceptable changes in parameters may make the Indian equipment eligible for consideration. As Requests for Proposals (RFP) are issued to foreign original equipment manufacturers as well, they prefer direct bidding. They decline joint ventures with Indian companies as it helps them to guard their technology and perpetuate their monopoly with consequent financial gains. All trials are carried out on 'No Cost No Commitment' basis. Whereas foreign vendors can incur the expenditure involved, many upcoming indigenous companies do not possess the necessary financial strength. This acts as a major disincentive.

Functional Issues

Due to the very nature of its usage, defence equipment has to meet highly exacting standards. There can be no failure in the face of the enemy. Regrettably, many Indian vendors have not fully grasped the import of this requirement and find the quality control regime to be extremely irksome. Every producer seeks economies of scale and assured continuous orders. Unfortunately, Indian procurement regime precludes both. RFPs are issued for one-time piecemeal quantities without indicating the envisaged total requirement over a period of time. Additionally, no long term commitment is made regarding regular flow of orders. This deters Indian companies from committing resources for establishing production facilities as the venture can prove both expensive and risky.

Lack of Mutual Confidence

The Indian public sector has got used to a position of pre-eminence. Its hold over defence orders is total. It thrives because of its monopolistic clout and not because of any displayed excellence. It is fully aware of its weaknesses and knows that it cannot survive an open competition with the private sector. This sense of insecurity makes it wary of any move to facilitate the entry of the private sector and it tries all stratagems to block it. On the other hand, many functionaries feel that the private sector is out to make a quick buck and lacks required perseverance. They tend to view the private sector as traders rather than committed manufacturers who can endure the travails of long drawn procurement procedure. According to them, anyone desirous of entering defence industry has to be fully aware of the fact that defence orders take inordinately long to materialise and vacillation invariably proves unproductive.

The Communication Gap

There is a total absence of an effective institutionalised interface between the MoD, the services and the private sector for regular interaction at the policy making level. There are a number of 'groups' or 'partnership forums' in place, but their utility is limited to exchange of views only.

Procurement Agencies are Unaware of Industry's Potential : The procurement agencies are extremely keen to encourage indigenous production and limit imports to the minimum inescapable requirements. They, however, are unaware of the capabilities and potential of different private sector companies, as the competence of Indian companies has not been authentically catalogued as yet. They do not know whom to invite for submission of proposals. It is much easier to acquire details of numerous foreign producers.

There is no data bank of Indian industries available with the MoD. Requests for Proposals (RFPs) are issued only to a few highly visible companies, while many others lose by default. Although, the Acquisition Wing has been tasked to create the necessary data bank, the process has hardly taken off as yet.

Industry Lacks Knowledge of Defence Requirements and Procedures : On the other hand, many private sector companies have the capability to manufacture the whole range of defence requirements but do not know whom to approach to ascertain details. They are ignorant of the procurement agencies, their policies and procedures. This ignorance makes them wary of dealing with the defence. To compound the problem, there are over 150 different defence procurement agencies with different procedures. There is no system of centralised notification of requirements and vendor registration. Due to this lacuna, a new entrant finds the whole environment highly dissuasive.

The Way Forward

The present process of interaction between the Government, public sector and private enterprises should be continued, albeit with renewed vigour and purpose. All joint committees should be represented at the level of decision makers, so that follow up action can be taken in a time bound manner.

Structural Reforms

A representative of the designated industry association should be a permanent invitee to the Defence Acquisition Council, depending on the security sensitivity of agenda points. His inputs as regards the technical prowess of the private sector will prove invaluable while deciding whether to import technology or not. Similarly, selected agenda points of Defence Procurement Board, Defence Production Board and Defence Development Board should be circulated to the industry association for advice. These steps will go a long way in integrating the private sector.

INDUSTRY ON ACQUISITION PROPOSALS

The Acquisition Wing should indicate broad parameters of equipment under procurement to the industry association six months prior to the issuance of RFP. The association could circulate this information amongst the concerned companies for their advance knowledge. This will give adequate time to the interested companies to carry out technology scan and scout for foreign collaborations, if required. Equipment Directorates of the Services Headquarters should seek advice of the industry before finalising parameters. The industry, with its massive pool of knowledge, will be able to help the authorities in getting a better understanding of the latest technological advancements worldwide and in India with their degree of stabilisation. Comments received from the association should compulsorily be put up to the approving committee. In some non-critical cases, indigenous capability may even influence the formulation of parameters. To help the Indian companies in taking decisions regarding investment of resources, RFP should invariably indicate the total requirement envisaged over the years. This could be without any firm commitment as such.

Support to Indigenous Industry

Most nations support indigenous producers by giving them purchase and price preference. Foreign producers should be given incentives for collaborations with Indian companies. It could even be made mandatory, as has been done by Great Britain under its Industrial Participation policy. Policy on grant of waivers for deviations from parameters must make a distinction between an Indian and a foreign producer. Easier grant of waivers, albeit within acceptable limits, to Indian companies will encourage them to commit resources more willingly. Even commercial terms should be made more favourable to the local vendors as the lower life-cycle cost of indigenous equipment must also be factored in.

Presently, the payment terms are unfavourable to the Indian producers. Foreign vendors are released full payment of their dues on submission of proof of dispatch (against performance and warranty bonds-each equivalent to 5 percent of contract value). However, Indian companies get payment only after the issuance of inspection note by the designated inspectors. This may take a few months, thereby increasing the cost of the capital involved. This incongruity needs to be addressed.

Facilitation Service

There is an urgent need to have a mechanism in place to facilitate the participation of Indian private sector in defence industry. Such a mechanism can serve twin objectives. First, it could assist in the assessment of a company's current technical/manufacturing prowess and its potential for the development of defence products. A directory of credible defence manufacturers should be compiled with details of all assessed companies. This directory should be made available to all the defence procurement agencies to assist them to identify companies for issuance of tenders. The directory could also help foreign producers to locate potential Indian partners for collaboration.

Secondly, advisory service could be extended to companies as regards the availability of opportunities for the supply of their current products to the defence. The service could also suggest defence products which a company can manufacture with marginal addition to its facilities. Related areas for development/diversification could also be indicated. Thus, this service can acquaint a company with the prevailing business opportunities and guide it as well.

PUBLIC-PRIVATE SECTOR PARTNERSHIP

The public sector possesses excellent infrastructure, manufacturing facilities and a highly experienced task force. It will be a waste of national resources if these assets are duplicated by the private sector. The private sector, on the other hand, can bring in latest technology, managerial practices, marketing skills and financial management. Therefore, a well-blended fusion of both will result in synergising of their strengths through economies of scale and prove mutually beneficial. A strong and fruitful relationship can be built with mutual accommodation. The public sector should not regard private players as a persistent irritant and adopt a confrontationist attitude towards them. Similarly, the private sector must not seek to replace the public sector. Such an approach may be perceived by the public sector as a threat to their primacy and existence. It may make them close their ranks and resist all interaction with the private sector. That shall be counter-productive.

The Government has to realise that both public and private sectors are national assets and harnessing of their potential is essential if India wants to achieve self reliance in defence production. It should not play favourites and treat both as equal partners in progress.

The then Defence Minister of India, Mr Pranab Mukherjee, in his address at New Delhi in June 2005 had stated: "The Government is committed to the development of a vibrant and proactive defence industry in India. It should be ensured that the available capability, infrastructure and resources including intellectual capital are harnessed to the fullest extent as our national assets and optimally utilised in achieving this objective." He further advocated a strong and healthy partnership between the public and private sector for enhancing the defence capability and in sustaining a powerful domestic industrial base for the future.

During the last three years, a serious and concerted effort has been made by the Government to reform and streamline the entire acquisition process. The Government has come to appreciate the potential of the private sector and wants it to complement the efforts of the public sector. A number of praiseworthy initiatives have been taken and policies reviewed. Yet, the results on ground have very little to show. There has been no appreciable inflow of anticipated foreign funds. Even today all major defence deals are signed with foreign producers. The public sector continues to get bulk orders under transfer of imported technology. The private sector continues to be a peripheral participant with the production of some low-tech items and indigenisation of some components.

The present process of interaction and integration should be continued, albeit with renewed vigour and purpose. All joint committees should be represented at the level of decision makers so that the follow up action can be implemented in a time bound manner. There is no point in having committees and joint task forces if their reports are going to gather dust with no follow up action. Technological prowess of the private sector should be given due recognition and considered a national asset. The objective of achieving self-reliance will remain elusive unless the private sector is duly integrated and its potential fully harnessed to build a viable indigenous defence industrial base. The Government has to create an environment wherein the private sector feels assured of just business opportunities, level playing ground and fair play.

And finally, India plans to spend USD 100 billion on capital expenditure during the 7th Plan Period (2007-12). Imports account for close to 70 percent of capital expenditure and offsets are required equal to 30 percent of import contracts. Thus, India expects offset trade worth USD 21 billion during the next five years. Currently, Indian defence exports amount to paltry USD 50 million annually, i.e. USD 250 million in five years. From USD 250 million to USD 21 billion, it will be a quantum jump of enormous proportions. The public sector cannot handle it by itself. The private sector has to be closely integrated and its potential fully harnessed for beneficial absorption of the projected offset business.

6

Defence Budgets and Plans

In the budgets estimates for 2002-03, Rs 67,200 crore (and a net of Rs 65,000 crore) was provided for revenue and capital expenditure under Defence Services Estimates. Going by present trends, there is likely to be a big surrender of funds in the Revised Estimate (RE). In 2001-02, about Rs 5,000 crore was surrendered at the RE stage, and the actual expenditure was still less. In relative terms, the situation was not much different in 2000-01.

The shortfall has been more pronounced in capital expenditure. Despite adequate funds allocation, the expected expenditure on modernisation has not taken place due to inadequate planning, exposing the weak links between the planning effort and budgets. Under the capital head, a total of Rs 21,410.63 crore was allocated in this year's budget, from which a significant amount is likely to be surrendered. One wonders what would have happened had the allocation for capital expenditure been around Rs 26,000 crore, as was recommended by the Ministry of Defence (MoD) to the Finance Ministry (MoF), and brought out by the report of the Standing Committee of Parliament. Even for 2001-02, the Committee viewed seriously the unspent funds of Rs 5,000 crore, out of which Rs 3,000 crore was for capital expenditure for procurement of new weapons systems. Proposals for a "Non-lapsable fund" made by MoD to MoF has not evoked any positive response from the latter. This, however, is no solution. Let's face it: our budgetary system, by focusing attention on one year only, does not allow for proper planning of expenditure. Beyond a point, procurement procedures cannot be simplified as the amounts involved are large, commitments required to be made for several years in advance and every attempt made to procure the best system suited to our requirement. Further, it should be a transparent system to avoid allegations of mismanagement. So the clamour for simplifying procurement process should cease.

Rather, we should institute a budgetary system that aids planning for modernisation. It would be of immense help to Service Headquarters in their planning exercise to meet future conflict scenarios if they were assured of a steady and continued allotment rather than receive generous allotments for a few years followed by a dearth of resources or vice versa. This allocation should be on monetary terms rather than be linked to an uncertain factor like a percentage of GDP, so that expenditure plans can be formulated for a sequence of future years.

How different would have been the position if in 1999-00 itself, MoD had received indications about the likely allotment of funds up to 2003-04. In the UK, for instance, under the Public Expenditure Survey (PES) procedure, every autumn, the House of Commons is provided with the government's public expenditure White Paper with projections of the total defence expenditure for the next three years. In the US, the defence department generates a five-year resource programme and eight years of forces, so Congress can see the future financial implications in obligational terms of projects just starting. The UK model has more to commend itself to the Indian situation: there is more commitment to future budgets under the Public Expenditure System than under the US programme, and is a contribution to budgetary planning at the highest level. This provides the required stability to the availability of resources for planning purposes. By publishing the PES, the government is committed to a planned level of defence spending for about three years.

The heart of the process is long-term planning, called Long Term Costing (LTC) which the MoD prepared annually, indicating their plans for the next 10 years. The LTC plan incorporates forecast of future force structure and is sent to the Treasury annually in May to be fed into the public expenditure system, which leads finally to the budgetary allocations. This is how the budget is systematically liked to expenditure plans.

What has been the Indian experience of linking budget to plans? The first Five Year defence plan was formulated for 1964-69, followed by the Second Plan (1969-74). There were also roll-on plans. Plans were formulated, reviewed and modified, keeping in view the change in the security environment, hike in oil prices, etc. Finalisation of plans have generally been delayed because of a significant gap between Services' projections of requirements and the resources actually available. The Seventh Plan could be finalised only in the last year of the plan and the Eighth Plan (1992-97) was not finalised at all. There was a huge gap between plan outlays and resources allocation. Though the Seventh Defence Plan had visualised an outlay of Rs 71,938 crore, the aggregate allocation during the five years amounted to Rs 58,188 crore only. Since the Eighth Plan was never sanctioned, no comparison can be made between the amount allotted under budgets and the envisaged plan outlay for 1992-97.

The allocation for defence is, in principle, inseparable from allocation for other purposes and prospects of availability of resources now and in the future. A proper framework for expenditure plan for all Central government activities for the next three years can be put in position by following a system like the PES in the UK.

As far as operating expenses are concerned, a certain degree of planning is now possible because of the New

Management Strategy (NMS), which has led to the institution of Authority and Responsibility Centres and Budget Centres with significant delegation of powers, on the UK model. But it must be realised that without instituting a public expenditure system, which provides indications about likely budgets for the next 3-4 years, it is not possible to derive maximum benefit from the new system. Each budget-holder should know what is likely to be his budget for the next 3-4 years in order to plan his expenditure properly. For the first time, this year there will be a Volume II to Defence Services estimate, which will show the allocation of funds budget Centre-wise and would be used for internal control purposes by MoD. This is a good step forward.

For planning defence expenditure, multi-year budgeting is imperative. In the US in 1987, in response to a recommendation by the Packard Commission, the Department of Defence has shifted to a two-year budget while still retaining its five-year planning horizon.

The formulation of Five Year plans at periodic intervals, which lose its relevance because of the changing security scenario and technological progress and which provides no basis for a budget may be given up as it serves no worthwhile purpose. Rather, a long-term plan for force structure and supporting services should be introduced and updated every year in the pattern of LTC. This should be the basis for introducing a multi-year budgeting system in India for the defence sector. This would indeed be the next logical step after the introduction of the Authority and Responsibility Centres on the UK pattern. The linkage between plan and budget should be firmly established in a systematic manner.

NATIONAL SECURITY, DEFENCE POLICY AND PLANNING

It is generally acknowledged that the approach to national security requires a comprehensive view of various political, social, economic, technological and strategic aspects. National security implies not only safeguarding territorial boundaries but also that the nation is able to build a cohesive, egalitarian, technologically efficient and progressive society with a good quality of life.

Compared with national security, defence policy is more focused, concerned with the protection of the state and its citizens from direct and indirect (proxy) military threats and actions of other states. In defence planning, the emphasis shifts to national security concerns that are mainly military in nature. There are two concepts at this level: deterrence (including coercive diplomacy) and defence (dissuasion).

Deterrence refers to policies designed to discourage the adversary from taking direct or proxy military action, by raising the cost so that it outweighs the gains that he may wish to attain.

Defence (dissuasion) policies are designed to reduce the capability of the adversary to cause damage—and own costs and risks—in the event deterrence fails. Deterrence and defence are two interwoven strands of defence policy. Defence planning involves the conceptualisation of plans and decisions for the execution of defence policy. Long-term planning for defence is essential for the following reasons:

(a) The existence of a highly fluid strategic environment, which results in continuous shifts and changing profiles of threat and power equations.

(b) To ensure judicious allocation of resources and cost effective utilisation.

(c) Revolution in Military Affairs (RMA), i.e. advances in technology, which result in weapons and equipment systems becoming obsolete at a fast rate.

(d) Lead time required to raise and prepare defence units; to produce or acquire and introduce new weapons and equipment systems.

(e) The changing nature of conflict and reduced reaction time.

(f) Coordination problems between defence, economic, science and technology, infrastructure and industrial activities, as well as among the Defence Forces.

The defence planning process attempts to match the budgetary resources likely to be made available for the requirement to establish the defence capability necessary to face the threats and challenges. This exercise is undertaken in two phases: (a) What should be the proportion allocated to the defence effort as against other areas of national security concerns and economic growth? This exercise involves a 'visionary' analysis of external and internal security threats (often linked) and challenges. In order to minimise adverse affects of high military expenditure on socioeconomic development, it is necessary to harmonise national development planning with defence planning. (b) Optimisation of allocated resources, i.e. distribution of resources within the Ministry of Defence (MoD) based on Force planning (Force and weapons mix, command and control, logistics and human resources management) by the Defence Services to combat current and future threats, and development of required capabilities by the Defence Research and Development Organisation (DRDO), defence production and other agencies concerned.

The quantum of indigenous production and the requirements to be procured from outside are decided in this phase. The objective is to achieve maximum defence capability from the given resources. Both allocation and distribution are closely linked. They need to be reviewed periodically but not so frequently that the planning process becomes ad hoc. In India's case, this is done at five-year intervals.

DEFENCE PLANNING AND SERVICES

Before independence, the defence services worked on a system of contract budget. Defence expenditure was pegged at Rs 55 crore per year, which was more than half of the Central Government's revenue. There was no serious threat from outside (except during World War II, when a fresh agreement was signed) and this amount was more than adequate to maintain the establishment.

The savings were not allowed to lapse but put away in the Defence Reserve Fund that was utilised to finance measures for re-equipment of the Defence Services, thus freeing the Government from having to provide fund money greater than the contract amount. Expenditure on defence rose steeply soon after independence. However, there was no planned effort and defence programmes consisted mainly of outright purchases from abroad, drawing heavily on available Sterling reserves. In the late 1950s, some efforts were made to initiate domestic weapons production by the Ministry of Defence when Mr. Krishna Menon was the Defence Minister. The Sino-Indian conflict in 1962 aroused a new defence consciousness in the country. After taking care of immediate postwar requirements, systematic defence planning started in 1964. Defence requirements were assessed on a five-year basis and the First Five Year Defence Plan (1964-69) was drawn up. This plan took into account the resources available and assistance which could be expected from friendly foreign countries. The plan was primarily based on an expansion and modernisation programme considered necessary by each Service in the light of the respective threat perception assessed. It also proposed a defence production base that would gradually reduce the country's external dependence, provide for improvements in border roads and communications, and a modest expansion of DRDO. The Government recognised the imperative need to synergise 'defence' and 'development' instead of planning each on a separate and unrelated level. The MoD emphasised the "inevitable need to harness all resources of the country for the country's defence and for the defence effort to derive full sustenance from the country's economic development plans".

Thereafter, the National Development Council authorised the Chairman of the Planning Commission to review the needs of both development and defence. A Planning Cell was established in 1965 in the Ministry of Defence 'to deal with the wider aspects of defence planning'. The new system was intended to facilitate medium and long-term defence planning and to maintain constant liaison with the Planning Commission and other ministries. It was expected that the MoD would derive maximum advantage from the development effort by being able to place its priorities for consideration along with the overall economic and industrial plans drawn up by the Planning Commission. The experience of the First Five Year Defence Plan showed that the development of weapons and equipment was a long drawn out process. The Government realised that there could be no forward movement in attaining self-sufficiency in weapons and equipment unless these requirements were planned over a reasonably long period, long enough to cover the span of development and production of new weapons systems and other fighting tools.

The inadequacy of foreign exchange reserves was another hindrance in planning and implementation. In order to mitigate some of these drawbacks, the Second Five Year Defence Plan (1969-74) was instituted on a "roll-on" basis. After a year, an additional year was added so that the Defence Services would have before them a revised and updated five-year plan. In this context, the MoD commented: "Opportunity is taken by this annual exercise to take note of and reflect the change in priorities, the shifts in emphasis and the latest concepts and programmes to reorient the plan within the scheme of resources so that the aims and means are most effectively balanced." This system was expected to facilitate the planning of projects that took five years or more and to revise or eliminate projects, depending on the prevailing foreign exchange situation and availability of domestic resources.

For a period of five years, firm assurances were to be given on the availability of resources. This, unfortunately, never happened. In 1971, it was impossible to adhere to the discipline and the pattern of the roll-on plan. Instead of roll-on annual revisions, immediate requirements dominated the Government's attention that pre-empted plan efforts. In its 1971-72 Annual Report, the MoD acknowledged that having a Planning Cell in the ministry was an insufficient and unsatisfactory method of meeting a crisis.

The Planning Cell was not taken seriously in the crucial stages of economic planning and the argument that defence needs would be adjusted in the over-all allocation of resources was proved wrong. In 1974, an Apex Group headed by the Union Minister for Planning again suggested that steady long-term defence programmes would be more cost effective and economical rather than fluctuating allocations due to periodic economic and security crises. In order to integrate defence planning with the overall economic planning effort, defence and economic development plans were made co-terminus.

Defence Planning Machinery

Most of the defence planning machinery and planning methodology was developed in the decade 1964-74. The Joint Intelligence Committee (JIC) was established in the Cabinet Secretariat to provide external and internal threat assessments. Inputs for this purpose were to be provided by all Intelligence agencies of the Government. The Service Chiefs were to assess the broad military aims and a strategy, coordinated in the Chiefs of Staff Committee, was to be approved by the Defence Minister. However, this was seldom done. Each Service ended up planning its own force level, choice of weapons and equipment, and build-up of infrastructure. In 1977, the Government formed a Committee for Defence Planning (CDP) to "undertake regular assessments relevant to defence planning in the light of all factors having a bearing on national security and defence". However, this committee could not function smoothly nor meet the desired goals.

Planning units were also established in the Department of Defence Production and DRDO. A Planning and Coordination Cell was created in the MoD to coordinate and compile various plans into a 'Defence Plan' for Cabinet approval. As the bureaucrats in the ministry had no professional knowledge or background, this cell could only compile different requirements without any analysis. In Army Headquarters, the Deputy Chief of Army Staff was made responsible for preparing the Army plan. A Perspective Planning Directorate was established in the late 1970s. Naval and Air plans were prepared in the respective Planning Directorates. Financial considerations, nonexistent at this level earlier, were introduced through Finance Planning Sections attached to these Directorates. In 1986, the Directorate General of Defence Planning Staff (DGDPS), comprising officers from the three Services, DRDO, and Ministries of Defence and External Affairs, was established under the Chiefs of Staff Committee (COSC) to coordinate and harmonise defence planning. Civilian officers from the Ministries probably did not find the job professionally satisfying and were gradually withdrawn, thus leaving the DGDPS a tri-Service set up.

All these measures enabled each Service headquarters to prepare defence plans in a more rational manner. But due to lack of clear political direction and each Service primarily planning for itself, joint planning, coordination between Services and other departmental plans of the MoD, were largely ignored. After the Kargil conflict in 1999, the Group of Ministers (GoM) and later the Cabinet Committee on Security (CCS) approved several reforms. An Integrated Defence Headquarters (IDH) was established and the DGDPS was merged with it. The creation of the post of Chief of Defence Staff (CDS), whose tasks would include ensuring intra and inter-Services prioritisation of defence plans and improvement in joint functioning of the Defence Services, was recommended. The reforms also included establishment of a Defence Intelligence Agency and creation of Defence Equipment Production, Research and Planning councils in the IDH and MoD, respectively. Unfortunately, the CDS, who would be the cornerstone of integrated operational planning for defence, has not been appointed.

Analysis of the Planning System

Despite several years of planning efforts, defence planning in India is characterised by seesaw bouts of frenzied activity followed by long periods of relative inaction. Five-year defence plans have rarely been formally approved before commencement. The Tenth Defence Plan, now in its third year, is yet to be accorded formal government approval. Adhocism is the order of the day, leading to knee-jerk responses and haphazard planning, making India a reactive rather than proactive nation in matters pertaining to national security. Whenever India's major adversaries plan a big defence purchase, there is an outcry for similar acquisitions, resulting in piecemeal decisions regardless of long-term impact and overall requirements.

The Defence Forces are forced to follow "a case-by-case" approach to modernisation and procurement of arms, ammunition and equipment to replace obsolescent items, in many cases long after their life cycle is over and they cannot be maintained in a cost effective manner. The Army's Vijayanta tanks, MiG-21s of the IAF, and IL-38 maritime reconnaissance aircraft of the Navy are some examples. Weapons development, procurement and absorption are complex processes. A lead-time of 15-20 years is required to plan and execute major projects. Despite this, for several years, a large amount of the capital acquisition budget has been surrendered. In the prevailing era of strategic uncertainty, the changing nature of warfare demands a judicious mix of threat and capabilities-based forces that can operate efficiently as combined arms, joint Services teams and components of multinational coalition forces.

CONCEPT OF NATIONAL SECURITY POLICY AND STRATEGY

The concept of national security rests mainly on the proposition that many foreign and domestic political, economic and military issues are interrelated, each with implications on the other. In India's case, this has been highlighted by insurgencies and other political events, particularly in border-states, and other outside pressures, which are brought to bear on the country's economy and technological progress from time to time.

A response to this type of environment calls for a highly focused national security policy and strategy. Effective guidance on national security and defence policy objectives is fundamental to the defence planning process. National security is a relative matter without a firm criteria but unless firm national security objectives are set and a defence policy evolved, there can be no military doctrine or balancing of defence effort with other national objectives and priorities such as maintaining a viable economy and supporting development of society. The lack of a cohesive national security strategy and defence policy has many implications. First, it results in the absence of clear political direction regarding politico-military objectives, which is the very basis of sound defence planning. Secondly, there is inadequate coordination of defence plans and economic development. Finally, science and technology policies for defence, general industrialisation and other development programmes are not coordinated properly to achieve security goals and objectives.

Defence Perspective and Integrated Planning

A Defence Plan has to be prepared on the basis of a 15-year long perspective planning system, such that the first five years of the plan are very firm (Definitive Plan), the second five years less firm (Indicative Plan) and the third five-year term tentative (Vision Plan). There has to be a reasonably firm allocation of financial resources for the first five years and an indicative allocation for the subsequent period.

Perspective planning needs to be done in the Integrated Defence Headquarters, where military, technical and R&D experts take an integrated view of future threats and challenges. This has to be based on future battlefield scenarios, and array of forecasts, evaluation of strategic options and force mixes, and analysis of potential technical and industrial capabilities. Based on this, the respective Service should work on their perspective plans and the R&D and Defence Production/Supplies experts should spell out their requirements in terms of effort, technology and indigenous production.

As stated earlier, the CDS, who would be the cornerstone of integrated operational planning for defence, has not been appointed. India's defence planning, therefore, continues to be Service based. Often, the threat perception of one Service is at variance with that of another Service. What emerges is essentially a sum of total of Service or department wise programmes. The focus is not on overall goals or priorities but on what is required by a particular Service. In its endeavour to lay the groundwork for an increased share of the budget, each Service tends to exercise its own priorities, favouring its own plans to the detriment of joint plans.

Subjects like surveillance, air defence, electronic warfare, and amphibious operations, which relate to more than one Service, do not get adequate attention. Integrated planning for defence is essential for creating balanced force structures and for the successful execution of all military missions.

In fact, it is the most effective manner of ensuring effective defence. According to Charles Hitch, "the revolution in military technology has not only changed the character of our military programmes, it has also to a significant degree blurred the lines of demarcation among various Services". Most major military missions today require the participation of more than one military service. Therefore, the principal concern now must be centred on what is required by the defence establishment as a whole to perform a particular mission—not what is required by a particular Service to perform its individual part of that 'mission'. The areas of commonality in modern weapon systems are immense and growing rapidly. Communications, guidance systems, missiles, radars, lasers—even traditional equipment such as guns, fuses, ammunition and vehicles are common. Integrated defence planning is necessary in view of escalating costs of these weapons and equipment.

Self-reliance in Defence Technology

The DRDO has a network of 51 laboratories and establishments. The Scientific Advisor (SA) to the Raksha Mantri (RM) is the Secretary of this Department. The DRDO has a staff of 30,000, including 6,800 scientists and engineers. It receives approximately four to six per cent of the defence budget annually. The DRDO is engaged in the pursuit of self-reliance in critical technologies relevant to defence. It formulates and executes a programme of scientific research, design and development for the induction into the Armed Forces of state-of-the-art weapons and other equipments.

In April 1984, the DRDO envisaged a programme "to transform the Department into a leader of international class with the mission to capture and retain commanding heights in critical technologies". A 'mission mode' organisational structure and approach was approved by the Government with a view to increasing the element of self-reliance from the current 30 per cent to 70 per cent by 2005. This goal, however, is nowhere in sight. The Department has developed more than 1,100 items of weapon systems and equipment with a production value of over Rs 6,000 crore. But it has not been able to make any major contribution to the state-of-art weapons and equipment. Most of its programmes, like Prithvi (sea borne version), Trishul (short-range surface to air missile), Akash (medium-range surface to air missile), Nag (anti-tank missile), Light Combat Aircraft with Kaveri engine, Pinaka (multiple-barrel rocket system), MBT Arjun, Electronic Warfare equipment, new radio sets for the Army, Sonar system for Navy, and many other items, are way behind schedule.

Because of the failure to deliver the required weapons and equipment, defence planning and Force structuring by the Services has suffered continuously. The DRDO's inability to deliver in time has caused a crisis of confidence and constant dissatisfaction in the Services. In order to ensure smooth progress towards self-reliance in defence technology, the Government must undertake a periodic performance audit of DRDO projects to reinforce efforts in areas of success and weed out projects that are unproductive.

OUTCOME AND PROGRAMME BASED SYSTEM

The contents of the general, as well as, the defence budget of the Government of India have normally been widely discussed and debated. However, the focus mostly has been on the magnitude of the budget rather than the system of budgeting.

Yet it is the system that needs to be the focus of discussions and requires reforms. Over a period of time, the budget documents had become quite static in terms of structure, content and communication of results. With the demands of those needing information from the budget changing with time, reforms in the structure and content of the defence budget had become overdue.

A budget is an instrument of policy. Through the annual financia statements it can translate a long term or medium term plan into action. The questions that arise are: what do we expect out of the budgeting system? And does it facilitate a meaningful translation of the intended objectives as reflected in the budget estimates? The perception about what the Defence Budget: Towards an Outcome and Programme Based System 709 defence budget should contain also depends on various categories of users. The institutions/persons looking into the budget can be divided into the following three main categories:

- Parliament, which votes the budgetary appropriations and also reviews the performance through the appropriation accounts and audit reports. Preceding the vote on the budget, Parliament has the report of the Standing Committee on Defence, which examines the demands for grants in detail.
- The administrative ministry, the executive arm and supporting institutions working with it. The administrative ministry formulates the budget and, after necessary backing of the Finance Ministry, gets the approval of Parliament to enable it to operate.
- A mix of users such as experts in the field, institutions, beneficiaries, academics and the common citizens who are interested in the information, especially the value for money derived from the actual expenditure.

To meet the changing needs of the diverse sets of users, the defence budger needs to change both its format and contents with time. Yet systemic changes in structure, form and content of the budget have been slow to come about in India. Changes have been made from time to time but essentially in amplification of contents or deletion of certain items, or addition of new service relating to expenditure. We, therefore, need to know how far and why it has not been feasible to introduce new concepts.

The Defence Services Estimates (DSE) have an amalgam of outlays that can be converted in terms of outcomes into tangibles and some intangibles. As far as the defence budget is concerned, it is clear that the Parliament, the executive, defence analysts and the tax payers would be interested to know the outcomes. They would be keen to know the quantum of funds provided for air defence, the cumulative total of such allocations in the budget over a period of time and the results achieved in providing protection against potential air attacks. While evolving any modifications in systems, it is necessary to know what is needed in the Indian context by various users.

Having recognized the inherent advantage of a budget that can reveal what it has achieved in terms of intended objectives, the question arises as to whether the existing structure and content need a total substitution, partial modification or supplements in order to serve as a conclusive document for evaluation of the outcomes. The past legacy also needs to be tackled in any overhaul or change in the existing system. The legacies are located in the content of the basic administrative and accounting data generated from the source levels, the mode of transmission, the organisational entities involved in the processing of the data, the relationships between these entities, the command and control, the technology used and, most important, the manpower resources, both in terms of skills and the numbers at the appropriate levels. Other relevant factors are: reluctance to exchange information in an institutionalised manner and an exaggerated sense of secrecy in publishing and disseminating information.

This article attempts to delineate feasible reforms to make the budget speak for itself in terms of intended objectives and the outcome or value for money realised out of the expenditure incurred.

The Defence Existing System

The Defence Services Estimates (DSE), as a document, has evolved over a period of time to its current structure. Though its structure has largely remained the same in form and contents, it has had modifications. It is believed by many that, as a public document, its existing format is adequate to convey the objectives of the government. The comments/ reactions to a budget presentation are made in terms of judgement on magnitude of allocations for army, navy, air force, DRDO and for new services, etc. However, a growing number of people, especially in the ministry and service headquarters, well-informed defence experts and academics have persuasively argued for a change. Many Members of Parliament have often sought more information, than what is available in the existing document.

The criticism of the present system is that it is largely input oriented. Specifically this means that it focuses on expenditure in generic terms, i.e., in terms of pay and allowances, stores, transportation, etc., and not in terms of targets and its actuals.

The budget is also devoid of details in a number of major components of expenditure. The figures of expenditure on certain categories such as 'stores', 'works', etc., are such that it is not clear as to why and for what the funds are provided. The budget is divided in terms of 'revenue' and 'capital'. Even in this regard, the classification was until recently carrying legacies of the past and did not reflect the basic nature of certain items. In several areas, assets of a capital nature were being classified under revenue. Consequently, capital assets were underpitched, especially in respect to the army. The omnibus nature of items under capital expenditure indicated as 'other equipment', 'aircraft', etc., do not reveal adequate information on specific items of expenditure, even where these are of large magnitude. The word 'maintenance' nowhere figures under Revenue Budget but is covered under 'pay and allowances', 'stores', etc.

With substantial increase in funding for defence, the need for adequate information has become of great importance for interpretation of the budget. At present, information on the budget is available to the executive/parliament through the following three main reports:

- The Appropriations Account
- The audit report of Comptroller and Auditor General
- Reports of Parliamentary Committees – especially those of the Standing Committee on Defence and, in

certain cases, the reports of the Public Accounts Committee, based on the audit reports.

The Appropriation Accounts signed by the Controller General Defence Accounts (CGDA)/Secretary Defence (Finance) and by the Defence Secretary gives the actual expenditure against allocations under various minor and sub heads. The reasons for variations of actuals against allocations are also indicated. However, it does not throw adequate light on physical achievements (outputs) in respect to a bulk of the items since the document is not intended to be an account on performance. However, there are exceptions. For two organisations-military farms and military engineering services-assessment of performance is given in separate sections.

Under the present system, getting an overall picture of budget in financial/physical terms and the actual performance is not easy and requires a lot of derivation, collation of data/ information and enormous effort on the part of the ministry/ services/departments. A document reflecting outcomes of at least major items provided in the budget would make the whole task easier apart from serving the basic and very important task of effective management of schemes and achievement of objectives.

By and large, the existing structure of the DSE with classification and sub-heads such as 'stores', 'works', etc., cannot facilitate the understanding of what is the outcome intended from the money spent on various items of expenditure related to defence. Even in an important area of maintenance of aircraft, it is difficult to derive from the budget that if Rupees "X" have been allocated for maintenance of an aircraft type "A", whether the required level of maintenance has been achieved. This information becomes available much later when an Audit Para is raised and even becomes an item in the report of the Public Accounts Committee (for example MiG-29). The existing budgetary system has another deficiency. For instance, allocations made for a gun are spent and the expenditure reports also reflects this position but the guns may still not be inducted for the purpose for which they were procured. The existing system may show good financial progress with almost entire payments having been made in respect of an item, but the crucial phase of testing, which is vital towards achieving the final outcome, could drag on. Successful tests of many systems do not necessarily lead to a successful outcome or their timely induction into the armed forces.

The DSE reveals very little about allocations even of a non sensitive nature. There are only one line entries in the budget documents for amounts running up to a few thousand crore of Rupees.

There are a number of other weaknesses in the system. The time taken for transactions does not get reflected in the financial information reports pertaining to a budget, and a continuous update of information on liabilities incurred by various sanctioning/spending authorities is not available An equally serious shortcoming is the inability to fully disseminate information to the concerned authorities and the absence of a synergised effort among various wings under the MOD for creating a comprehensive integrated report that would reflect the financial-cum-physical programmes.

Steps have been taken from time to time to make the existing DSE and the annual compilation of accounts more meaningful. In 1987, a reform was initiated in segregating pension from the DSE and ordinance factories from the army budget, with the objective of making this production organisation into a separate cost centre. Further reforms took place in 1992, based on the report of the task force (under A. K. Ghosh) which added over 150 categories in the classification of accounts, revealing more on the content of the expenditure, so that certain specific activities could be made transparent. It is clear that a well evolved coding section, in vogue since the1930s and subsequently enhanced by computerisation in 1971, has enabled further expansion of codes, meeting the growing need for giving information on expenditure related to an item.

GROUP OF MINISTERS REPORT AND FURTHER ENHANCEMENTS

Following the submission of the Kargil Review Committee Report, Government of India instituted a comprehensive review of the National Security System. This review was carried out by the Group of Ministers (GOM) constituted on 17 April 2000. The GOM further set up the following Task Forces:

- Task Force on Intelligence Apparatus
- Task Force on Internal Security
- Task Force on Border Management
- Task Force on Management of Defence.

To overcome some of the shortcomings in the system of budget the Task Force on Management of Defence recommended certain steps to improve matters. A Study Group on Budgetary Reforms (set up under the Task Force on Management of Defence) was constituted in August 2001, with the following terms of reference:

- To reveal the form and content of DSE;
- Examine the expansion of budgetary classification to promote programme-based budgeting;
- Reveal the classification of expenditure between revenue and capital in respect of defence services/ departments.

The Study Group on Budgetary Reforms, in its Report submitted in January 2002, suggested that the existing DSE may include additional inputs under certain heads of accounts in the various detailed demands for grants. The estimates for the defence research and development organisation were also segregated from the army and a separate major head opened. Thus the demands for grants were expanded from five to six.

Based on the Study Group's recommendations, an additional volume, called DSE Volume II, has been introduced for better budget management. With the additional details provided, internal management control by the services/departments/MoD/MoD (Finance) has improved. It is important that the existing scope and content of the budget documents are enhanced before taking up more complex tasks. The significance of opening budget centre heads and additional classification categories needs no emphasis. The Group, consisting of representatives of all the services and departments, recognised that the first step in implementation would be an evolution of a comprehensive financial information system in respect of all the three services and the departments and the real time availability of budget centre data pertaining to budgetary allocations, progress of expenditure and committed liabilities. Meanwhile, to make the existing classification between 'revenue' and 'capital' more meaningful, it was recommended that guidelines be drawn up for identifying items which are appropriately capital but are being placed under revenue. The Study Group also recommended the expansion of budgetary classification in the DSE to provide better budgetary control, which will facilitate the future formulation of a programme budget. For purposes of expenditure monitoring and feedback controls, the group also recommended a more detailed classification with a separate volume covering all categories of expenditure, right down to the services and departments with budget centre-wise allocations. These are now available in Volume II of the DSE, which is an internal document. The gap in the existing document is sought to be bridged to some extent by the DSE Volume II.

The introduction of DSE Volume II has enabled the stakeholders to get a feedback on activities related to various budget centres. Put in simple language, this volume is a document that shows where the money is allocated, on what it is to be spent and by whom. This format is applicable to all the three services, ordnance factories, DRDO, etc., and has made monitoring, control and evaluation of the results of budgetary allocations more meaningful. This is an important step towards better management. It would also be a step towards planned allocation down to the various cost centres, based on a plan of expenditure, linked to the performance of activities.

Concept of Defence Budget Centres

Alongside budgetary reforms, another committee was constituted to further expand the concept of accountability and responsibility, budget centres, and delegation of financial powers. The concept of budget centre allocation was recommended to be further expanded. This concept involves planning, programming, accounting, reporting and evaluation systems. The report of the Committee on Delegation of Financial Powers for the army, navy and air force emphasised that the following facts need to be taken into account:

- Responsibilities centre with clear objectives;
- Decentralised authority-cum-responsibility centres;
- Physical targets, linked to input and output in financial terms;
- Set of financially feasible and clearly defined objectives;
- A network of accounting and effective reporting systems.

The committee had the advantage of the framework already created by the first new management strategy concept was tried out in the naval dockyard, when B.V. Adavi was the Financial Adviser Defence Services (FADS). The concept of budget centres, along with integrated finance sector, was established in the services headquarters when A. K. Ghosh was the FADS. The budget centres, in concept and operation, facilitate generation of necessary inputs and outputs, which, in turn, enables evaluation of performance from field level and upwards. The measures implemented during the last decade and a half have gone a long way in enhancing the value of budget and supporting documents towards achieving better monitoring and control, and better insight of the results.

Content of Deficiencies

The content of the existing budget still falls short of a document oriented towards outcome. The recent reforms, additions and modifications would, no doubt, help all those who are deeply involved in the Ministry of Defence and service headquarters in managing expenditure and evaluating the results of the existing budget, with the additional facility of detailed accounts, papers and supporting documents. But to the rest of those involved/interested in not so intense a manner, some gaps in understanding the intended results of the outlay, outputs and outcomes remain. So it would appear the system of budget calls for a change.

The question arises: for whom the budget is made? It is principally for the services/defence departments, MoD and all the players who receive allocation of funds as per objectives and norms that get translated into policy and allocations when the budget is prepared. It is also for all those who have a stake in knowing whether the value for money has been realised. However, the problem is that the feedback mechanism is inappropriate for fully meeting the need for information and even the reports of various parliamentary committees are received too late for incorporation in the Budget. Even though the appropriation accounts are available on time, the performance evaluation is confined to only two areas of activities: military engineering services and the military farms. The system does not provide for concurrent/annual review of all expenditure. So, the budget as a whole gets neglected in terms of evaluation of the outcome. This is the position, in respect to the budgeting system for the defence though certain improvements have been built into the system over time, these are not adequate for a full scale evaluation of a large part of the budget.

At this stage, it would be appropriate to comment on the meaning of the terms 'performance budget', 'programme budget' and 'outcome budget'. Performance budget primarily indicates the physical progress of various schemes and programmes in relation to budget estimates. This was introduced by the Government in a number of Ministries, especially those handling development programmes, based on the recommendations of the Administrative Reforms Commission in 1969. Programme budgeting was first introduced in the US Defence Department as a system contrary to conventional budgeting. It describes and gives details of costs of all activities or programmes in a budget. Objectives, outputs and expected results are described fully as are the necessary input costs, such as of raw materials, equipment and staff. The sum of all activities or programmes constitutes the programme budget. The major task is to consolidate all activities that could be classified as a programme mission, such as training, coastal defence, etc.

Programme based budgeting requires linkage between plan and programmes, and input and output. As A. K. Ghosh has stated in his book India's Defence Budget and Expenditure Management in a Wider Context, the terms "performance budgeting and programme budgeting has been used interchangeably as both concepts are based on functions and activities and the emphasis is on results." He further states, "The time dimension is of immense importance for expenditure management in defence, which is emphasised by programme budgeting. Programmes are inherently forward-looking. Performance, on the other hand, is based on past activity and evaluation of the past performance becomes a focal point of attention."

However, as Ghosh himself states that confusion has somewhat been removed in the UN manual, which has viewed performance budget as an all inclusive concept, embodying programme formulation as well as measurement of the performance of work in accomplishing programme objectives.

The outcome budget, as the Ministry of Finance in its memorandum dated 30th December 20053, stated, is a pre-expenditure instrument. It helps to realise the ministries' vision through clearly defined outcome/output as a supplement to the current system built around postexpenditure scrutiny. The need for this has been felt as there is a lack of clear cut one-to-one relationship between the final budget and the performance budget as it was evolved earlier and inadequate setting of physical targets for the ensuing year. Development of outcome budget is not as complex as of a programme budget and can be built around the existing systems with some modification and expansion.

FORCE STRUCTURE AND CAPABILITY BUILDING IN DEFENCE

The main determinant of defence capability is the force structure. So force planning becomes the key element in capability planning. When Program Budgeting or its variant Programme, Planning and Budgeting System(PPBS) was introduced in sixties in U.S. Defence, the Five Years Defence Program (FYDS), ten Major Force Programs (MFPs), were its central foci. Defence budgets were allocated among these MFPs to achieve optimal allocation of resources. The ten MFPs were so defined that they expressed the principal missions the military needed to perform. Without defining the missions and tasks, and allocating resources for carrying the military tasks, capability planning cannot be attempted. The most important ingredient of capability planning is force structure planning. In India, we are yet to attempt force structure planning through our five year plans. The main drivers of cost in defence are the strength and composition of forces. If we want to use budgeting for building up desired defence capabilities, then an affordable force planning should be its main focus for all the three Services.

In determining appropriate force structure, there has to be a well conceived and well debated defence strategy. National security strategy would have to relate 'means' to 'ends'. There is no strategy in the absence of choice about 'means' and 'ends', or their relationship. In a democratic society, difficulties are often faced in coming to grips with the 'ends' rather than the 'means' of strategy.

This is why there is absolute necessity of periodic comprehensive Defence Reviews, in defining the 'ends' and establishing relationship between 'ends' and 'means' towards formulating a defence strategy and broad allocation of resources in a multi-year perspective. We are yet to undertake such a review.

It may be worthwhile in this context to quote from the report of the Estimates Committee of the Parliament (1992-93) on defence force levels: "The committee is apprised that the force level under the Ministry of Defence is determined by the dynamic perspective of the security scenario coupled with the annual availability of resources within the plan period, competing demands of other priority sectors, the technological developments and other systemic inputs. They are shocked to find that the question of force level which is inherently linked with perspectives on national security should be dealt with on such vague and unpredictable considerations (emphasis added)."4 The issue is still unresolved.

Policy decisions regarding broad military tasks and missions to be aimed at are to be taken to provide a basis for approving a force level and a force structure, which can be addressed though a Defence Review - which is long overdue. Nothing is more urgent than having a Defence Review from the point of view of public interest and policy, if the government wants to address the unresolved issues as brought out in the Report of the Estimates Committee of 1993 on defence force levels, manpower etc.

Without it defence capability building may take an ad hoc character and may not meet the desired objectives. Naturally, defence budgeting would also take an ad hoc character, as it is very much evident.

CAPABILITY PLANNING AND PROGRAMME OF BUDGETING

Programme Budgeting (PPBS) introduced in 1960s in USA laid the foundation for capability-based planning. While it has undergone a number of changes over the past four decades, but the core element and the basic process still provides the basis for allocation of resources for capability building. After the operation of PPBS for nearly two decades, many analysts pointed out that the first 'P', which stood for strategic planning, was missing. Some of the reforms brought about in mid-eighties, were really concerned with the front end of planning - meaning strategic planning.

The Group of Ministers (GoM), in their report on Reforming the National Security System (2001) stated that, "Aneed has been felt for a review of the form and content of the Defence Services Estimates and the expansion of the budgetary classification to promote programme based budgeting, while ensuring compliance with security requirements." They also stated that "optimal allocation of resources cannot be achieved unless greater emphasis and attention is given to the process of budget formulation and implementation, including forecasting, monitoring and control." But they did not emphasize the need for strategic planning and the need for linking budgeting process to it. In fact without it, budgeting process cannot be improved.

Unfortunately, the GoM did not go into the implications of adopting programme budgeting nor did they emphasize that programming process should precede budget making to bring about optimal allocation of resources. As David Novick pointed out that "planning and programming are aspects of the same process; they differ only in the emphasis."5 Planning here does not mean the Five Year Plans, as we formulate them, a list of schemes. It is an activity concerned with selection of best course of action among various alternatives given the limitation of resources. To quote Novick again, "Planning is the production of the range of meaningful potentials for selection of a course of action through systematic consideration of alternatives. Programming is the specific determination of the manpower, materiel, and facilities necessary for accomplishing a program. In addition, except in the very short term where dollars are in effect 'given', programming entails interest in dollar requirements for meeting the manpower, materiel, and facility needs." 6 By adopting the programme budgeting concept in this sense, budgeting for desired defence capability became possible. The GoM did not get into these aspects of programme budgeting. Thus, a great opportunity of reforming the defence budgetary process in India to develop defence capability was lost. They got more concerned with defence procurement process, with a view to expedite it and recommended organizational changes - which were promptly adopted. Procurement planning cannot substitute for defence planning which calls for consideration of alternatives to achieve defence objectives. Without strategic planning to back it up, defence procurement takes an ad hoc character.

BUDGETING FOR DEFENCE CAPABILITY

Budgeting for defence capability has to have a close link with strategic planning process for national security. Resource allocation under capability based planning would look for capability gaps on the basis of objectives to be attained. Budgeting should aim at allocating funds on a priority basis for meeting the capability gaps, based on strategic consideration. There should be a close link between Defence Strategy and Defence Budgeting. In a sense defence budgeting for capability is defence strategy. This is because defence capability building is not done for its own sake. Capabilities are developed to achieve national military objectives and operational objectives, and budgeting is the means to do so. Defence budgeting has to be viewed as a resource allocation process for building up required military capability for carrying out military tasks based on operational objectives. Important elements of defence capability building viz. manpower, training, ammunition and various other stores meant for operation and maintenance purposes, are in the revenue side of defence budget. When capability building is the objective, the entire defence budget has to be considered for allocation to develop specific defence capabilities. In capability planning major emphasis is given on operational concepts and operational challenges and resource allocation has to be done on that basis.

Defence Capability Plan and Defence Budgeting

Budgeting for desired defence capability would very much be dependent on a well-conceived Defence Capability Plan. Till the 10thDefence Plan we have not specifically adopted capability based planning in defence. The aim of the Five Year Plans has been to modernise defence forces. The projections of the Ministry of Defence for 10th Plan were reviewed thrice between March 2003 and July 2004 bearing in mind the needs of defence modernisation. As per 11th Report of the Standing Committee on Defence on Demand and Grants (2006-07), the Ministry of Finance had finally agreed in principle to the projections made by the Ministry of Defence of Rs. 4,18,101 crores for the 10th Defence Plan 2002-07. "However, the total allocation for the 10th Plan on the basis of annual plan allocation comes to Rs. 3,64,000 crores. Hence, there has been a gap of Rs. 5,41,000 crore between the indicative figure given and the total allocation made by the Ministry of Finance for the 10th Plan."7 This in fact, with reference to original projection, was around Rs. 1,29,000 crores.

It is clear that the projections made by Ministry for the plan are not taken very seriously. In capability based planning there has to be a closed link between planning and budgeting as the desired capabilities are required to be achieved within a given time frame, to meet specific challenges. So the most important lesson for budgeting for capability building is that projected five year budget should have in–principle approval from the Government, say of the Cabinet Committee on Security(CSS). It cannot be left to be a debate between Ministry of Defence and ministry of Finance. Capability Plan should be based on it.

It has been reported keeping in view the experience of 10th Defence Plan, the 11th Defence Plan (2007-12) has been drawn up keeping in view the financial constraints with the aim of filling up defence capability gaps. The aim and objectives to be achieved in the 11th Defence Plan by the three Services, as intimated by the Ministry of Defence to the Standing Committee on Defence while discussing Demands for Grants 2006-07, are briefly as under:

Army - Development of capability to attain military objectives in a short, high intensity war against nuclear backdrop. Continued up gradation of capability for countering proxy war/insurgencies and other emerging internal security challenges.

Navy - Impetus on improving the capability in the area of airborne maritime surveillance, anti-submarine warfare, air defence capability through induction of aircraft, integral helos and UAVs (Unmanned Armoured Vehicles). Arresting the force level decline of submarines and networking platforms for more effective maritime operations.

Air Force - The formulation of 11th IAF Plan (2007-12) has been driven by the imperative of keeping an equal focus on several vital issues: strategic reach, enhancement of firepower of combat forces, enhancement of air lift capability and operating infrastructure with due regard to the perceived security concerns and technological environment. The broad thrust of the plan has been on containing the adverse effect of force depletion to the extent possible.

What confuses a layman is that goal of capability planning for each Service is different. The element of 'jointness' in capability planning is missing. While Army would be developing capability to attain military objectives "in a short, high intensity war", Air Force in its capability plan does not mention anything of this "high intensity" war or how it would support Army to attain military objectives in such a war. The thrust of the plan is containing adverse impact of "force depletion". Navy in its capability plan aims at all round improvement in capability and arresting force level decline but does not mention about developing specific capability based on operational concepts. Budgeting for each Service based on this kind of planning would have different thrust and would not lead to optimal allocation of resources for attaining strategic objectives.

DEFENCE STRATEGY, CAPABILITY BUILDING AND FORCE PLANNING

Defence strategy, force planning and capability building are closely interrelated. Deliberations and methodology adopted for capability planning in USA in the context of Quadrennial Defence Review, 1997 (QDR '97) as also subsequent QDRs, clearly indicates the interrelationship. The QDR took a "capabilities analysis" perspective by emphasizing the need to have operational capabilities for a highly diverse set of military contingencies. It drew on the ideas in Joint Vision 2010 and revolution in military affairs.

But equally important, the capability planning in QDR'97 was based on the assumption that defence budget was likely to remain constant in real terms during the plan period. For capability planning the assumption about likely availability of budgets for next five years or more is absolutely essential. If it is expected to grow then the assumption about the rate it is likely to grow annually at is very important for capability planning. Assumption might relate to real term growth in defence budget and if that was not possible, growth may be assumed in numerical terms. For defence planning in India, it will require decision at the level of Cabinet Committee on Security (CCS). Finance Ministry on its own cannot give this kind of commitment. So the most important point relating to budgeting for defence capability is that it calls for long term budgeting.

In Australia, for example, the 2000 Defence White Paper committed the Government to increase defence spending by an average of 3 percent real growth a year from 2000-01 to 2010-11.

In 2006, the Australian government decided to increase defence spending by 3 percent in real terms per year until 2015-16. Because of the long term commitment of funding it became possible to earmark $2.2 billion to acquire heavy airlift capability enabling rapid deployment of combat vehicles, helicopters and supplies, as also to earmark $1.5 billion for a ten year period for networked Army and increase in its size.

Long Term View of Funding is Necessary for Determining Affordability

When considering phasing out of two or more new aircraft, the analyst may have to look 20 years or more into the future to have some assurance that he is recommending an affordable acquisition plan since, "In the long view of fighter modernization, long-term averages of budgets and expenditures assume more importance than what happens in the next year or two."10 Affordability is assuming increasing importance as a design consideration for new fighter aircraft, even in US defence considerations.

One cannot confidently predict the size of future defence budgets. But it is not impossible to make projections about allocation for defence and the likely share of Air force, Army and Navy keeping in view past trends of allocation for defence budget and the share of respective services in the defence budget. Any projection for defence budget for next ten years, assuming more than 9 percent annual growth on the present level, given the operation of FRBM Act, would appear optimistic. In making projections for long term one has to make conservative estimates.

It may not be possible to maintain the present high level of allocation for capital expenditure which has now touched almost 43 percent of defence budget, as no rationalization of expenditure on support services has taken place. Keeping in view past trends, percentage of allocation for revenue budget would have to increase from the present levels, particularly with implementation of recommendations of Sixth Pay Commission. Without change in force levels in terms of manpower, it may be difficult to sustain a capital budget of more than 35 percent on the average during next ten years. One can even consider the possibility of sustaining a capital budget at 37-38 percent with changes in force level and other reforms during next ten years.

On the basis of such possibilities one can attempt to calculate likely availability of funds for various segments of defence capabilities. For this, each Service has to work out the competing needs for capital expenditure out of its share of capital budget and the affordability of various aspects of modernization. For the Air Force, for example, in the current context for capability building, one has to assess broad possibility of affordability of fighter aircraft modernization.

BUDGETING FOR DESIRED DEFENCE CAPABILITY

The Defence procurement policy and procedure as brought out in DPP- 2006 (Defence Procurement Policy, 2006) indicated that for policy decisions relating to acquiring of weapons and systems, we are basing them on capability planning in the context of operational requirements. It talked in terms of existing 'capability gaps', and examination of alternative means of overcoming them, while processing a case for policy decision.

Capability planning has various implications from resource allocation angle and particularly for defence budgeting, which are yet to be addressed in a systematic manner. An attempt has been made below to highlight some of the issues and the possible ways to tackle them.

Budgeting as a means for obtaining optimum defence capability would call for reform in the defence budgeting process in three important aspects. First, the budgetary process has to be changed so as to treat defence budgeting as a part of decision making process for optimum resource allocation for achieving specific defence capabilities. The process should be so designed that choice could be exercised in allocating limited means for achieving identified 'objectives' with a view to achieving maximum effectiveness in defence spending. To develop optimum defence capability, the objective should be clear.

Second, the budgeting process should be closely linked with the defence planning process. Budgeting should be treated as the execution portion of defence planning cycle, so that there is close coordination between capability planning and budgeting. This will call for extended time horizon for defence budgeting as also change in the format of defence budget. Third, attention should be focused on the end products of defence budgeting through the concept of programmes for capability building, making it an output-oriented budget. In this context, it is good to remember, that for optimum capability building through objective-based defence planning, a relationship is required to be established between the identified objectives and the various activities to enhance military capabilities.

Military capabilities are capabilities to perform specified tasks. Therefore, the basis for resource allocation decisions in the capability based Defence Plans, should be military tasks that are required to be performed. It is the military tasks conceived in the framework of objective- based approach that would provide the basis for development of programmes for those tasks. Programmes by themselves have no sanctity, unless they are linked to the performance of military tasks that have been identified as necessary for carrying out national security policy. There should be explicit link between aims of policy and military forces required to achieve the aims. Programmes should be considered as providing that link.

In the capability based approach, defence forces must be manned, equipped, and trained to carry out the identified military tasks, for which they are assigned. So the programmes should be developed on a composite basis, taking into account all the elements required to develop capabilities to carry out specific tasks. Cleary, in the capability based approach, programmes cannot merely be conceived as equipment acquisition programmes, as we often tend to do, and make our Defence Plans as equipment acquisition plans. Defence Plans have to be much more than that.

So, what we are following today is a truncated approach to defence planning, which may not be the right approach to develop optimum defence capability. Because of the basic importance of military tasks to provide the building blocks for defence programmes, there should be an adequate planning and resource allocation mechanism in Service Headquarters. We have not adequately emphasized upon it, as our planners have mostly concentrated on acquisitions of equipments and systems. Programme planning and budgeting for capability building to achieve identified objectives have to take place at the level of Service Headquarters, within the overall guidance provided by formulation of military policy and strategy at the Ministry and higher level. The policy objectives, however, cannot be set at the Service Headquarters level.

Planning and Programming

When Arthur Smithies, in his seminal work in the nineteen fifties, first conceived of budgeting as a part of decision-making process, he conceived a process consisting of six stages: determination of policy objectives, planning, programming, budget formulation, budget or program execution, budget or program review. What was the role of planning in the decision making process, as conceived by Smithies? In his words: "Planning, as the term is used here, means the preparation of alternative plans that will further particular policy objectives in varying measure and are within the reasonable bounds of feasibility."1 His definition of programming was "Programming denotes a further step in the direction of finality and feasibility, and may involve selection among alternative plans or a combination of elements from a number of plans."2 Basic decisions that greatly influence the size of budget are required to be taken at the programming stage. To quote him once again, "the distribution of the defence program among the three Services are budgetary questions, since the national objective is to obtain the most efficient use of resources devoted to defence. While these questions are largely settled before a budget is prepared, the programming decisions should be based on the relative costs of the various defence alternatives."3 Costing of programmes again assumes central importance both for decision making and budgeting. That is why for budgeting for defence capability, programming stage should be properly designed and should precede budgeting.

Arthur Smithies has been quoted for two reasons. First, to indicate that in quest for rational allocation of resources, setting of policy objectives followed by planning and programming are essential steps, before budgeting is attempted. Secondly, these steps have their validity in any rational system of decision making in resource allocation, and were visualized much before PPBS was introduced in US Defence in the sixties. One may criticize PPBS for various reasons, but that does not make the concept of planning and programming invalid. Their validity is derived from need for rational allocation of resources for achieving optimum defence capability.

GENERAL DEFENCE BUDGET AND SECURITY PREOCCUPATIONS

India's security preoccupations are determined by the dynamics of the global and regional strategic and security environment. The post-Cold war international situation and the terrorist attack on Indian Parliament and on the twin towers in the United States on 9/11 have brought into sharp focus the concern of the international community on global security issues and challenges, though significant differences of perception and action on specifics remain. India's strategic location, its long coast line and distance island territories and the continuing acts of terrorism from across her borders, require India to maintain a high level of vigilance and defence preparedness. Against this background, the Committee have examined this year's budget estimates of the Ministry of Defence.

The requirements for the Civil expenditure of the Ministry of Defence Secretariat, Defence Accounts Department, Canteen Stores Department, Defence Estates Organization, Coast Guard Organisation, JAK LI (w.e.f. BE 2005-06) etc., and Defence Pensions, are provided for in two separate Civil Demands for Grants of the Ministry of Defence, viz. Demand No. 21 – MOD (Civil) and Demand No. 22 – Defence Pensions. These are not included in the overall Defence Allocation of Rs. 83000.00 crores in Budget Estimates 2005-2006. The requirements of the Border Roads Organisation are provided for by the Ministry of Surface Transport.

The 'running' or 'operating' expenditure of the three Services and other Departments, viz. Defence Research and Development Organisation (DRDO), Director-General of Ordnance Factories (DGOF), Directorate General of Quality Assurance (DGQA), National Cadet Corps (NCC), Directorate General Aeronautical Quality Assurance (DGAQA) and Directorate of Standardisation are provided under the first five Demands, which cater to the Revenue Expenditure, while the sixth, viz. Capital Outlay on Defence Services, caters to the expenditure incurred on building or acquiring durable assets. The Demands No. 23 (Defence Services – Army) caters to the Revenue expenditure of Army, NCC, and DGQA, and Demand No. 24 (Defence Services --Navy) caters to Navy and Joint Staff.

The Revenue Expenditure includes expenditure on Pay & Allowances, Transportation, Revenue Stores (like Ordnance stores, supplies by Ordnance Factories, rations, petrol, oil and lubricants, spares, etc.). Revenue Works (which include maintenance of buildings, water and electricity charges, rents, rates and taxes, etc.) and other miscellaneous expenditure. The Capital expenditure includes expenditure on lands, construction works, plants and machinery, equipment, tanks, Naval Vessels, Aircraft and Aeroengines, Dockyards, etc. The expenditure on items which have a unit value of Rs. 10 lakhs and above and a life span of 7 years or more, is debited to the Capital Heads.

Approval of Parliament is taken for the 'Gross' expenditure provision under different Demands for Grants. Receipts and Recoveries, which include items like sale proceeds of surplus/obsolete stores, receipts on account of services rendered to State Governments/other Ministries, etc. and other miscellaneous items are deducted from the gross expenditure to arrive at the net expenditure on Defence Services.

IMPACT OF EXPENDITURE CUT ON DEFENCE PREPAREDNESS

The representatives of the Ministry of Defence in their deposition before the Committee have stated that the austerity instructions of Ministry of Finance have inter alia entailed a mandatory cut in the Budgetary Allocation for non plan non salary expenditure as well as the expenditure on petrol/oil/lubricants and travel; revision of non-tax receipts so as to ensure recovery of the cost of services; ban on the creation of posts, reduction in the number of sanctioned posts; restrictions on purchase of new vehicles; restrictions on foreign travel and on entertainment/hospitality expenses; review by the administrative Ministries/Departments of release of funds to those Autonomous Institutions having substantial balances utilized with them and kept in deposit with the Banks, reduction in a graded manner or release of deficit grants to those Autonomous Institutions which have potential of raising funds. Elaborating further on the issue a representative of the Ministry of Defence inter alia stated as under: "When we say shortages of 'human resource', we are referring to shortages across the board. It is categorized in different categories, shortages in the Officers cadre, shortages in the sailors cadre and shortages in the civilian cadre – the three different cadres. But, overall, there is a shortage.

10 per cent cut applies across the board to all the categories of civilian manpower. We are not allowed to fill up the posts even if we have vacancies available to us. As and when the posts fall vacant, we are not allowed to fill them up. This is the Government's policy and therefore, we have to cut down on the manpower across the board. The point at this stage which would help considerably is that, at least, all the new acquisitions which we make, particularly when it comes to major acquisitions or a big project like the Karwar Naval Base, then we cannot operationalise those assets unless we have the requisite manpower available to us.

The other issue is that the technical manpower takes a long time to train before it becomes useful. So, if the Base is to be commissioned, say, next year, it does not help to recruit the manpower at this stage. It should have been done three or four yeas earlier. It would help considerably if for the new projects, we are given the requisite manpower at the time of sanction. For replacements, for which if there is some old asset which is being paid off, then we are showing savings in any case before we ask for the manpower".

The Defence Secretary while explaining the cumulative affect of the pruning of Defence expenditure has stated that : "Over a period of time the vacancies or shortages have built up to a stage that it became 10 plus 10, 20 per cent. But it should not have. As I explained, the Navy is heavily dependent upon the civilian manpower for its dockyards and there are technical people, the bulk of them. Secondly, for example, there are two major establishments which are going to be readied shortly". Regarding the Ministry's endeavours to change the perception of Ministry of Finance and lift the restrictions on recruitment, the Defence Secretary has added that : "It is not on account of lack of efforts on the part of us in the Ministry of Defence. We have been trying to persuade the Ministry of Finance that the Navy should be allowed to recruit. As the hon. Chairman was saying, the Defence forces should not be treated at par with any other civilian organisation. However, till now we have not succeeded".

The Secretary, Defence (Finance) supplementing on the above stated as under: "In addition to the last directive, the Ministry of Finance said that if three people retire, only one will be recruited. This has to be done for the next five years. That is why Navy has to come to a stage where they are now. They had already shortages because earlier they were not allowed to fill up the posts".

Replying to a query whether the Ministry down sizes the funds at RE stage on its own or it is done as per the directives of the Ministry of Finance, the Secretary Defence Finance has stated that: "It is not that we were not able to spend but we were asked to surrender".

Supporting the above contention, the Defence Secretary has further stated that : "Last year we had got these committed liabilities. They had their deficit problems. So they said that we will take about Rs. 5000 crore out of your budget. We told them that this is our committed burden and all these things will pass on to the next year".

With reference to a question regarding our capabilities to meet any threat in the region, the Defence Secretary has stated that: "I presume the question is about our capabilities vis-à-vis our immediate neighbour on all sides. There again, with individual neighbours the kind of deployment and forces they had or likely to or capable of deploying, we feel confident enough to be able to face that. However, if one or more of these neighbours were to combine their efforts and to pose a joint threat, then it would introduce some element of uncertainty or complications. Even there to some extent, we are able to handle than but then the neighbours also have their neighbours. Therefore, it is no inconceivable that they would get assistance from others. Therefore, in these kinds of things, there are a number of imponderables. But as far as the present assessment against the immediate neighbour on either side of our country is concerned, we feel that we can take on a threat without compromising on our security or territory or in any case to be able to inflict more damage to the other side so as to see that we are not divorce of".

The Committee are deeply concerned to note that the Ministry of Defence was compelled to surrender funds to the tune of Rs. 5,000 crore, Rs. 9,000 crore and Rs. 5,000 crore at the Revised Estimates stage of 2001-02, 2002-03 and 2003-04 respectively, to meet the deficits. The budgetary ceilings imposed by the Ministry of Finance in the year 2005-06 have led to the downsizing of the total projected capital requirements of the Defence Services from adequately Rs. 44123.86 crore to Rs. 34375.14 crore which fails to address the security concerns of the nation. The arbitrary caps on budget utilization over a period of time have taken a toll of almost all sectors of Defence like manpower in the Navy, the ongoing modernization, infrastructure development, procurement of equipment/acquisitions, indigenisation and R&D initiatives. The across the board cut applied by the Ministry of Finance on Defence expenditure without undertaking any exercise to check the ramifications of their decision on defence preparedness calls for an immediate review. The Committee feel that there should not be any cut or reduction in the defence budget by the Ministry of Finance at any stage.

Closely related to the issue of Defence Preparedness and the ability to meet the threat perception is the quantum of funds available to our services. It is seen from the above that our Defence allocations as a percentage share of GDP since 1988-89 (year wise) have been between around 2 to 3 percent.

However, considering the present defence expenditure of some of our neighbours and the present security scenario, the Committee feel that there is a need to fix a minimum percentage of our GDP which should be made available to defence forces at all costs every year. The Committee are aware of the fact that the precarious finances entail the Government to consciously fixed the level of Defence expenditure as a percentage of GDP after assessing the prevailing the threat perceptions and the present and future operational and modernization requirements of the services.

The Committee, therefore, strongly recommends that 10% cut applied by the Ministry of Finance across the board over the years should be immediately reviewed to check further depletions of our Military assets. The Committee also desire that the Ministry of Defence should re-priorities their plans to ensure the optimum utilization of the available assets.

The Committee are surprise to observe that in spite of its earlier recommendation, which was agreed to by the Government on setting up of Defence University i.e. National Institute for Defence and Strategic Studies/Central Defence University, No budget provision is made in this budget. The Committee strongly feel that this may be made on priority.

DEFENCE PLANNING AND PROCESS

As regards the planning process, the Government has taken a number of measures to improve the structure, process and procedure relating to defence planning based on the recommendations of Group of Ministers on 'Reforming the National Security System'. The preparation of Long Term Plans, Five Year Defence Plans and Annual Budgetary proposals have been brought under the newly established Integrated Defence Staff (IDS) to bring about greater inter-service co-ordination in planning. The IDS also interacts closely with Defence (Finance) in the formulation of Plans and Budgets. The Government has set up a Defence Acquisition Council headed by the Raksha Mantri and consisting of Raksha Rajya Mantri (s), the three Service Chiefs and Defence Secretary, Secretary (Defence Finance), and Secretary (Defence Production) to assist the Raksha Mantri in taking decisions in the totality of the new planning process, including capital acquisitions and major modernisation projects. The Government has also set up a dedicated institutional structure for defence procurement, the Defence procurement Board, headed by the Defence Secretary for acquisitions on the capital account. Planning processes have been further tightened under budgetary pressures and the need to establish greater synergy and jointness amongst the Armed Forces. This has also necessitated greater co-ordination in planning and procurement among the three services.

The Ministry in its written note submitted on the current status of the implementation of the 10th Plan has inter alia stated that: "The projections of the Ministry of Defence for the Tenth Defence Plan were reviewed thrice between March 2003 and July 2004 bearing in mind the needs of defence modernization and the likely constraints to the availability of funds for defence in the Tenth Plan. The Ministry of Finance have now agreed in principle to the latest projection made by the Ministry of Defence of Rs. 4,18,101 crore. However, a firm indication of annual outlays for the remaining year of the 10th Plan has not yet been given by the Ministry of Finance.

Meanwhile, in the absence of a formal approval of the allocation for defence in the Tenth Plan, defence planning has been harmonised with the allotments for defence in the annual budgets of the Government. Actual expenditures in 2002-2003 and 2003-2004 were Rs. 55,620 crores and Rs. 60,300 crores respectively. An allocation of Rs. 77,200 crores has been made in the Budget Estimate for 2004-2005 against a projection of Rs. 90,928 crores. About, Rs. 11,000 crores additional funds have been allocated beyond the Budget Estimate for the capital head.

The projected expenditure in 2005-2006 and 2006-2007 are Rs. 1,00,960 crores and Rs. 1,10,251 crores respectively. However, an amount of Rs. 83,000 crores only has been allocated in the Budget Estimate (B.E.) for the current financial year 2005-2006.

While some compromises are inevitable in the absence of a formally approved Plan, every effort has been made to ensure that the annual budgets have been utilized in accordance with the Plan projections of the Ministry of Defence and that any negative impact on ongoing modernization, infrastructure development and procurements of equipment is minimized. Ongoing projects and commitments have been reviewed and prioritized so that the main objective of the Tenth Defence Plan to carry forward the process of modernization of the Armed Forces is not adversely affected. A modest outlay of over Rs. 950 crores has been made for new schemes for the Army. (No increase is being sought)".

In response to a query regarding the existence of a core plan the Ministry though a written reply has inter alia stated that : "There is no formal draft core plan to make up for the delay in the finalization of the Tenth Defence Plan. Meanwhile, in the absence of a formal approval of the allocation for defence in the Tenth Plan, defence planning has been harmonised with the allotments for defence in the annual budgets of the Government. While, indigenous production/ Research and Development is being made in accordance with the decisions flowing from the Defence Acquisition Council, defence procurement is being made in accordance with annual acquisition plans for the three services as approved by the Defence Procurement Board. Adequate measures have been taken to minimise any adverse effect on ongoing modernisation schemes. On-going projects and contractual commitments have been reviewed and prioritised to minimise the effect of any shortfall in actual allocation vis-à-vis projections, both in respect of modernisation plans and in essential procurement.

Keeping in view, the rising competing demands on limited resources, the budgetary framework has been fine-turned in such a manner to ensure most effective utilisation of Government resources".

While presenting a detailed picture on the entire planning exercise that has been undertaken in the recent past, the representative of Ministry has stated as under: "In the year 2001-02, projections for the 10th Plan were examined in the Ministry of Defence. These projections were made by the different Services and the Departments. They added up to Rs. 4.97 lakh crore. In January, 2002 the Ministry of Finance indicated the likely availability of Rs. 4.21 lakh crore. So, there was a gap of about Rs. 75,000 crore. Therefore, the Chief of Integrated Defence Staff and Chief of Staff were requested for giving their views. They recommended slightly reduced allocation of Rs. 4.61 lakh crore. In February 2003, in consonance with the recommendations, it was done. The matter was again taken up with the Finance Ministry in March 2003. But we did not have received any response from them thereafter.

We had to carry out a review of our projections. This was because if some scheme was supposed to be sanctioned in the first year of the Plan, it will involve expenditure in the first, second, third years and leading up to the fifth year. If, for the first two years, projected allocations are not utilized, there is no way the original amount, which was projected for the entire five years could be spent in the last three years.

It is because in defence acquisition, we are not really buying things off the shelf and paying out for the whole thing. So, if you take a case of some scheme or project costing Rs. 5,000 crore in five years with simplistic allocation of expenditure of Rs. 1,000 crore each year, and if in the first two years, it is not sanctioned and in the third year it is sanctioned, we are not going to have anything in the first two years, but the expenditure will be Rs.3,000 crore in the remaining three years and not Rs. 5,000 crore. When we received the projects, we reviewed what would be and what would not be sanctioned. Then the revised figures came to something like Rs. 4,18,000 crore as indicated. But they did not give us any annual allocations, not capacity utilization, etc".

On the lessons learnt and the measures that are being implemented to overcome the nagging delays of Defence Planning, the Defence Secretary deposed that : "Presentation of the fourth year Budget is made to the Parliament. As has already been mentioned, there is the Ministry of Defence and there is the Ministry of Finance which are the players in this exercise.

The exercise for preparing the plan is undertaken by us well in time, much before the start of the year in which the next Five Year Plan is going to start. For example, for the 11th Plan, to answer your question, we have already started the exercise. For doing that planning as to what would be needed, considering the gaps that is there in the Tenth Plan – if any exercise of this nature is to be undertaken – we might have a wish list; it might represent a large figure. But we still have to have some kind of an indicative figure from the Ministry of Finance saying that we have asked for this much amount, which may not be available, but we can have so much amount at the outer limit, beyond which we cannot go. This kind of an indication is no forthcoming. This is what happened in this current year. If you contrast it with the situation of the Ninth Plan, as the Chairman was enquiring, the Ninth Plan was approved on 1st January, 1998.

Therefore, it was approved in the first year. It was a very major achievement and they indicated a total allocation of Rs. 2,20,000 crore. The Annual Budget, as it took place during those five years if you total up those they came to Rs. 2,43,000 crore. That means the annual allocation was more than the indicative figure of the Plan. That was a situation which was quite in contrast to what is prevalent just now where, firstly, the figure itself was not known to us till December – finally what we wanted and how much they can give. This went till December of 2004.

If we were to juxtapose the Tenth Plan indicative figure of Rs. 4,18,000 crore divided by four years, which are known, it is nowhere. There was no relation. Therefore, this figure becomes an academic figure. That is the point that we have been discussing, that is the outlays have to be finalized at the beginning of the plan and secondly Annual Allocation should be conforming to the overall outlay".

Adding further on the issue, the Defence Secretary has also stated that : "As has been mentioned earlier, how initial projections of Rs. 4,97,000 crore was done at the beginning of the Tenth Plan (2001-02).This was also communicated to the Finance Ministry with the break up. They needed it in a particular format. It was given in that format. Subsequently, they had indicated Rs. 4,97,000 crore is too much and we may plan within Rs. 4,21,000 crore. There was a gap of about Rs. 75,724 between the projection and what they had indicated. By that time certain time had elapsed. We were involved in an internal exercise of readjusting. In December 2004 they indicated Rs. 4,18,000 crore, which was what we had projected earlier".

Explaining the details of the ongoing measures to formulate the Eleventh Defence Plan and how these initiatives have a bearing on the implementation of annual plan programmes, the Defence Secretary has briefed the Committee : "As I just said, we have started our exercise of preparing the Eleventh Plan which means that the Integrated Defence Staff which gets inputs from all the three Headquarters puts together the long-term perspective plan requirements of each service and makes them into one composite plan called the Defence Plan. It sees whether there is any overlapping of capabilities or whether there is any repetition or commonalties.

So, it does such modifications and vetting and then it is projecting that requirement to the Ministry where we see whether it is all right or whether it needs any change or not.. Accordingly, we pass it on to the Ministry of Finance for approval. Of course, we have discussions with the Ministry of Finance because they might also like to understand the details. So, that dialogue is there.

Our request is, if the Ministry of Finance were to give its indications well before the start of the first year of the Eleventh Plan, then that would help everybody to know what is going to be the situation during the five years of the Eleventh Plan. Secondly, we do need some kind of a figure to show that this is the total figure and whatever amount it might be would be divided in the five years in this fashion in the Annual Budget so that the Annual programmes can then be fine tuned to adjust to the availability. Otherwise, there is likely to be a mismatch between what we might project and the money availability".

When asked whether the Ministry of Finance had intimated the details of the 10th Plan allocations in time, the Defence Secretary has stated that : "It was towards the end of the third year. This was one part of the problem. The second part, as I said, is annual allocations are nowhere matching even this figure. Therefore, how do we do the Planning? We do not know what will be the figure for the fifth plan. Budget has been submitted for the fourth year. It totals up to Rs. 2 lakh something".

The Ministry of Defence in its written Action Taken Reply on the recommendation of the Committee on long term planning of three Services contained in the First Report on Demands for Grants of the Ministry of Defence for the year 2004-05, has stated as under : "A draft Long-Term Integrated Perspective Plan (LTIPP) covering the 15-year period from the Tenth to the Twelfth Plan (2002-2017) was formulated in June 2004 in consultation with the three Services. Since more than two years of the current Tenth Plan period have already elapsed, a new approach paper has been made formulating a Long Term Integrated Perspective Plan (LTIPP) covering the period from 2007-2022. This Plan is expected to be finalised by the Integrated Defence Staff by the last quarter of 2005."

The Committee are unhappy to note that the Ministry of Finance has failed to finalise the 10th Defence plan even after three years of the plan have passed. Non-finalisation of the 10th Defence Plan at its beginning by the Ministry of Finance has created a great deal of uncertainty about the availability of adequate finance for the acquisition of the vital equipment, modernization, etc. The Ministry of Defence had projected a demand of Rs. 4,97,000 crore in 2001 for the Tenth Plan. However, the Ministry of Finance has given indicative figure of Rs.4, 18,000 crore in December 2004,without any firm commitment. The total allocations in the first four years of Tenth Defence Plan just come to about Rs.2, 76,300 crore which is nowhere near their requirements. This gap between the demand and allocations, has adversely affected the defence planning and our preparedness. The Committee take a serious note of this and want the Government to finalise the Tenth Plan immediately and take steps to utilise the committed amount in full. The Committee would like to be apprised of the fmalisation of the Plan as well as the follow-up steps being taken to utilise the total allocation of the Tenth Plan.

The Committee also observe that due to non-finalisation of the Tenth Plan in time, the long term perspective plan of the Forces has got affected and is presently at the fmalisation stage with a revised plan schedule spanning from 2007-2022. The Committee, while expressing their displeasure over the present situation, recommend that the Ministry of Defence should reorient the plans and strive to adhere to the schedules envisaged. As regard the 11th Plan, the Committee desire that it should be finalised at least an year before the plan period starts.

It is high time that the Government prepared a road map for self-reliance. The Committee strongly feels that India should not be taken as a weapons/arms market by the global suppliers and action in this direction should be visible by the end of Tenth Defence Plan and 11th Plan should entirely be devoted to self-reliance.

The Committee has also observed that the surveillance capabilities of our forces are in adequate. This is primarily due to non-availability of low-level radar systems with the three services. The Committee feel that all round effort should be undertaken by the Government to ensure that the entire country is covered. The Committee feel that the Ministry should explore all possibilities of acquiring the required radar systems in adequate numbers without any delay.

7

Future Trends in Military Expenditure and Arms Transfers

Towards the end of the millennium the decline in world military expenditure had slowed down and there were indications that the trend would be reversed in the early 2000s. Expenditures on arms procurement in the European NATO countries has been increasing by 14 per cent since 1995. Defence plans in some of the major spender countries also point towards future increases.

The USA, which accounted for more than one-third of world military expenditure in 1998, presented a defence budget for fiscal year 2000/2001, which represented a 1 per cent increase in real terms, while procurement expenditure is planned to increase by 19 per cent over the five year period 2000-2005. Russia appeared in 1999 both politically and economically prepared to halt the rapid fall in its military expenditure and announced a planned 50 per cent increase in arms procurement. In Europe new requirements are arising out of new doctrines of military intervention in areas of conflict, which are likely to lead to increased military budgets. In Asia the simmering conflict between China and Taiwan has already resulted in increased military budgets and the 1997 Asian financial crisis has not had a strong impact on military expenditure in these countries. In Africa, where military expenditure has been on a long-term decline, the bottom was reached in 1995 after which there has been a gradual increase—probably more than SIPRI data show, because of the hidden cost of armed conflicts in the region. Overall, therefore, unless current plans are changed, it can be expected that the first years of the third millennium will become a period of increasing military expenditure.

As regards future trends in arms transfers, most observers agree that although the early post-cold war decline in the volume of international arms transfers has been halted, there will not be a return to the previous, cold war, levels of arms transfers within the near or medium-term future. In the three major arms-importing regions— Asia, Europe and the Middle East—there are no indications of a significant future growth in their arms imports. The financial crisis in Asia, which started in August 1997, has resulted in the cancellation of orders and arms import programmes in the affected countries. While some of these economies are now recovering, and are likely to revive some of their cancelled programmes, this will not suffice for a return to previous levels.

In Europe, the Central and East European countries have expressed significant requirements for new arms imports, but they lack the financial means to implement these. In the West European countries the change from territorial defence forces to forces for military action in conflicts abroad is likely to lead to demands for new equipment for peacekeeping forces. However, this emerging demand will be met both by domestic production and imports, and while the degree of imports is difficult to assess, it is not a matter of the huge quantities of cold war imports of large and sophisticated weapon platforms.

While the demand for weapons in the Middle East continues to be significant, there is a general consensus that Middle East arms purchases are not likely to return to previous levels. This is due to (*a*) domestic pressure to spend more of oil revenues on social programs to accommodate growing populations, (*b*) the turbulence in oil markets which has led to new caution in making major economic commitments for the future; and (*c*) problems of absorbing weapons already received.

DETERMINANTS OF MILITARY EXPENDITURE AND ARMS CHANGES

The determinants of military expenditure include both the driving forces for increasing military expenditure and the various forms of constraints which set limits on these forces. Actual military expenditure trends can be seen as a synthesis of these two types of determinant: the driving forces, seeking to maximize military expenditure, and the constraints. The main conventional rationale for military expenditure is related to international security, to protect state and people against external armed aggression. However, with the end of the cold war this factor is diminishing in importance. The prevalence of international armed conflict has decreased dramatically. Most major armed conflicts are internal today. At the global level there is little similarity between the patterns in global military expenditure and in armed conflict: military expenditure is concentrated to the industrial world, but the majority of armed conflicts are located in the developing world.

However, this is not always true at the regional and national level. In a study of 40 African countries covering the period 1960-91, a positive correlation was found between wars and military expenditure in 71 per cent of the countries. Also, if the level of military expenditure is compared with national output, it is clear that most of the countries with the highest ratio of military expenditure to national output (GDP) are countries involved in major armed conflict.

While security-related factors and the prevalence of armed conflict belong to the driving forces of military expenditure, these also include non-security related factors. Political and economic factors, often purely domestic in character, also act as driving forces. Nation building and the positioning of states in the international power structure are to some extent based on the build-up of a strong defence establishment. Military forces are not used exclusively for territorial defence but also for domestic repression of a country's own population, i.e. to secure the power of regimes without a democratic power basis. Driving forces of an economic nature are best exemplified by those of the military industrial complex, that is, the interplay of interests of the arms industry, government and the military establishment, and manifesting itself in, for example, the lobbying of arms-producing companies, the inter-service rivalry and the efforts of politicians to support military contracts to their local home electoral constituencies. During the cold war, the main driving force for high and rising military expenditure was the competition for strategic military superiority between the United States and the Soviet Union, reinforced by exaggerated threat perceptions on both sides (political) and the pull from the military industrial complex in both countries (economic and political).

The constraints on high military expenditure are mostly economic in nature but, at least in democratic countries, there are also political constraints, in terms of competing demands on public resource allocation by the electorate. Economic constraints have been one of the most important factors behind the sharp reduction in Russian military expenditure The disintegration of the Soviet Union in 1991 and the subsequent transition of the economic, political and military system of its successor state, the Russian Federation, led to a dramatic reduction of Russian military expenditure. The largest cut in Russian military expenditure actually occurred in 1992, under the pressure of the liberal economic reforms of Finance Minister Gaydar. Later into the decade difficulties to implement adopted defence budgets into actual expenditures have continued to undermine Russian military expenditure plans. In Africa too, the long-term decline in military expenditure was the result more of scarce economic resources than of the absence of wars and internal conflicts, of which there were plenty on the continent, particularly in the Horn of Africa and in Southern Africa. Also in Europe, although to a lesser extent, the cuts in military spending have been reinforced by the coincidence in time with periods of restrictive overall budgetary policies.

In Asia and the Middle East, on the other hand, many countries have experienced little economic constraints, at least until recently. Thus, it has been possible to raise military expenditure significantly due to high economic growth rates in Asia, high oil revenues in some of the Arab Middle East states and large amounts of US military and economic aid to Israel).

Determinants of Arms Transfers

International arms transfers are determined by three broad categories of factors: politico-military, technological and economic. These factors all operate at the international, regional and national levels in the major supplier and recipient countries that dominate the arms trade. The arms transfer and production system can be perceived of as located at the intersection of three important sets of forces for change in international relations that are seldom considered together: the pursuit of wealth, power and victory in war. First, the production of and trade in weapons are to some degree subject to the same economic pressures as are non-military goods; second, attempts by states to change their position in the arms transfer and production system reflect shifts in the international power hierarchy; and third, war often provides a dramatic catalyst to military innovation and production.

The system itself is based on a three-tier structure of arms-producing countries. The first tier, which during the cold war consisted of the USA and the USSR. Their near-monopoly of modern military technology granted them a capability to use arms transfers as effective tools of foreign policy. The second tier, which consisted of 10-15 other industrial countries with less, but still significant, capabilities in arms production and innovation. Their motivation for participating in the arms transfer system is different from that of first-tier suppliers: low levels of domestic procurement and relatively small research and development establishments force a greater reliance on arms exports. Throughout the 1970s and 1980s sophisticated weapons were further diffused throughout the system to what became the third-tier: several states in the developing world (Brazil, China, Egypt, India, Israel and others) which sought to acquire not only the weapons but also the means of reproducing them, in order to establish a strong regional political or military presence. However, the advance of third-tier producers was hindered by their weak economic, industrial and technological infrastructures.

These states therefore relentlessly pursued arms exports in order to maintain their fragile defence industrial bases, although with limited success. During the post cold war period the system of world arms production and trade has maintained the three-tier structure, while the positions of the participating states have changed fundamentally. During the mid-1980s, the two superpowers each accounted for roughly one-third of global arms production, 13 second-tier, industrial countries accounted for another 25 per cent of the world total, while 15 third-tier states in the developing world accounted for the remaining 10 per cent.

By the mid-1990s there was still a strong concentration of world arms production. The 10 largest arms-producing countries accounted for close to 90 per cent of world arms production. The main change is that the first tier has been reduced to one country, the USA which alone accounted for almost 50 per cent while Russia, which took over most of the arms production of the Soviet Union, ranked fifth in size and accounted for only 3–4 per cent of global arms production. During the years since 1996, the concentration in global arms production has, if anything, become even greater.

The post cold war period has also seen another significant change in the international arms transfers and production system: towards a diminishing role for political factors and a growing role for economic factors.

This is primarily the result of (*a*) the end of superpower rivalry and its replacement by a unipolar system, in which foreign policy incentives have less relevance; and (*b*) the decline in domestic armaments markets in almost all arms-producing countries, including the only remaining superpower, the United States.

These two factors have contributed to an increased pressure for exports and intensified competition among weapon suppliers to win the few large contracts on the now smaller world arms market. Companies are lobbying for financial and other support from their home governments, such as for the promotion and marketing of their weapon systems. Governments are becoming increasingly involved in the negotiation of large arms deals and of the various types of offset offers which constitute a normal part of any large arms deal today. Such offset agreement are normally worth as much as the arms deal itself, often reaching more than 150 per cent of the original deal. Thus, while offsets are regarded as an unfair trading practice in most sectors of the civil foreign trade, in the international arms trade they constitute the norm.

Another indication of the strong export pressure in the current arms trade is the fact that governments also provide financial support for arms exports, in the form of export credit guarantees, but also in more direct forms. A recent study of US Government funding of foreign arms purchases from US corporations shows that more than half of US weapon sales are now financed by taxpayers instead of foreign arms purchasers. These subsidies included loans, grants and government promotion activities for US arms exports. Similar tendencies have been identified in other major arms supplier countries.

IMPACT OF GLOBALIZATION ON MILITARY EXPENDITURE AND ARMS TRANSFERS

Although the term 'globalization' did not appear until recently, the notion of globalization has existed for a long time. The concept is being used for a wide variety of phenomena and trends and the descriptions of current trends in globalization and the conclusions as regards its impact differ accordingly. There exists not one discourse of globalization but several. In a recent survey of the debate and the literature, five major discourses on globalization are identified, basically falling into the areas of economics, sociology, political science, culture and ecology. All these aspects of globalization, together with the globalization of technology, have an impact of the trends and patterns in military expenditure and arms transfers, directly or indirectly by their impact on the causes of military expenditure, arms production and arms transfers.

The process of globalization has gone through several phases during which the various aspects have assumed different importance. During the cold war period, the political aspects were predominant. The impact of this phase of globalization on trends and pattern of military expenditures and arms transfers was significant and is well documented. During the subsequent, current, phase of globalization, the politico-military dynamic of the cold war has been overtaken by a mainly financial phase. It began in the second half of the 1980s, with the enormous expansion of trading in foreign currency after the breakdown in the 1970s of the international Bretton Woods currency system, and has resulted in the abolishing of state controls of capital markets and opening up of new financial world markets, in privatizations of public enterprises and services, in a break-up of national champion monopolies, and in a general encouragement of global competition. Simultaneously with the globalization of financial and economic activities, the end of the cold war has meant a deglobalization of political action.

These factors, around the existence of which there is fairly broad consensus, have an impact on military expenditure and arms transfers in several ways, perhaps primarily through its effect on the arms industry. While the military sector has been the sector most resistant to privatization, commercialization and reduced political control, all these trends are currently affecting the production, procurement and international transfers of arms. The arms industry is increasingly being privatized and commercialized. The European arms industry is going through a process of internationalization, until now relatively limited and primarily through cross-border joint ventures, but more recently (during 1999) also through cross-border mergers of arms producing companies. European companies are also acquiring armsproducing companies in other continents, recent examples include Australia, South Africa and South Korea, while transatlantic military-industrial links are still rare in spite of the lively debate on both sides of the Atlantic about their potential.

The increasing privatization, commercialization, competition and internationalization of arms production, have resulted in an increased pressure from the arms industry to export their excess supply of weapons, and thus to increased commercialization also of the arms trade, in which marketing and generous sales terms play an increasing role. At the same time, increased internationalization means reduced possibilities for national governments to implement national arms export regulations, since companies can choose to export their products from a business unit in another country with more liberal export regulations. For this reason, national export laws are becoming increasingly irrelevant. This points to the need for common or international export rules.

However, globalization may render also international control more difficult. The globalization of technology in general, and in the context of a gradual closing of the gap between military and civil technology, will make it increasingly difficult to control the international transfer of militarily relevant technologies in the future. The challenge is to achieve international limitations in the transfer of military technology without resorting to controls which will inhibit international transfers of all types of advanced technology, that is, also civil technologies which would benefit economic growth in the recipient countries.

A relatively new development is the impact of globalization on armed conflict and the financing of these. The fragmentation and decentralization of the state has produced a new type of wars and with it increasingly financing of wars outside traditional government defence budgets. As described by Mary Kaldor, these new wars take place in the context of extreme globalization, under which territorially-based production has more or less collapsed and production continues only of a few valuable commodities (diamonds, emeralds, drugs), which provide a source of income for whoever can provide 'protection'. These wars are fought by various types of fighting units, public and private, state and non-state, including regular armed forces or remnants thereof, paramilitary groups, self-defence units, foreign mercenaries, and regular foreign troops, usually under international auspices. During these conditions governments, like privatized military groups, need alternative sources of funding for their military activities, many of which involve criminal activities. These fall into the following categories: 1) 'Asset transfer', i.e. the redistribution of existing assets to benefit the fighting units (such as loot, robbery, hostage-taking, and deriving profits from control over market prices); 2) 'war taxes' or 'protection' money from the production of primary commodities and various forms of illegal trading; and 3) external assistance, in particular for imports, such as (a) remittances from abroad to individual families, b) direct assistance from the Diaspora living abroad; (c) assistance from foreign governments; and 4) humanitarian assistance diverted by governments and warring factions for their own use. For countries involved in such new wars, data on government military expenditure are irrelevant for measuring military expenditure. What is more important is that the set of social relationships which are formed by these systems for financing wars constitute strongly resisting factors for the ending of war.

Privatization of security is an increasing trend also in countries which are not involved in regular armed conflict but where there is a demand for more security services than the government can offer. There is an emerging group of private security companies whose main task is the provision of security in many Third World countries, especially in Africa. The demand for private security services has emerged from a combination of factors, including from western governments seeking to reduce defence budgets, African governments in search of security, international mining corporations and rebel movements. They provide a variety of services, ranging from guarding installations, protecting convoys, supporting humanitarian assistance operations to performing reconnaissance and intelligence services, providing logistical and transport support, military training, strategic planning, and engaging in combat. These companies have developed to fill the need for security in the current context of conflict in Africa, in weak states with limited government legitimacy and with limited economic resources, and in which the international community is increasingly reluctant to intervene.

INDIA'S UNENDING DEFENCE EXPENDITURE

Despite criticism from various circles that India is not investing more to tackle development issues as millions remain mired in poverty; the Indian government's ambitious modernisation plan for its military is in full swing. In February this year, Indian military procurement units descended on the DefExpo 2010 trade fair in New Delhi. Inaugurating the Indian Defence Exhibition, Defence Minister A.K. Antony said that India's defence expenditure, which is 2.5 percent of its gross domestic product (GDP), is going to increase. He pointed out, “our defence industry is open up to 100 percent for Indian private sector, while foreign direct investment is allowed up to 26 percent.” Antony further indicated that our government is committed to rapid modernisation of armed forces. Over the next 12 years, India is set to spend a whopping US$200 billion on defence acquisitions to replace its outdated inventory. In this regard, on February 15, 2010, a report of the Indian strategic defence magazine (India Strategic's DefExpo) revealed that 70 per cent of the inventory of the Indian armed forces is 20-plus years old, and needs to be replaced with the modern technology.

It explained that nearly half of this funding ($100b) will go to the Indian Air Force (IAF), which would need to replace more than half of its combat jet fleet as well as the entire transport aircraft and helicopter fleet. The army needs new guns, tanks, rocket launchers, multi-terrain vehicles, while the navy needs ships, aircraft carriers and new range of nuclear submarines.

In three from 1994 to 1997 India's defence budget was increased from 20 percent to 24.4 percent. For the financial year 2001-2002 defence has been allocated Rs 620,000.00 million. This amount shows an increase of Rs 75,000 million as compared to previous year's revised estimates of Rs 544,610 million. In 2009, India increased its defence budget by a whopping 28.2 percent or Rs 130,000.00 million. Some experts estimate that military spending will increase further, totalling as much as 200 billion dollars over the period to 2022.

India's military has planned a massive upgrade of its mainly 1990s-era weapons systems which is mostly from the former Russia. The plans include the purchase of 126 new combat aircraft to replace an ageing fleet of MiG-21s..The US has emerged as a potential military supplier to India since the two countries signed a deal of civil energy technology in 2008, which lifted sanctions on New Delhi in order to import nuclear technology. India is likely to become a major customer for the US military-industrial complex over the next few years. During the recent visit of the US Secretary of State Robert Gates to New Delhi, American Defence officials, however, have said that US weapons sales to India would not be a focus of the trip. Regardless of such denials, the key reason for the Gates' visit can be found in the fact that India is planning to raise its military budget by 50% to almost $40 billion, making military expenditure 3% of the annual GDP. In contrast to India's planned defence expenditures, Pakistan's entire 2009-10 budget amounts to little over $30 billion.

India, the largest arms buyer among emerging nations, accounted for 7.5 per cent of all international arms sales between 2000 and 2007. It has spent billions of dollars in the past few years on purchases of planes, radars and ships from Britain, France, Germany and Russia and Israel.

In recent years, India has bought reconnaissance aircraft from US aerospace major Boeing worth 2.1 billion-dollars, medium range missiles for 1.4 billion dollars from Israeli Aerospace Industries, and signed an upgrade service contract with the Russian Aircraft Corporation to upgrade its MiG-29 squadrons for 965 million dollars. Several deals are planned for the near future including one of the largest arms contracts of recent times—a 11-billion-dollar project to acquire 126 multi-role combat aircraft.

It is mentionable that after 9/11, both India and Israel which had openly jumped on Bush's anti-terrorism enterprise are acting upon a secret diplomacy, targeting Pakistan China, Iran and Syria. In this context, Indo-Israeli secret diplomacy could be assessed from the interview of Israel's ambassador to India, Mark Sofer published in the Indian weekly Outlook on February 18, 2008. Regarding India's defence arrangements with Tel Aviv, Sofer had surprisingly disclosed "We do have a defence relationship with India, which is no secret" and "with all due respect, the secret part will remain a secret."

As regards joint exercises, Sofer replied, "Certain issues need to remain under wraps for whatever reason."

Notably, India's 'The Tribune' wrote on September 10, 2003, "India and Israel took giant leaps forward in bolstering the existing strategic ties", and Tel Aviv has "agreed to share its expertise with India in various fields such as anti-fidayeen operations, surveillance satellites, intelligence sharing and space exploration." With the support of Israel, New Delhi has been acquiring an element of strategic depth by setting up logistical bases in the Indian Ocean for its navy. In fact, India wants to become a mini-superpower of the region and hence it uses the pretext of deterrence against Pakistan and China. In this context, New Delhi with the support of US and Israel has presumed peace-loving Pakistan and China as their arch enemies, but it does not admit officially.

In May, 1998, when India detonated five nuclear tests, Islamabad was compelled to follow the suit through its own atomic experiments. But Pakistan which so far relied upon the minimum nuclear deterrence has again been forced by India's unending spending on arms purchases to counterbalance the former. In this regard, Pakistan has signed a number of agreements with China. Nevertheless, currently, more than half of India's budget is allocated for military, paramilitary, various security forces and debt servicing. That leaves less than half for everything else including infrastructure development projects, education, healthcare, poverty alleviation, and various human services. New Delhi' s latest arms buildup will leave even less for what India needs most to lift hundreds of millions of its citizens from abject poverty, hunger illiteracy and disease.

Indian civil society organisations, while complaining of excessive defence spending indicated that the government spends 2.35 per cent of GDP on defence, but only 1.72 per cent on the social sector. The defence budget for 2009-2010 is 29 billion dollars, up 34 percent over the previous one.

Indian defence analyst Ravinder Pal Singh, while calling New Delhi's unending defence spending at the cost of poverty-alleviation—with security requirements competing with socioeconomic concerns for money calls it guns-versus-butter question.

Even some of Indian officials are surprised in relation to Indian defence expenditure which has no bounds. For example, an official of the country's finance ministry remarked, "There is a dilemma...poverty needs to be eradicated to prevent men from taking to the guns...but more funds for security means less money for poverty alleviation." Meanwhile, a report of United Nations pointed out that India ranks 134th of 182 countries on the United Nations Development Programme's Human Development Index. It estimated that 50 per cent of the world's undernourished population lives in India. Nearly 31 per cent of the billion-plus Indians earn less than a dollar a day.

Secretary General of the Control Arms Foundation of India Binalakshmi Nepram said, "When people are dying of poverty and bad sanitation, what protection will arms provide them?" On the one hand, international community has been making strenuous efforts for world peace in wake of global financial crisis and war against terrorism, on the other, India has initiated deadly nuclear arms in South Asia where people are already facing multiple problems of grave nature. Majority of South Asian people are living below the poverty level, lacking basic facilities like fresh food and clean water. While yielding to acute poverty, every day, some persons commit suicide in India, Pakistan, Sri Lanka etc.

Setting aside regional problems, and resolution of Indo-Pak issues-especially thorny dispute of Kashmir, Indian rulers state that they don't have any aggressive designs. But it becomes a big joke of the 21st century, reminding a maxim, "armed to the teeth, but no enemy", if we take cognisance of India's unending defence expenditure.

THE MILITARY-INDUSTRIAL COMPLEX IS RUINING THE ECONOMY

Everyone knows that the too big too fails and their dishonest and footsy-playing regulators and politicians are largely responsible for trashing the economy. But the military-industrial complex shares much of the blame. Nobel prize winning economist Joseph Stiglitz says that the Iraq war will cost $3-5 trillion dollars.

Sure, experts say that the Iraq war has *increased* the threat of terrorism. See this, this, this, this, this, this and this. And we launched the Iraq war based on the false linkage of Saddam and 9/11, and knowingly false claims that Saddam had WMDs. And top British officials, former CIA director George Tenet, former Treasury Secretary Paul O'Neill and many others say that the Iraq war was planned *before* 9/11. But this essay is about dollars and cents. America is also spending a pretty penny in Afghanistan. The U.S. admits there are only a small handful of Al Qaeda in Afghanistan. As ABC notes: U.S. intelligence officials have concluded there are only about 100 al Qaeda fighters in the entire country.

With 100,000 troops in Afghanistan at an estimated yearly cost of $30 billion, it means that for every one al Qaeda fighter, the U.S. will commit 1,000 troops and $300 million a year. Sure, the government apparently planned the Afghanistan war *before 9/11*. And the Taliban offered to turn over Bin Laden. And we could have easily killed Bin Laden in 2001 and again in 2007, but chose not to, even though that would have saved the U.S. hundreds of billions of dollars in costs in prosecuting the Afghanistan war. But this essay is about dollars and cents.

The methods of awarding contracts for research and development reflect an even sharper departure from regular business practices. Again, some of the basic ideas may have been produced by cooperation between the prospective contractor and the scientific branches of the armed forces in which such requests originate. However, eventually the job is put out for proposals (which are major engineering tasks in themselves). The need to produce proposals has had a profound effect on the employment structures of military contractors. Technical proposals must be quite detailed. In them the prospective contracting firm gives an overview of its understanding of the job, describes the methods it would use to solve the problems, and tries to impress the government with an elaborate presentation of previous experience. That kind of exercise resembles the proposals that universities submit as part of grantsmanship more than any normal kind of business negotiation. In any case, the details of facilities and managerial organization that bidders must include in proposals of this sort go far beyond what a business would normally submit in contracting privately. (The government's power over the firm's internal affairs affects not only what is made but also methods and quantities as well, as will be explained later.)

A good technical proposal alone, however, is not all there is to winning a contract. To be considered eligible to submit a bid, a firm must be on the list of approved bidders. Inclusion in a list depends upon various considerations; one factor appears to be that certain firms are thought of as "belonging" to a particular unit of the armed services. For one of these regular bidders, it might be considered real diversification to supply a different command within the Air Force, or perhaps the Navy rather than the Army. In practice, each firm functions as an unofficial division of the Pentagon conglomerate or one of its parts.

The relationship between a contractor and its military sponsor is a peculiar one. For the company, having once won a military contract puts it in a position tantamount to engagement, or at least going steady. Once a unit of a company has become dependent upon military orders, its military controllers view with disfavor any efforts to diversify into commercial areas. The company is supposed to stay true to its military benefactor and grateful for a glance of favour. This outlook epitomizes the usual negative reaction of military industrial contractors to the subject of possible conversion or diversification away from dependence on the military.

How to Make It

The control of the "state management" over methods of production is at least as pervasive as its control over products. The ASPR takes four pages to list the areas over which the government exercises direct control. More than just technical surveillance of the item is concerned; one would expect technical standards to be imposed for any specialized, technically oriented equipment. Machine firms, for example, are certainly used to having customers' inspectors on the premises to see how the job is progressing. Engineering firms doing work on contract have customers' representatives among them to keep track of the design and procurement. Technical specifications often go into considerable detail on materials to be used and standards for quality, inspection, and performance.

However, the government control over military contractors goes much further than that. Not only are technical aspects covered in minute detail, but aspects of the operation of the firm (such as wage structure, insurance, benefits) are also fair game for the government to evaluate and inspect. (These considerations affect quantity of output required as well.) To some degree, this watchfulness on the part of the government could be attributed to the fact that the contracts are on a cost-plus basis. But the functional controls appear to go beyond even that. The subcontractors are all subject to similar rules, varied according to the nature of their work. The controls may apply only to the prime contractor if the item being supplied by the subcontractors is a standard one, similar to their usual commercial product. The control structure is so marvellously pervasive that it is worth studying carefully. Many a firm made up of many divisions would consider such a centrally determined and controlled list of characteristics an extremely onerous form of centralization of the kind that has been heavily criticized in textbooks on management. Be that as it may, this control is certainly unparalleled elsewhere in the American economy.

How Much to Build

Concerning the quantity of items to be manufactured for the military, three considerations diverge radically from determinants in the commercial sector. As mentioned, the functions of research and production are kept separate. This means that regardless of what organization did the research, another may eventually be responsible for production. This separation is conducive to inefficiency, wasted lead-time, and even outright flaws of production. Costs and quantities may be disproportionate to effort, and accurate projections of amounts are out of the question.

The government gains further control as it prescribes precisely how much of each item is to be produced. Normally, private management jealously guards the prerogative of deciding the quantity to be produced. The decision is reached by assessing such factors as the needs of the market to be served and its prospects for expanding, or the likelihood of new markets or market segments opening. The most important single variable in making the decision is the physical scale of manufacture.

In military procurement, however, the firm enjoys no such discretion. Unless the government alters its requirements, there is no way of changing the quantities. Although it may at times be possible for a firm to alter specifications slightly, there is no way of changing the size of the market except by political process. A limited market thus sets limits on production.

But perhaps most important, in a military setting the quantity to be procured cannot be determined rationally. The quantity depends upon a great many extrapolations, particularly in a time when (as government leaders are constantly assuring us) the product is designed solely to deter something or other, rather than to be used. Such overkill as has been endemic to military procurement for more than 25 years precludes using market saturation as an overall limit, so items are ordered to some extent just to maintain the industrial base. Some of that reasoning appears to hark back to the dear dead days of Rosie the Riveter in World War II, when a major war could be won on the production lines of America. Here, of course, enters the military predilection for refighting an old war.

The Department of Defence cannot and should not assume the responsibility for creating a level of demand adequate to keep the economy healthy and growing. Nor should it, in developing its programs, depart from the strictest standards of military need and operating efficiency in order to aid an economically distressed company or community. This principle is, of course, violated continually; at any rate, whenever a weapon is proposed, its proponents invariably contend that it will produce jobs, and politicians present it as a plum for their constituents, even though most other activities are well known to produce more jobs for a given investment. Keynesianism is evidently alive and well at the Pentagon, whatever stern supply-side or monetarist precepts are in favour elsewhere.

At What Monetary Value

One of the tiresome cliches of recent times is, "If they can send a man to the moon, why can't they... ?" It makes its way into all kinds of discussions of industrial change, and even into advertising copy. It was used for the original promotion of Brim, the decaffeinated coffee, with the reassuring voice-over, "Consider it done."

The principal fallacy in this comparison, of course, is that there is no way of determining ahead of time how much a trip to the moon ought to cost, whereas other technically oriented developments (such as techniques of desalinating seawater) require precise economic parameters if they are to compete. In the case of weapons, as with lunar flight, no such assessment is possible in a rational way, even though it is obvious that there is some limit to the resources that can be devoted to military purposes. The price that society is willing to pay for progress is thus essentially a political decision. It simply is not an economic decision that can be based on needs and demand; decision makers, whether managers of enterprises or individual citizens, cannot verify possible results in advance.

Even if competition were fully feasible, however, the fact is that for many years, some 80 percent of all contracts have been negotiated rather than being put out for competitive bidding. Even with bidding, the specifications for the job (especially in research contracts, but also in manufacturing) are often written after the buying agency has consulted with a favoured prospective bidder. Any other firm whose proposal is solicited is thus trying hopelessly to guess the punchline of an incompletely told joke.

Such a firm, referred to as playing second fiddle in a one-man band, has no real chance, but must nevertheless bear the very real costs of competing. The different form of pricing of military economics is imposed upon society mainly through the system of using cost-plus-fixed-fee contracts, customary in military procurement. In settling a price for a negotiated contract, the prospective contractor and the contracting officers have a mandate to base their final agreement on reasonable costs plus a standard fixed fee for profit. During World War II, contracts based on cost plus a fixed percentage led to considerable abuse; such contracts have Long been illegal. However, now considerable leeway is allowed for engineering changes; these are the main cause of cost overruns. Once a large amount of money has been expended on a project that falls short of expectations, it becomes difficult and embarrassing to simply abandon it. Instead, more and more money is pumped into it by way of engineering changes—which in many cases include a provision for additional profit. The job thus seems to continue, in Jonathan Swift's apt phrase, "driven on equally by hope and despair."

All of these special considerations have had the effect of starkly distinguishing the military industrial firm from the conventional private enterprise. The latter is, broadly speaking, a cost-minimizing and profit-maximizing entity, regardless of long-range and short-range effects. By contrast, the military industrial firm maximizes sales or subsidy. The contract structure itself is a disincentive for cost saving. Occasionally the government has made attempts to provide incentives for performing on time and within budget. For some contractors this has meant juggling costs between various accounts so that as many accounts as possible could qualify for the incentive payments. This finagling is of great concern to the government auditors (who, consistent with the general head-office-versus-division arrangement, are a strong presence among the major military contractors). The emphasis in such firms on maximizing subsidization is the reason that they stockpile engineering talent. As long as it can reasonably be charged to a job in house, the stockpiling costs nothing extra—and having the resources available may help in securing a new contract. Overemployment is thus endemic in the military industrial firm.

8

Approach to Defence Procurement and Industrialisation

The approach that India has adopted in defence procurement and defence industrial development is similar to that followed other less developed countries (LDCs). Within this general model, however, the country's experience can be divided into three stages. The first was from independence in 1947 until the early to mid-1960s. The second went from the period following the Sino-India war (1962) and second Indo-Pakistan (1965) conflict until the mid-1980s. And the third went from the mid-1980s until the present day. In the first period, India only possessed the ability to make things such as shells and other ammunition, small arms, guns and explosives; it also had a limited aircraft and ship maintenance capabilities based in Bangalore and Calcutta. Thus, it had to look abroad to foreign defence equipment suppliers, such as the United Kingdom and France to meet its needs.

During the second stage, efforts were made to build up domestic production, mostly through assembly under license from the Soviet Union and the United Kingdom. (This programme was centred on the PSUs). During this period, the range of activities undertaken by defence sector was also deliberately widened to include previously peripheral items such as clothing. The third period started with large purchases from the Soviet Union by the former Prime Minister Rajiv

Ghandi's government (1984-1989). During this period, India consistently spent over 3.3 per cent of Gross Domestic Product (GDP) on building up its armed forces. By the end of the decade, India had the fourth largest armed forces in the world, the fifth biggest airforce, and the sixth biggest navy. Likewise, India became the world's largest importer of conventional weapons, spending $US12.2 billion in the period, of which Russia was the largest supplier.

By the end of the 1980s India was assessed as being able to assemble Complete Knock Down (CKD) and Semi-Knóck Down (SKDs) purchased from foreign companies and production under license. Furthermore, gradual improvements were also made in and greater attention paid to the country's defence research and development capability, as well as systems integration for the in-country assembly of weapons. Between the financial year 1991-1992 and the FY 1994-1995, for example, funding for military R&D increased by 36 per cent to UD$430/454 million. And in 1995 India announced its intention to double the share of the defence budget allocated to defence R&D to ten per cent of the total defence budget with a view to reducing the imported content of defence goods to 30 per cent by 2005. Broadly speaking the decision to allocate increased funds to defence R&D came at the expense of funding for more traditional procurement programmes. The move towards defence indigenisation and the tensions associated with it in the 1990s did not occur in a vacuum; indeed it arguably happened earlier than India either predicted or was ready for.

For example, the 1991 economic crisis that best the economy forced India to reduce defence spending as a percentage of GDP, from four per cent in the late 1980s to below three per cent in 1994, while the amount of funding allocated to procurement was slashed. The end of the Cold War and the collapse of the Soviet Union, meanwhile, led to the end of the supply of cheap and subsidised weaponry from Moscow. As the previously centralised Soviet arms industry was now spread across the new Republics, India also found it increasingly difficult to acquire spare parts for much of this equipment. Against this backdrop, indigenous R&D was apparently seen (*or at least presented as*) a way around the problem. India's approach to defence industrial development from Independence onwards is also closely related to its approach to economic development generally.

Crucially, a significant proportion of India's defence production and R&D base is entirely under state control. This is the result of the Industrial Policy Resolutions of 1948 and 1956. These placed the development of all key sectors of the economy, such as machine tools, railways, iron and steel and defence production, under state control. (Both the Mazagon Docks and the Garden Reach Shipbuilders were brought under public ownership in 1960). The large-scale participation of private sector companies in defence production, in the meantime, is limited to providing components to the PSUs. Even though the manufacture of components, assemblies and sub-assemblies was opened up to the private sector in 1991, the Indian armed forces procure 250 per cent more from the public than the private sector. A survey of 500 top companies in Indian in the same year also reported that only 30 of them had (or are currently) involved in defence contracts.

DISPUTES TO INDIA'S CURRENT DEFENCE PRODUCTION

India's experience of developing its defence industry and research and development capability over the past decade has been mixed.

The country's ordnance factories are capable of providing the Indian military with a significant proportion of their ammunition and low level material needs. In the period 1992/93-1997/98, for example, India only imported 11 per cent of its total ammunition needs. India is also planning to open a 40th Ordnance factory in the near future. Furthermore, speaking in the Indian Parliament, the *Lok Sabha*, on 4 July 2000, George Fernandes, the Indian Defence Minister, stated that the country's ordnance factories recorded a surplus of Rs 780 crores (a crore is ten million rupees) during the period 1999-2000. In addition to this, Fennandes stated that due to last year's Kargil conflict, output increased from 33 per cent to 900 per cent for ammunition items; 20 per cent to 108 per cent for clothing items; and 76 to 233 per cent for cables.

More generally, an overall increase in output value of 34.6 per cent in 1999-2000, as compared to the value of issue in 1998/99. The picture for the PSUs is similar. Output in the sector has been rising rapidly since the 1980s, and all the companies have started to move into profitability. According to the latest MOD, moreover, the value of production in 1998-1999 (Rs 7205.55 crore) registered growth of 15.57 per cent over that in 1997-1998 (Rs 6234.75 crore). In addition to this all the defence PSUs reportedly earned a profit in 1998-1999.

Set against that is the fact that these two elements of India's defence industrial base continue to receive large amounts of money from the government in the form of government loans. Between them they also employ in the region of 300000 people. The picture is further complicated by the fact that almost half the production of the PSUs goes to the civil sector; a small proportion of the Ordnance factory production also goes this way. (Put another way if is arguable that, certainly in the case of the PSUs, it is the production of equipment for civil use rather than for military use that is actually making money). Against this backdrop, questions have been raised about their efficiency and ability to meet production targets, as underscored by the fact that it has taken Garden Reach Shipbuilders 12 years to build the Indian Naval Ship (INS) Brhamaputra; three times longer than it would take Russia's cash strapped shipbuilders to do.

Traditionally, the price of purchasing systems and platforms from the PSUs has also worked out more expensive than purchasing them from abroad. For example, back in 1956 it was estimated that the cost of independently producing under license the HS-78 plane would be in the region of US$320000; come the end of the 1970s it stood at $1.5 million per unit.

Indigenous R&D

The success of India's indigenous R&D efforts is even more questionable: despite considerable investment through the 1990s nearly all major programmes implemented in the 1980s are experiencing time and cost over-runs.

The IGMDP: Covering the Prithvi and Agni short and medium/long range ballistic missiles, the Nag anti tank missile, and the Akash and Trishul surface to air missile, this programme has scored a number of notable and high profile successes. For example, the Prithvi has been tested regularly since 1988 and three versions of the missile (150km, 250km, and 350km ranges) are now believed to be in (or close to) production. The Agni was first tested in 1994 and in a 1998 missile test the missile flew close to 2500km. According to some reports, moreover, the missile is now operational. The Aksah, Nag and Trishul, meanwhile, are expected to enter service soon. However, none of these missiles are entirely indigenous. Some reports suggest, for instance, that five to ten per cent of the technologies used in the Prithvi are imported from abroad

The Arjun: India's experience of designing an indigenous tank has been less successful. Take the example of the Arjun tank. Originally, expected to be in operation service by 1985 the tank has suffered from continued problems, such as problems with the engine overheating. Limited production of the tank has now started; however the Indian Army has cut back on the number of tanks that it is ordering.

The LCA The story of the LCA is almost identical to that of the Arjun tank. The programme has experienced delays since its inception in 1983 for a variety of reasons. And the first flight-test, originally scheduled for 1996, is now not expected to take place until some time in 2002. The cost of the programme, in the meantime, has increased from Rs560 crores. This increased to Rs2188 crores in 1993, when approval was given to enter the Full Scale Engineering Development Phase-1.

Other Programmes: The picture is much the same for a number of other less high profile programmes, such as the Pinaka, MBRL. This was initiated in 1986 with a budget of Rs25.6 crores. This was subsequently increased to 49 crores. The system underwent troop trials in October 1999, moreover, but is still waiting for acceptance by the Army before entering full production.

A similar story emerges for products such as the Indian Small Arms System (ISAS). The only product deemed to have been a complete success is arguably the ALH. The failure of many of India's R&D programmes and its reliance on the outside world for key technologies is confirmed by a number of by external assessments, such as the United States government Military Critical Technologies List (MCTL). For example, India's capability to manufacture, gas turbine engines, and human crew systems (aeronautic systems technology) is not even considered worthy of a mention in the MCTL.

Likewise, its ability to manufacture the systems necessary to ensure that a combat vehicle is superior to the technology that it is confronting. India scores a little better in the area of Marine Systems Technology, where it is rated to have limited Sub-surface and Deep Submergence Vehicle Capability. One area where India is deemed to have been successful is in the area of Means of Delivery Technology for nuclear and other non-conventional weapons, where it is rated as having a sufficient Theatre Ballistic Missile Capability (TBMC), some ICBM capability; and a sufficient Cruise Missile capability. By way of a comparison, outside the core-areas of competency that it has developed, India's defence production and R&D capabilities do not compare that favourably with other developing countries such as China, which has managed to develop its defence industry across a broader spectrum.

Consequences and Responses

India's inability to meet its top end defence needs have been compounded by the approaching obsolescence of a number of platform and systems; a problem that has been made even worse by the fact that Indian has not made any major defence purchases for the past ten years.

Last year's crisis in Kargil has also impressed the need to introduce new equipment on the armed forces-according to the reports, for example, the Indian military assessed Pakistan's Ukranian T-80s as being 'almost a generation ahead of what we had'.

In response, as far as major systems and high-technology products are concerned, the government has reversed the pattern of the 1990s and shifted the balance of procurement funding away from its home grown programmes and back towards external procurement. This re-evaluation started in the late 1990s and has progressed since there.

Thus in 1996-97 and 1997-98 the DRDO's share of the defence budget decreased in real terms for the first time in that decade. At the same time, India announced its decision to purchase 40 SU-30MK fighter/bombers from Russia in India's largest ever defence deal. Likewise, even though India announced that it would increase its defence budget by 28 per cent to $13.94 billion (2.5 per cent of GDP) in 2000-2001 this March, funding for domestic R&D was only raised by 5.2 per cent; the percentage of the defence budget allocated to defence R&D has also slipped to 4.4 per cent of the total budget. At the same time, while this year's defence budget has seen the amount of money for R&D fall in relative terms, the funds for the purchase of defence equipment from abroad have been steadily increased since 1998.

Reviving the Russian Link

Despite the challenge to their defence relationship that occurred following the end of the Cold War and the economic crisis in India, Russia and India still managed to maintain close defence ties throughout the latter part of the 1990s. For example, the two countries signed a long-term defence cooperation programme in 1994; a number of agreements for the upgradation of Indian defence equipment were initialled; India also agreed to buy 40 SU-30MKs in 1997; and according to the Russian Vice Premier Liya Klebarov, defence sales to India account for between 20 and 25 per cent of the annual total export of Russian military goods, making it India's largest arms supplier. It comes as little surprise to find, therefore, that much of the money allocated for procurement will be spent in Russia. Although many of the deals have been under negotiation for some time, the October visit of the Russian president, Vladimir Putin, appears to have broken the logjam. Thus, although the details still have to be finalised, India and Russia officially agreed to extend their defence cooperation programme until 2010. Furthermore, India announced its intention to buy Russian arms worth more than $2 billion. Intended purchases include, additional Su-30 long range fighter bombers, a number of which will be made under license in India, more than 300 T-90 Main Battle Tanks (MBTS), one third of which will also be made in India, the ageing Soviet-era aircraft carrier, the Admiral Gorshkov, which will be provided for free but would cost $500 million to refurbish; an, as yet, unspecified number of MiG-29s for the ship; and a number of Smersh MRBLs.

European and Other Suppliers

India has also looked to solidify its links with European suppliers. For example, although the details of the deal have yet to be finalised the British based company BAE SYTEMS is also believed to have secured the deal to provide India with the Hawk advanced jet trainer aircraft. (India has been negotiating this purchase for over a decade). France has also been particularly successful, recently concluding an agreement to sell India additional Mirage 2000 fighters. Outside Europe, India has established a close defence procurement relationship with Israel, which is thought to have provided it, among other things, with equipment suitable for border surveillance. Furthermore, reliable sources have suggested that the Phalcon early warning plane (AEW) that Israel was building for China but recently agreed not to sell to Beijing after pressure from the United States will be delivered to India. South African arms exports have also managed to carve out a small niche for themselves in the country. A number of Eastern European nations are also looking to provide India with new equipment and to help it upgrade its existing inventory. Quite simply, these purchases will fill those gaps that have appeared in India's armed forces in recent years.

DEFENCE OFFSETS: DEMONSTRATING DETRIMENTAL TO THE SERVICES

Post Kargil, Indian defence imports had been ranging between three to six billion dollars annually whereas defence exports had been stagnating at meagre 50 million dollars an year. Despite India's best efforts very little headway was being made on the export front. As a last resort, a proposal was mooted in 2004 to coerce foreign sellers to compulsorily buy Indian defence goods in exchange. While the proposal was being debated, an article titled "Offsets in Arms Trade: Need for a National Policy" appeared in Indian Defence Review (Oct-Dec 2004). It had suggested that India should have a national offset policy and all major defence deals must carry mandatory offset obligations. Defence Public Sector Undertakings (DPSU) and the Ordnance Factory Board (OFB) were quick to grasp the significance of offsets and modified their proposal from one of counter-trade to that of offsets.

As India has no national offset policy, Ministry of Defence (MoD) took the initiative to evolve its own defence offset policy. Initially announced in early 2005, the policy was made a part of Defence Procurement Procedure-2005. As the primary aim of the policy was to boost exports from the public sector, it allowed discharge of offsets either through FDI in Indian public sector undertaking for defence industrial infrastructure or direct purchase of products/components/services from DPSU/OFB/other industry identified by MoD. Interestingly, the task of monitoring implementation of every offset contract was to be assigned to a DPSU or OFB.

The above policy was subjective in intent. The private sector protested strongly against the unfair treatment meted out to it, forcing MoD to revise the policy in 2006. Scope for direct purchase of defence goods and services was enlarged to include the whole Indian defence industry. It also allowed FDI in Indian defence industry and defence R&D. Further, it defined Indian defence industry to include DPSU, OFB and any private defence industry manufacturing defence products under an industrial licence granted for such manufacture. As no major manufacturing activity was taking place in private sector under licence, the policy continued to favour the public sector.

As was expected, industry associations were not satisfied and appealed to MoD for a level playing field. Bowing to pressure, MoD removed the mandatory requirement of an industrial licence for private companies in 2008. Now, the only stipulation to being an offset partner is that the Indian company should not have more than 26 percent foreign holding. Before examining the effect of offsets on the services, it is essential to understand three aspects that have a profound bearing on the modernisation plans of the armed forces, i.e. objective of seeking offsets, receipt of technology against offsets and cost of demanding offsets.

OBJECTIVE OF SEEKING OFFSETS

Offsets are universally accepted as a powerful leverage to obtain compensatory benefits by asking the seller to undertake well-designated activities to satisfy vital economic necessity or fill critical technological void. Therefore, before embarking on offsets every country identifies and spells out objectives that are proposed to be achieved through offsets. Thus, the objectives are always nation-specific and in consonance with national aspirations and long-term vision. In the absence of well evolved objectives, offsets lose focus and prove highly wasteful. An aimless offset policy can neither contribute to the growth of indigenous industry nor provide long term economic benefits.

India may be the only country whose defence offset policy has no stated objectives. MoD has not considered it necessary to explain as to what it intends to achieve through offsets and the roadmap for the same. However, as offset policy is a part of Defence Procurement Procedure-2008 (DPP-2008), it can be reasonably inferred that its objective would be in line with the objective spelt out in DPP-2008, i.e. achieving self-reliance in defence equipment. Additionally, India has been reiterating its resolve to reduce the current proportion of imports from 70 percent to 30 percent. If that be so, primary thrust of the Indian policy should be to seek infusion of technology to strengthen its indigenous defence industrial base.

However, contrary to all rationale, the Indian offset policy has been formulated to continue dependence on imports. India has not considered it necessary to direct offsets to pre-designated areas of its choice. It has abrogated the right to select methodology, areas and offset programmes in favour of the vendors, thereby rendering India's needs inconsequential. It is natural for every foreign vendor to opt for programmes that cost the least and are easy to fulfil-Indian needs do not count at all.

EXTRACT OF TECHNOLOGY AGAINST OFFSETS

Every country that strives to develop indigenous industry seeks technology through offsets to bridge the gap and use acquired technology as a take off platform for indigenous development of more advanced technologies. More than 35 percent of all offsets worldwide relate to technology transfer. Transfer of Technology (ToT) is rightly called as the engine that drives offsets.

For technology transfer, all countries adopt a two-step approach, as given below:-

Identification of Critical Technologies. These are technologies that are considered essential for stimulating and expediting the growth of indigenous industrial competence. For economies of scale, sought technologies should not be product-specific but have much wider application across a large range of systems. Ability to absorb identified technology and monitor its transfer is another major consideration.

Persuasion of Vendors to Offer Required Technology. To persuade vendors to part with the technology sought, a system of assigning different multiplier values to various offset programmes is put in place. Multiplier value is a factor applied to the actual value of an offset transaction to calculate the credit value earned. For example, by undertaking an offset programme worth Rs 100 crores with a multiplier value of 3.5, a foreign vendor would earn offset credits equal to Rs 350 crores. By assigning differential weightage to offset programmes, buyer nations provide sellers with incentives to offer offsets in targeted area of buyer's choice.

Despite repeated assertions of wanting to make India self-reliant in defence production, India does not accept technology against offsets. This aspect will be dealt with subsequently.

Offsets and Cost Penalty

One of the major misconceptions is that offsets are free add-ons. Nothing can be farther from the truth. Offsets certainly do not come for free as foreign vendors have to incur additional expenditure to fulfil them. There are a number of factors that affect offset overhead costs and it is not feasible to fix an exact yard-stick. Value of an offset is always expressed in terms of percentage of the value of the main contract. It is generally seen that offsets up to 50 per cent inflate the cost of the main contract by close to 10 per cent. Similarly, 100 and 200 per cent offsets may result in cost escalation by 15 and 20 percent respectively.

The graph on the following page shows:-

- Cost penalty is not directly proportional to offset percentage. Cost penalty varies with the type of programmes undertaken.
- Initial cost of establishing infrastructure and initiating offset programmes is considerable. Once the process becomes functional and gets streamlined, rate of increase in cost penalty drops.
- Cost penalty tends to plateau after offset percentage reaches 200 percent. It implies that beyond this stage, both the offset provider and the receiver remain engaged in programmes which make commercial sense to both.

It may come as a surprise to many that the US allows its defence producers to charge offset costs even for government to government Foreign Military Sales (FMS). Although the US Government considers offsets to be detrimental to free and fair trade, it appreciates the need for companies to recover offset costs as they are considerable.

The Defence Federal Acquisition Regulation Supplement (DFARS) of May 1995, allowed US companies to recover full cost necessary to 'implement an offset agreement' in connection with FMS purchases. Subsequently, the scope was widened by using the term 'offset costs', thereby facilitating recovery of full expenditure incurred in fulfilling offset obligations.

It proves the point that fulfilment of offset obligations costs a company considerable expenditure which it can not absorb and has to recover by factoring it in the sale price.

Offsets and the Indian Services

When the idea of demanding offsets was initially floated in official circles, most service officers thought it to be a harmless appendage to the procurement procedure. Very few were fully aware of its implications. Many welcomed it in the hope that offsets would result in giving an impetus to the Indian defence industry. Being terribly uncomfortable with the continued dependence on foreign vendors and the resultant uncertainties, the services did not grudge encumbrance of offsets in order to make India self-reliant. However, the services were in for a shock. The Indian offset policy is anything but self-reliance centric.

India allows three routes for the fulfilment of offset obligations and they are:-

- Direct purchase of or executing export orders for defence products or services provided by Indian defence industries. For the purpose of defence offsets, services mean maintenance, overhaul, upgradation, life extension, engineering, design, testing of defence products, defence related software or quality assurance services.
- FDI in Indian defence industries for industrial infrastructure for services, co-development, joint ventures and co-production of defence products and components.
- FDI in Indian organisations engaged in research in defence R & D.

An examination of the viability of the above three routes is very revealing. At the face of it FDI route appears highly viable but when considered in the light of upper cap of 26 percent, the dissuasiveness of the policy becomes apparent. A foreign investor is expected to invest his resources in a venture where he has no significant control, strict capacity/ product constraints, no purchase guarantee and no open access to other markets including exports. The FDI policy was announced in May 2001 and has elicited no response. Therefore, options (b) and (c) above mean little.

Export of defence goods and services is thus the only possible method to fulfil offset obligations under the Indian policy. It amounts to compensation trading which is considered to be the least beneficial form of offsets.

Export of goods and services provide temporary and illusory gains, as has been the experience the world over. New markets dry up soon after the offsets are fulfilled, leaving created infra-structure idle and bereft of orders. Therefore, such trading does nothing to either strengthen the defence industrial base or promote technology upgradation. In other words, a potent tool like offsets is wasted on one-time exports.

Undoubtedly, the services have been taken for a ride. Offsets have added to their disquiet and anxieties without any boost to indigenous defence industry. A look at the following major concerns of the services will reveal the intensity and magnitude of the dilemma faced by them:-

- Offsets impose a cost penalty on all procurements that carry offset obligation clauses. This implies that the outflow from the defence budget gets proportionately increased. For example, for a deal that mandates 50 percent offsets, the defence budget will have to pay up to 10 percent extra in costs.
- Simultaneous signing of offset contract can result in a loss of focus, away from the main contract. DPP-2008 lays down that at every stage of evaluation, offset proposals would be examined along with the main technical and commercial proposals to confirm compliance. A competent vendor may get eliminated by default if his offset proposal is found unsatisfactory.
- Offset obligations have to be fulfilled co-terminus with the main contract. The policy allows imposition of penalty and its recovery by way of deduction from the bank guarantee of the main contract or the amount

payable to the vendor under the main contract. Further, failure to implement full offset obligations during the period of the main contract makes the vendor liable to be disqualified for participation in future defence contracts. With such punitive provisions in place, any default in offset programmes can delay the main contract and even jeopardise it.

- Offsets are notorious for corruption as they are often formulated in broad and imprecise terms, leaving enough leeway for multiple interpretations and manipulations. Furthermore, offset contracts are never monitored as closely as the main contract. Allegations of malpractice in offsets can put a foreign vendor under cloud and affect his commitment to timely completion of the main contract. Additionally, MoD may be forced to debar the vendor to exhibit its zero tolerance for dishonest activities, thereby endangering the main contract as well.

DEFENCE BUDGET

A military budget (or military expenditure), also known as a defence budget, is the amount of financial resources dedicated by an entity (most often a nation or a state), to raising and maintaining an armed forces. Military budgets often reflect how much an entity perceives the likelihood of threats against it, or the amount of aggression it wishes to employ.

It also provides an idea of how much finances could be provided for the upcoming year. The size of a budget also reflects the entity's ability to fund military activities, with factors including the size of that entity's economy, other financial demands on that entity, and the willingness of that entity's government or people to fund such military activity. Generally excluded from military expenditures is spending on internal law enforcement and disabled veteran rehabilitation.

According to the Stockholm International Peace Research Institute, in 2010, world military expenditure for the world amounted to 1.630 trillion US$.

HISTORIC EXPENDITURE

1897

In the *Saturday Review* magazine in February 1898, indicates that the percentage of tax revenue spent on military budgets as follows:

- United States: 17%
- Russian Empire: 21%
- France: 27%
- British Empire: 39% (40 million pounds or 2.5% of GNP.)
- German Empire: 43%
- Empire of Japan: 55% (132 millions of yens.)

2003

In 2004, the yearly report by the Stockholm International Peace Research Institute showed that the purchase of military products by NATO member nations during the year 2003 rose 11 percent relative to 2002 (6.5 percent in volume). In some countries, this budget had been increased to the level maintained during the Cold War. The military budget of the United States lead this increase; U.S. purchases accounted for 47% of world military expenditure in 2003. A total of about US$415 billion. Additional funding for the War in Iraq and the supplementary expense of US$83 billion accounted for much of the increase; other spending only accounted for 3.5 percent of the increase.

The military budgets of The United Kingdom, France, Germany and Italy represented about 15% of world military spending. France and the United Kingdom increased their equipment expenses, so as not only to act in US military operations with the same technological level of their ally, but equally to be able to act independently in smaller military campaigns. (Such as was seen in the Libya).

Among non-NATO nations, Japan spent US$46.9 billion in 2003, The People's Republic of China, US$32.8 billion, and Russia, US$13 billion. As a percentage share of world military spending this represented 5%, 4%, and 1%, respectively.

PERMANENT WAR ECONOMY

The concept of permanent war economy originated in 1944 with an article by Ed Sard (alias Frank Demby), Walter S. Oakes and T.N. Vance, a Third Camp Socialist, who predicted a post-war arms race. He argued at the time that the USA would retain the character of a war economy; even in peacetime, US military expenditure would remain large, reducing the percentage of unemployed compared to the 1930s. He extended this analysis in 1950 and 1951.

The CEO of General Electric and vice-chairman of the War Production Board, Charles Edward Wilson ("Electric Charlie," not to be confused with "Engine Charlie," Charles Erwin Wilson of General Motors) had already argued for the continuation of large scale military spending in a speech at the Twenty-Fifth Anniversary Dinner of the Army Ordnance Association on January 19, 1944.

Although he did not use the term "Permanent War Economy" he did argue for an institutionalized war economy—i.e. a semi-command economy to be directed by corporation executives, based on military industry, and funded by government. Wilson argued for this system for purely military reasons. He did not make any argument for a "military Keynesianism". The term refers to the economic component within the military-industrial complex (MIC) (aka. "the Iron Triangle") whereby the collusion between militarism and war profiteering are manifest as a permanently subsidised industry. Wilson warned at the close of World War II that the US must not return to a civilian economy, but must keep to a "permanent war economy."

Marxist Theory

The term has also been used to refer to a Marxist theory which seeks to explain the sustained economic growth which occurred in the decades following World War II, especially amongst developed countries. Marxists developed the theory when the anticipated stagnation of capitalism which had previously followed World War I did not recur. When post-WWII economic growth came to an end with the 1973 oil crisis and gave way to a new period of deepening stagnation, Marxists viewed this as a typical development of late capitalism.

The theory of the permanent *arms* economy (as it is called in order to be distinguished from other not necessarily Marxist *war* economic theories) commences with a difference between the period after the First and the period after the Second World War. Whereas after the First World War state expenditures for arms were soon cut back to peace levels, after the Second World War state expenditures on arms remained very high due to the developing Cold War and the arms race. These continuing strong expenditures on arms are according to the theory of the permanent arms economy the reason for the long boom up to the early 1970s. Military spending was around 16% of gross domestic product (GDP) in the 1950s in the USA after 38% in 1944 during World War II. This spending rate has been in a slow decline since then and finally in the mid-1990s it was only at about 2%. During the Vietnam War in 1968 it was 9% and in 2003 it was 4%. This strong decline in military spending during the 1960s and 1970s meant the end of the permanent arms economy and the return of capitalist crisis.

The different versions of the theory differ in the way to explain the exact mechanism how armaments expenditures did stabilise the capitalist economy. A more "Keynesian" version is to be distinguished from an approach, which is based on the law of the tendency of the rate of profit to fall.

Military Keynesianism

The stabilising effect of armaments expenditures on the economy is more or less explained the same way as "non-military" Keynesians explain the effects of their policy. Therefore, additional explanations are needed as to why it is necessary to use military expenditures instead of just civilian useful state expenditures. Several reasons are put forward :

"Legitimation crisis of late capitalism": According to Jürgen Habermas capitalism will suffer from a "legitimation crisis" if there is too much state intervention, because this will lead people to ask for more. Capitalism will no longer be perceived as a system ruled by quasi-natural laws, but as something that can be formed by politics. An external threat to be countered by government expenditures on arms, however, avoids this danger for the ruling class.

The balance of forces between the working class and the capitalist class will be shifted in favour of the working class if there is too much spending on social welfare and other items benefitting working class people.

The end of military Keynesianism came when competitors to the US, like Germany and Japan, the countries that had lost the Second World War, were not allowed or could avoid building their own military machine. They were increasingly allowed to export arms, however. Finally the US could no longer play the role of the world Keynesian but had to prepare for competition with nations like Japan and Germany. This resulted in cutting back on arms expenditures, thus bringing back crisis to world capitalism.

The law of the tendency of the rate of profit to fall

Other Marxists like Chris Harman or Michael Kidron oppose any Keynesian explanation. For them the decisive cause is the "siphoning off" of profits away from private investment expenditures to armaments expenditures, which count as "consumption" in the System of National Accounts. Harman emphasises that contrary to Keynesian assumptions arms expenditures were not financed by public debt but by taxes. Governments were able to keep public debt in check even though they had huge outlays for arms. Armaments expenditures did not work along Keynesian lines but because they interfered with the workings of the law of the tendency of the rate of profit to fall.

Karl Marx assumes that the value composition of capital c : v rises with technical progress and as a means by capitalists to raise labour productivity. This means that the rate of profit must eventually fall, if the rising value composition of capital is not counterbalanced by a rising rate of surplus value s:v. (The value composition of capital is often called organic composition of capital, which is, however, defined by Marx in Das Kapital, volume I, as the value composition of capital insofar as it reflects the movement of the technical composition of capital.)

If, however, profits are not spent on constant capital, but used for something else, the rise of the value composition of capital is slowed down if not stopped altogether. This raises the question, why capitalist should be prepared to give away parts of their profits if this does not serve directly their own interests, but "only" the interests of the system as a whole. The fall of the general rate of profit itself induces changes, however, which make it easier for the state in alliance with larger capital groups to intervene. So, the falling rate of profit is linked to the tendency of concentration and centralisation of capital (as described by Marx in Das Kapital, volume I). Firms become larger and larger. Large firms take over small firms. Concurrential capitalism becomes monopoly capitalism. The nature of capitalist competition changes. Firms no longer compete with each other inside branches but across branches. As a result it is no longer necessary to "outproduce" competitors. The demand for investment goods drops. Capacities of investment firms lay idle. These overcapacities in the investment goods industry threaten to trigger a downward spiral thus deepening the crisis.

That is why it is crucial that demand for armaments goes to what Marx called department I, the investment goods branch. This is the very department, which due to the changing character of competition with monopoly capitalism lacks demand for its products.

Weapons are technically close relatives of investment goods like machines. The demand for weapons by the government can therefore stabilise production of the investments goods industry, thus fending off a downward spiral into depression.

The government buys goods of the surplus production and can realise surplus value for single firms. In this way it can stabilise capitalism. The government cannot, however, create surplus value.

Expenditures on arms are economically "consumption" or waste, not investment. But this surplus value would not have been realised anyway, due to lack of demand for investment goods, which is a characteristic feature of monopoly capitalism. What the government can do is to fend off a downward spiral which often is triggered by lack of demand, causing lay-offs, reducing demand even further and so on. Due to armaments expenditures by the government the general rate of profit does not fall even further due to vicious circles but at least gets some stabilisation. (Karl Popper in his The Open Society and Its Enemies, vol. 2 "Hegel and Marx", gives a brief sketch of Marx's economic theory and the role expenditures on arms might play, if consumption of workers does not keep up with production.)

By this mechanism crisis could be postponed until the early 1970s, when finally the internal contradictions of the logic of capital also took hold of the permanent arms economy with rising rates of inflation, increasing government debts and so on. Also with this version of the theory, the free riders like Germany or Japan forced the US to cut back on armaments expenditures.

Capital Export

A similar effect can result from capital exports. Again profits are siphoned off from private investment. Marx (volume III of "Das Kapital") mentions capital export as a countervailing tendency for the tendency of the profit rate to fall. The reasons, he puts forward, are that if capital finds in other parts of the world areas with lower costs and higher profit rates, capital exports increase the average rate of profit. It is Henryk Grossman (and Marx's "Grundrisse"), who argues that capital exports in themselves are a cause, which postpones a crisis, which otherwise would follow from the rising value composition of capital and the tendency of the rate of profit to fall.

Question of Deliberate Policy

Some authors emphasise that the permanent arms economy was not something planned by capitalists. It was like a lucky fate, which came upon monopoly capitalism by special circumstances, which cannot be repeated at will or by planning. This contrasts with the view of the German Marxist Alfred Sohn-Rethel who with a rather similar theory claims that the idea of an arms economy was applied rather deliberately in the Germany of the 1930s to fend off a crisis for German capitalism. Based on analyses which were in fact influenced by Marxist theory, German capitalists came to the conclusion – according to Alfred Sohn-Rethel – that only arms expenditures as a kind of waste could "save" German capitalism for the moment. Thus, they decided to opt for Adolf Hitler and his promises of increasing military expenditures.

A Different View

The case made by some Marxists, that military spending is necessary and useful for capitalism, has been contested. The central arguments against this position have been made by economists like Seymour Melman, Lloyd J. Dumas and John Ullmann. It should be noted that, without giving a specific reference, Melman states, in the 1974 edition of Permanent War Economy published by Simon and Scuster (p. 16), that "The concept of a "permanent war economy" formulated in 1944 was soon made a reality." The reference is almost certainly to Sard's article in February of that year in Politics. The critique centers on whether or not military spending has a "use value," i.e. a productive use within the economy. On the one hand, the macroeconomic stimulus of arms spending may be positive in the short run, when comparing such spending to the absence of any form of procurement. On the other hand, military spending represents serious opportunity costs. First, the economic benefits of spending in non-military areas may be greater, i.e. have greater multiplier effects. For example, an investment in a tank or plane is rapidly depleted and after the tank or plane is invented, leads to no further economic use value. Moreover, when the state fails to invest in key resources, this creates opportunity costs with respect to "socially necessary" or world competitive infrastructure investments. These costs are evident in depleted infrastructure, reduced spending on education, failure to develop massive investments in alternative energy and transit systems, and outbreaks of violence (such as riots) caused by uneven development.

The counter-argument is that military advances provide spin-off benefits for civilian technologies. Additionally, military spending may represent an overhead charge for an economy, allowing a nation to function without fear of invasion. Essentially, military spending ensures the property rights of a nation's citizens: an essential element of a capitalist system.

PRIVATE MILITARY COMPANY WITH SPECIAL REFERENCE TO US AND IRAQ

A private military company (PMC) or (private military or security companies) provides military and security services.

These combatants are commonly known as mercenaries, though modern-day PMCs refer to their staff as security contractors, private military contractors or private security contractors, and refer to themselves as private military corporations, private military firms, private security providers or military service providers. Private military companies refer to their business generally as the private military industry or The Circuit, in an attempt to avoid the stigma often associated with mercenaries. The hiring of mercenaries is a common practice in the history of armed conflict.

The services and expertise offered by PMCs are typically similar to those of governmental military or police forces, most often on a smaller scale. While PMCs often provide services to train or supplement official armed forces in service of governments, they can also be employed by private companies to provide bodyguards for key staff or protection of company premises, especially in hostile territories. However, contractors who use offensive force in a war zone could be considered unlawful combatants, in reference to a concept outlined in the Geneva Conventions and explicitly specified by the US Military Commissions Act.

P. W. Singer author of *Corporate Warriors: The Rise of the Privatized Military Industry* says about private contractors "In geographic terms, it operates in over 50 different countries. It's operated in every single continent but Antarctica." In the 1990s there used to be 50 military personnel for every 1 contractor, now the ratio is 10 to 1 (Singer). Singer points out that these contractors have a number of duties depending on who they are hired by. In developing countries that have natural resources, such as oil refineries in Iraq, they are hired to guard the area. They are also hired to guard companies that contract services and reconstruction efforts such as General Electric. Apart from securing companies, they also secure officials and government affiliates. Private military companies carry out many different missions and jobs. These include things such as supplying bodyguards to the Afghan president Hamid Karzai and piloting reconnaissance airplanes and helicopters as a part of Plan Colombia. They are also licensed by the United States Department of State, they are contracting with national governments, training soldiers and reorganizing militaries in Nigeria, Bulgaria, Taiwan, and Equatorial Guinea. The PMC industry is now worth over $100 billion a year.

According to a 2008 study by the Office of the Director of National Intelligence, private contractors make up 29% of the workforce in the United States Intelligence Community and cost the equivalent of 49% of their personnel budgets.

In 1985, LOGCAP was established primarily to preplan for contingencies and to leverage the existing civilian resources. However, it was not until three years later before it was first used. In support of a United States Third Army mission, the United States Army Corps of Engineers (USACE) used LOGCAP to contract for the construction and maintenance of two petroleum pipelines systems in Southwest Asia.

Later, USACE awarded the first contract under LOGCAP umbrella concept to Brown and Root Services (now KBR) in August 1992 as a cost-plus-award-fee contract, which was used in December that year to support the United Nations forces in Somalia.

Some contractors have served in advisory roles, that help train local militaries to fight more effectively, instead of intervening directly. Much of the peacekeeper training the United States provides to African militaries is done by private firms, and with the increasing absence of Western military support to international peace operations, the private sector is commonly utilized to provide services to peace and stability operations from Haiti to Darfur.

The Center for Public Integrity reported that since 1994, the Defence Department entered into 3,601 contracts worth $300 billion with 12 U.S. based various PMCs within the United States, specifically during the initial response after

Hurricane Katrina in New Orleans. Domestic operations are generally under the auspice of state or federal agencies such as the Department of Energy or the Department of Homeland Security rather than the Department of Defence. Driven by increasingly greater fears of domestic terror attacks and civil unrest and disruption in the wake of disasters, more conventional security companies are moving into operations arenas that would fall within the definition of a PMC.

The United States State Department also employs several companies to provide support in danger zones that would be difficult for conventional U.S. forces.

On December 5, 2005, U.S. Secretary of Defence Donald Rumsfeld held a lecture dubbed "The Future of Iraq" at Johns Hopkins Paul H. Nitze School of Advanced International Studies. During a Q&A session afterwards he was asked a question by graduate student Kate Turner regarding PMCs:

Turner: "There are currently thousands of private military contractors in Iraq and you were just speaking of rules of engagement in regards to Iraqi personnel and US personnel. Could you speak to, since the private contractors are operating outside the Uniform Code of Military Justice, can you speak to what law or rules of engagement do govern their behavior and whether there has been any study showing that it is cost effective to have them in Iraq rather than US military personnel. Thank you."

Rumsfeld: "Thank you. It is clearly cost-effective to have contractors for a variety of things that military people need not do, and that for whatever reason other civilians, government people, cannot be deployed to do. There are a lot of contractors, a growing number. They come from our country but they come from all countries, and indeed sometimes the contracts are from our country or another country and they employ people from totally different countries including Iraqis and people from neighboring nations. And there are a lot of them. It's a growing number. Of course we've got to begin with the fact that, as you point out, they're not subject to the Uniform Code of Military Justice. We understand that. There are laws that govern the behavior of Americans in that country. The Department of Justice oversees that. There is an issue that is current as to the extent to which they can or cannot carry weapons, and that's an issue. It's also an issue, of course, with the Iraqis. But if you think about it, Iraq's a sovereign country. They have their laws and they're going to govern, the UN resolution and the Iraqi laws, as well as U.S. procedures and laws govern behavior in that country depending on who the individual is and what he's doing. But I personally am of the view that there are a lot of things that can be done for a short time basis by contractors that advantage the United States and advantage other countries who also hire contractors, and that any idea that we shouldn't have them I think would be unwise."

Application of UCMJ to PMCs

The FY2007 Defence Budget appropriation bill, amended the UCMJ to allow for prosecution of military contractors who are deployed in a "declared war or a contingency operation." "SEC. 552. CLARIFICATION OF APPLICATION OF UNIFORM CODE OF MILITARY JUSTICE DURING A TIME OF WAR. Paragraph (10) of section 802(a) of title 10, United States Code (article 2(a) of the Uniform Code of Military Justice), is amended by striking 'war' and inserting 'declared war or a contingency operation'."

Farah Stockman of the *Boston Globe*, (7 January 2007) wrote: "Previously, the code applied to 'persons serving with or accompanying an armed force in the field' only during a war, which US courts interpreted to mean a war declared by Congress. No such declaration was made in the Iraq conflict. Now, Congress has amended the code to apply to persons accompanying an armed force during a 'declared war or contingency operation.' But the provision might also have unintended consequences, if the military chooses to use its new power to court-martial civilians. For instance, the language in the law is so broad that it can be interpreted as saying that embedded journalists and contract employees from foreign countries would also be liable under the military code. Other punishable offenses under the code include disobeying an order, disrespecting an officer, and possession of pornography in a combat zone."

International Legal Issues

In October 2007, the United Nations released a two-year study that stated, that although hired as "security guards", private contractors were performing military duties. Many countries, including the United States and the United Kingdom, are not signatories to the 1989 *United Nations Mercenary Convention* banning the use of mercenaries. However, a spokesman for the US Mission to UN Office in Geneva (UNOG) said that "Accusations that U.S. government-contracted security guards, of whatever nationality, are mercenaries is inaccurate."

Recruitment

Discharged military personnel make up the majority of Western contractors. The boom of the private security industry that took place in the 1990s can be traced back to the over 6 million military personnel that were discharged in that decade. Post Cold War military reduction has also expanded the recruiting pool for PMCs. In some cases, entire elite units, such as the South African 32nd Reconnaissance Battalion and the former Soviet "Alfa" unit have been reorganized into private military companies.

Some commentators have argued that there has been a recent exodus from many special operations forces across the globe towards these private military corporations. Units that have allegedly been severely affected include The British Special Air Service, the US Special Operations Forces and the Canadian Joint Task Force 2. Finding work in the industry is not difficult for most former soldiers as their personal network of fellow and ex-soldiers is enough to keep them informed of available contracts.

PMC Activities in Iraq

In December, 2006, in Iraq there are thought to be at least 100,000 contractors working directly for the United States Department of Defence which is a tenfold increase in the use of private contractors for military operations since the Persian Gulf War, just over a decade earlier. The prevalence of PMCs has led to the foundation of trade group the Private Security Company Association of Iraq. In Iraq, the issue of accountability, especially in the case of contractors carrying weapons is a sensitive one. Iraqi laws do not hold over contractors. Just before leaving office as head of the Coalition Provisional Authority, Paul Bremer signed Coalition Provisional Authority Order 17 where it is stated that:

> Contractors shall not be subject to Iraqi laws or regulations in matters relating to the terms and conditions of their Contracts, including licensing and registering employees, businesses and corporations; provided, however, that Contractors shall comply with such applicable licensing and registration laws and regulations if engaging in business or transactions in Iraq other than Contracts. Notwithstanding any provisions in this Order, Private Security Companies and their employees operating in Iraq must comply with all CPA Orders, Regulations, Memoranda, and any implementing instructions or regulations governing the existence and activities of Private Security Companies in Iraq, including registration and licensing of weapons and firearms.

PMCs supply support to U.S. military bases throughout the Persian Gulf, from operating mess halls to providing security. They supply armed guards at a U.S. Army base in Qatar, and they use live ammunition to train soldiers at Camp Doha in Kuwait. They maintain an array of weapons systems vital to an invasion of Iraq. They also provide bodyguards for VIPs, guard installations, and escort supply convoys from Kuwait. All these resources are called upon constantly due to the war in Iraq.

- Employees of private military company CACI and Titan Corp. were involved in the Iraq Abu Ghraib prison scandal in 2003, and 2004. The U.S. Army "found that contractors were involved in 36 percent of the [Abu Ghraib] proven incidents and identified 6 employees as individually culpable", although none have faced prosecution unlike US military personnel.
- On March 31, 2004, four American private contractors belonging to the company Blackwater USA were killed by insurgents in Fallujah as they drove through the town. They were dragged from their car in one of the most violent attacks on U.S. contractors in the conflict. Following the attack, an angry mob mutilated and burned the bodies, dragging them through the streets before they were hung on a bridge.
- On March 28, 2005, 16 American contractors and three Iraqi aides from Zapata Engineering, under contract to the US Army Corps of Engineers to manage an ammunition storage depot, were detained following two incidents in which they allegedly fired upon U.S. Marine checkpoint. While later released, the contractors have levied complaints of mistreatment against the Marines who detained them.
- On June 5, 2005, Colonel Theodore S. Westhusing committed suicide, after writing a report exonerating US Investigations Services of allegations of fraud, waste and abuse he received in an anonymous letter in May.
- On October 27, 2005, a "trophy" video, complete with post-production Elvis Presley music, appearing to show private military contractors in Baghdad shooting Iraqi civilians sparked two investigations after it was posted

on the Internet. The video has been linked unofficially to Aegis Defence Services. According to the posters, the man who is seen shooting vehicles on this video in Iraq was a South African employee of Aegis Victory team named Danny Heydenreycher. He served in the British military for six years. After the incident the regional director for Victory ROC tried to fire Heydenreycher, but the team threatened to resign if he did. As of December 2005, Aegis is conducting a formal inquiry into the issue, although some concerns on its impartiality have been raised.

- On September 17, 2007, the Iraqi government announced that it was revoking the license of the American security firm Blackwater USA over the firm's involvement in the deaths of eight civilians in a firefight that followed a car bomb explosion near a State Department motorcade. Blackwater is currently one of the most high-profile firms operating in Iraq, with around 1,000 employees as well as a fleet of helicopters in the country. Whether the group may be legally prosecuted is still a matter of debate.

Legal position

Two days before he left Iraq, L. Paul Bremer signed "Order 17" giving all Americans associated with the CPA and the American government immunity from Iraqi law.

A July 2007 report from the American Congressional Research Service indicates that the Iraqi government still had no authority over private security firms contracted by the U.S. government.

The new status-of-forces agreement makes it clear that Contractors are under the jurisdiction of Iraqi law.

Plans for the future

After the withdrawal of US troops from Iraq the US State Department is reportedly planning to more than double the number of its private security guards, up to as many as 7,000. Defending five fortified compounds across the country, the security contractors would operate radars to warn of enemy rocket attacks, search for roadside bombs, fly reconnaissance drones and even staff quick reaction forces to aid civilians in distress. The State Department plans to acquire 60 mine-resistant, ambush-protected vehicles (MRAPs) from the US military to expand its inventory of armored cars to 1,320 and to create a mini-air fleet by buying three planes to add to its lone aircraft. Its helicopter fleet, which will be piloted by contractors, will grow from 17 to 29.

PMC Activities Elsewhere

- In 1994 and 1995 South African based PMC Executive Outcomes was involved in two military actions in Africa. In the first conflict, EO fought on the behalf of the Angolan government against UNITA after a UN brokered peace settlement broke down. In the second action EO was tasked with containing a guerrilla movement in Sierra Leone called the Revolutionary United Front. Both missions involved personnel from the firm training 4-5 thousand combat personnel for the Angolan government and retaking control of the diamond fields and forming a negotiated peace in Sierra Leone.
- In 1999, an incident involving DynCorp in Bosnia was followed by a Racketeer Influenced and Corrupt Organizations Act (RICO) lawsuit being filed against DynCorp employees stationed in Bosnia. It alleged that: "employees and supervisors from DynCorp were engaging in perverse, illegal and inhumane behavior and were illegally purchasing women, weapons, forged passports and participating in other immoral acts."
- In 2000, the Australian Broadcasting Corporation's ABC Television international affairs program "Foreign Correspondent" broadcast a special report "Sierra

Leone: Soldiers of Fortune", focusing on the exploits of South African pilot Neall Ellis and his MI-24 Hind gunship. The report also investigated the failures of the UN Peacekeeping Force, and the involvement of mercenaries/private military contractors in providing vital support to UN operations and British military Special Operations in Sierra Leone in 1999-2000.

- On April 5, 2005, Jamie Smith, CEO of SCG International Risk announced the expansion of services from the traditional roles of PMCs of protection and intelligence to military aviation support. SCG International Air would provide air support, medevac (medical evacuation), rotary and fixed-wing transportation, heavy-lift cargo, armed escort and executive air travel to "any location on earth." This marks a unique addition and expansion of services to rival the capabilities of some country's armies and air forces.
- On March 27, 2006, J. Cofer Black, vice chairman of Blackwater USA announced to attendees of a special operations exhibition in Jordan that his company could now provide a brigade-size force for low intensity conflicts. According to Black, "There is clear potential to conduct security operations at a fraction of the cost of NATO operations". These comments were later denied.
- In mid-May 2006, police in the Democratic Republic of the Congo arrested 32 alleged mercenaries of different nationalities; 19 South Africans, 10 Nigerians and three Americans. Half of them worked for a South African company named Omega Security Solutions and the Americans for AQMI Strategy Corp. The men were accused of plotting to overthrow the government but charges were not pressed. The men were deported to their home countries.

- In 2006, a U.S. congressional report listed a number of PMCs and other enterprises that have signed contracts to carry out anti-narcotics operations and related activities as part of Plan Colombia. DynCorp was among those contracted by the State Department, while others signed contracts with the Defence Department. Other companies from different countries, including Israel, have also signed contracts with the Colombian Defence Ministry to carry out security or military activities.
- In December 2009, the Congressional Research Service, which provides background information to members of the United States Congress, announced that the deployment of 30,000 extra U.S. troops into Afghanistan could be accompanied by a surge of "26,000 to 56,000" contractors. This would expand the presence of personnel from the U.S. private sector in Afghanistan "to anywhere from 130,000 to 160,000". The CRS study said contractors made up 69 percent of the Pentagon's personnel in Afghanistan in December 2008, a proportion that "apparently represented the highest recorded percentage of contractors used by the Defence Department in any conflict in the history of the United States." In September 2008 their presence had dropped to 62 percent, while the U.S. military troop strength increased modestly.
- Also in December 2009, a House oversight subcommittee said that it had begun a wide-ranging investigation into allegations that American private security companies hired to protect Defence Department convoys in Afghanistan would be paying off warlords and the Taliban to ensure safe passage. That would mean that the United States is unintentionally and indirectly engaged in a protection racket and may be indirectly funding the very insurgents it were trying to fight. A preliminary inquiry

determined that the allegations warranted a deeper inquiry, focused initially on eight trucking companies that share a $2.2 billion Defence Department contract to carry goods and material from main supply points inside Afghanistan (primarily Bagram air base) to more than 100 forward operating bases and other military facilities in the country.

NGOs and Private Security Contractors

NGOs' rare use of private security contractors in dangerous regions is a highly sensitive subject. While rare, many NGOs have sought the services of private security contractors in dangerous areas of operation, such as Afghanistan, Somalia and Sudan due to the following reasons:

- Lack of knowledge/skills and time to adequately meet the challenges of deteriorating security environments; and
- Administrative costs of managing security in-house and potential to outsource the liability.

Quite often the contractors hired are local companies and mostly are unarmed personnel guarding facilities, only very rarely are international contractors or mobile armed security personnel used.

9

Economic Possessions of Military Expenses in Rising Country

THE ECONOMIC EFFECTS OF MILITARY EXPENDITURE

As discussed in Section 3 any analysis of the economic effects of military spending is contingent upon the theoretical understanding of its role in capitalist development. In undertaking empirical work it is possible to use casual empiricism, such as correlation analysis, to support arguments based upon theoretical reasoning, or to set up a simple reduced form model based upon an underlying theory. But the most satisfactory way is to specify a formal model to deal with the interactions of military spending and the economy and to estimate it and it is this approach which has dominated the literature. Much of the applied literature is located within a Keynesian theoretical framework which emphasizes the potential role of military expenses in increasing national output through income multiplier effects, in the presence of inadequate effective demand.

This framework was developed by Smith and Smith (1980) and has provided the basis for most of the subsequent studies of the economic impact of military expenses . It has been more successful as a means of studying the economic effects of military expenses in developing countries than those studies which adopted a neo-classical approach, which perceives the State as a class-neutral actor balancing the opportunity costs and security benefits of military expenses in order to maximize a well-defined national interest . Nevertheless, the neoclassical approach retains its adherents and recent examples include Adams et al. (1992), Linden (1992), Mintz and Stevenson (1992) and Landau (1994). There are also a number of studies which do not use such a formal approach but which are important in relating the issue to the process of development, for example Ball (1988). In the empirical literature the impact of military spending on economic growth has been identified theoretically as acting through a number of channels. The relative importance and sign of these effects and the overall impact on growth can only be ascertained by empirical analysis. The main channels are:

Capital: Military spending can have positive or negative effects on both savings and investment. It is argued that if increases in military expenses are funded by taxation, then if these expenses are reduced in the future savings propensities may increase. In developing countries, however, raising new revenue from taxation can be difficult, thus military expenses may be funded by increased money supply which may lead to inflation which can reduce savings. A direct impact can result from military expenses being directly at the expense of education and health, requiring increased private provision and lowering private savings .

Again the impact of military expenses on investment is an empirical question. On the one hand it is hypothesised that it can crowd out investment . On the other hand it can boost demand, output and profits and lead to increased investment (other forms of government expenses could also have the same impact). It is possible, however, that bottlenecks could prevent any significant positive effect. In addition, the effects of infrastructural investment by the military can be either to benefit industry, or be purely of military value remote and irrelevant to the civilian sector.

Labour: An important problem in developing countries is creating adequate skilled and educated labour as the economy develops. Military spending can have both positive and negative effects. The military can train soldiers and conscripts with valuable technical and administrative skills which they take into civilian life. It can also have modernising effect, with organisational skills and modern attitudes tending to break up social rigidities . On the other hand these effects may be insignificant and the military may attract scarce skilled labour and valuable resources away from the civilian industrial sector and place a fetter on growth. The transferability of skills may be limited and the military may be no more, or less, modern than civil institutions . Military spending might be at the expense of education and training expenses as discussed below.

External relations: The impact of military expenses on the Balance of Payments will depend upon whether or not a country produces arms and whether or not it receives military related aid. In most developing countries imports of weapons will place a huge burden on the economy, through using scarce foreign exchange, and will make trade deficits difficult to avoid. Indeed, Grobar et al (1990) suggest that arms imports in the early 1980s accounted for almost 10% of all developing country imports. This may be offset by military related aid, exports of arms and import substitution, but in general military spending is likely to be a burden on the trade balance. In addition, evidence suggests that military related debt in developing countries is substantial and that the financial burden of earlier arms imports via debt service has grown over time .

On the other hand the military may provide security from threats, encourage foreign investment, and have links with foreign powers with an interest in the region that can be beneficial to trade, investment and aid. However, this must be weighed against the possibility of involvement in conflict and the damaging effects multinational investment and aid can have on weak client economies .

Socio-Political: Military expenses may provide the conditions under which development can take place. The military may provide control and discipline of labour, reduce internal conflict, and be a modernising influence. As discussed above, they can impart discipline on conscripts, making them more suited to industrial labour when they leave the forces, and can provide skills which can be of value in the civil sector. It is, however, possible that the military sector and its technology is capital intensive and so far removed from the rest of the economy as to impart little of value in terms of spin offs. It may also take skilled labour away from the civil sector and military regimes may be conservative, corrupt and inefficient and a fetter on economic development.

Labour: An important problem in developing countries is creating adequate skilled and educated labour as the economy develops. Military spending can have both positive and negative effects. The military can train soldiers and conscripts with valuable technical and administrative skills which they take into civilian life. It can also have modernising effect, with organisational skills and modern attitudes tending to break up social rigidities . On the other hand these effects may be insignificant and the military may attract scarce skilled labour and valuable resources away from the civilian industrial sector and place a fetter on growth. The transferability of skills may be limited and the military may be no more, or less, modern than civil institutions.

The debate in the empirical literature on the economic effects of military spending started with the contribution of Benoit (1973, 1978) which purported to show that military expenses and development went hand in hand. Ball (1983) provided a comprehensive critique of Benoits work, undermining the conclusions drawn. This led to considerable research activity using econometric analysis to overcome the deficiencies, most of which has tended not to support Benoit, but there is still no consensus view.

There are three types of econometric studies: The first are the single equation analyses which use economic growth as the dependent variable and military spending (burden, per capita or absolute value) as the, or one of the, independent variables. Looney and Frederiksen (1983a) re-examined

Benoit's data, including more factors in the estimated equation and dividing the group of countries into resource constrained and not resource constrained. The significant relation for military expenses on growth only held for the resource unconstrained group (negative for resource constrained), similar results for an updated data set are found in (1983b). A number of studies using other data have followed and are outlined in the appendix. Overall, this approach has generally found a positive or insignificant effect of military expenses on growth.

A major problem with the approach is that it explicitly assumes that military expenses is exogenously determined and that the causality goes from military expenses to growth, both of which were brought into question by Joerding (1986). This concern is the result of a failure to derive the final equation, which can be thought of as a reduced form from an explicit structural model which would provide a causal chain. There was some discussion of the equations being interpreted as having an underlying but implicit structural model, with some, such as Lim (1983), deriving the estimating equation used from an explicit structural model. Other studies took an alternative path and investigated the causal links (using statistical definitions of causality referred to as "Granger causality" to distinguish the concept from theoretical causality) between military expenses and economic growth, with, in general, the studies finding no dominant result, Looney (1991), Chowdhury (1991), Kusi (1994) and the case studies of China, Chen (1993) and Hasan (1994) disagreeing. A further criticism of these models is that while the reduced forms may be interpreted as providing estimates of the net effect of military spending on growth, the specifications they employ, implicitly or explicitly, fail to pick up the indirect effects adequately.

Second, there are studies adopting simultaneous equation systems, which emphasise the importance of the interdependence between military spending, growth and the other variables. The majority of the studies including Deger and Smith (1983), Gyimah-Brempong (1989) Mohammed

(1992) and Scheetz (1991), tend to confirm the existence of negative impact of military expenses on economic development. On the other hand, a number of influential studies such as Dixon and Moon (1986) have suggested the existence of a positive impact on developing economies. The studies do vary in their use of data. Some deal with cross section averages (eg Deger and Smith, 1983), others with time series estimates for individual countries (eg Scheetz, 1983), while others are more comprehensive (eg Dunne and Mohammed, 1995). The Appendix presents other examples, including time series estimates for individual countries. As with the single equation approaches attempts have been made to investigate sample stratifications. Brauer (1993) restimates Deger (1986) study dividing the sample between arms producers and others and finds differences in the subsample results.

Third, there are studies which use macroeconometric and other forms of world models. A pioneering study by Leontief and Duchin (1980) used a macroeconometric model of the world economy to analyse the global effects of disarmament in the major powers and a transference of the resources to low income countries. The overall impact was found to be positive, though not particularly significant. Cappelen et al (1982) made similar findings. Gigenhack et al (1987) use the Systems Analysis Research Unit Model (SARUM) and an arms dynamics equation, of the action reaction type, to simulate the effects of different security scenarios. Other world models which have introduced forward looking expectations mechanisms find that reduced military spending will have positive effects if announced, even without the reallocation of the savings, through a real interest effect resulting from the fall in the budget deficit, Szymanski (1995)) This is in direct contradiction to Keynesian models which do not have the same real interest rate effect and indeed fail to find such an effect in their econometric analysis (eg Adams et al., 1995). There are also a few individual country studies for developing countries using relatively large macromodels for obvious reasons. One exception is Adams et al (1992), which finds a positive effect of military spending in the Philipines, using a Keynesian macroeconometric model, though not considering the opportunity cost.

The dominant approach to studying the economic effects of military expenses using Keynesian or neoclassical models has come under some attack. It fails to consider the particular nature of developing countries and the alternative development literature (eg Park, 1994). There have also been some developments of these models, Berthelemy et al (1994) have used models of endogenous growth based on Romer's work to analyse the impact of military spending on growth and to consider the welfare and security effects. Using simulation analyses for India and Pakistan the study suggests there are considerable economic costs to militarisation.

A further literature has developed which focuses on the opportunity cost of military spending, or the trade off between military spending and other forms of welfare expenses. While this approach is somewhat problematic, as it suggests that if money was not spent on military spending it would be spent elsewhere and it often does not allow for the fact that it is possible to have more of both with economic growth, there are some interesting studies. In general the share of military spending is analysed over time or across countries to see if any increase in military expenses matches falls in other forms of welfare expenses. There is no consensus, with some studies, eg Dabelko and McCormick, Verner (1983) and Looney (1986), finding weak evidence of military spending crowding out spending on education an health in developing countries over the 50s and 60s but Harris et al (1988) and Hess and Mullen (1988), not finding this result. Verner (1983) and Looney failed to find trade-off between military and other forms of government spending in Latin America, although by improving upon the data provided by international sources Scheetz (1992) found clear evidence of crowding out for Argentina, Chile, Paraguay and Peru as did Apostolakis (1992) using the usual data for the whole of Latin America. Davis and Chan (1990) found no significant impact for Taiwan. In addition, Gyimah-Brempong (1992) found that in Sub-Saharan countries governments tend to favour defence budgeting when budgets are tight and discriminate against them when budget resources are increasing.

There are a number of researchers who argue that despite the valiant attempts of researchers, the experience of the developing countries is so varied, the data is so poor, and the equations open to a number of alternative interpretations that further investigation requires case studies. While not disagreeing with the value of case studies as we have argued above it really depends on the question the researcher is asking. there have been a number of case studies and studies of more homogeneous groups of countries which have provides valuable results but they should really be seen as complementary to our understanding rather than substitutes. Recent examples are: Park (1994) of Korea, Dunne and Mohammed (1994) of Sub-Saharan Africa, Scheetz (1991) of Latin America.

Considering the applied studies outlined in the appendix the conclusion is that, while there is no clear consensus on the economic effects of military spending the most common finding is that military burden has either no significant effect, or a negative effect on economic growth. Certainly there are few studies post-Benoit that claim to have discovered a positive effect. Indeed, if we distinguish between the supply side models and those which have a demand side, there is some consistency in the results.

Models allowing for a demand side and hence the possibility of crowding out investment tend to find negative effects, unless there is some reallocation to other forms of government spending, while those with only a supply side find positive, or positive but insignificant, effects (Hartley and Sandler, 1995). This means that there is the potential for developing countries to cut military spending with, at worst, no harm to economic performance and, at best, higher economic growth. However, the macroeconomic nature of such results does tend to obscure the problems of structural adjustment which may occur within countries. The next section deals with these issues.

CHANGED STRATEGIC SURROUNDINGS

The end of the Cold War the changed strategic surroundings has presented an opportunity to reduce global military spending. In the developed world the end of the superpower arms race has, indeed, led to marked cuts in military spending, while in the third world the removal of superpower involvement in regional conflicts has reduced tensions, military and military-related aid, and the scale of conflicts. Although this has led to some reductions in military spending in the developing countries the situation is complex. There are still some countries increasing their expenses, mainly in response to local insecurities and local arms races, but also encouraged by the push for arms exports by the developed countries. It is also important to recognise that the cuts in military spending that have taken place do not necessarily imply a reduction in militarisation. Weapons have turn out to be cheaper in the increasingly competitive world market and the world remains a very dangerous place with many regional and civil conflicts. Nevertheless, there is the potential for marked reductions in military spending by some of the poorest countries in the world and present is evidence that a number of countries are taking the opportunity presented to them.

Given that reductions in military expenses release resources that can be used for other purposes, the possibility exists of tackling some of the major threats to human survival. Attention can be directed towards the problems of poverty and economic security, environmental degradation and environmental security. UNDP estimate that in developing countries the chances of dying from social neglect (malnutrition, preventable disease) are 33 times greater than from a war started by external aggression. Some of he worlds poorest countries use their scarce foreign exchange resource to purchase weapons and spend more on their military than on the peoples education and health. Indeed in 1992, world military spending equalled the income of almost half the world's population (UNDP, 1994). The cost of military security in terms of resources foregone from economic and social development is huge and this sacrifice has not necessarily been justified in terms of national security. The question is whether the resources made available will be used for these purposes. Certainly, the belief that reducing military spending will lead to a "peace dividend", as the economic benefit of reallocating military expenses to other uses has been termed is not accepted by all. Some people have argued that cuts in military expenses are more likely to result in a "peace penalty", because of the costs of adjustment. The experience of the developed economies is rather salutary, as they have generally failed to benefit economically from cuts in their military expenses. While this is mainly the result of failing to reallocate the savings made to other forms of expenses as part of a policy of conversion, rather than the lack of a peace dividend per se, it does suggest that care must be taken to develop policies to aid structural adjustment (Dunne and Willett, 1992, Hartley, 1993).

In the case of the developing world the circumstances differ but the issues are similar. In order to develop policies of disarmament, it is important to consider the role military spending plays in the economy and the likely economic effects of changes in such spending. It is only after such information is available that policies to help developing countries adjust can be developed, both at a national and an international level. This paper contributes to this understanding by providing a survey of the studies of economic effects of military expenses and the economics of disarmament and conversion for developing countries. Section 2 presents some information on the trends in military spending in developing countries and the potential for a "peace dividend". A discussion of the method and theoretical approaches used in analysing the economics of military spending in developing countries is presented in Section 3. Section 4 then provides a review of the empirical literature on the determinants of military spending in developing countries, followed by a review of the applied literature on the economic effects of military spending on developing countries in Section 5. A survey of the issues involved in the process of disarmament in developing countries is then undertaken in Section 6, allowing a discussion of the requirements of policies for disarmament and conversion. Finally, section 7 draws some conclusions.

TACTIC AND HYPOTHETICAL APPROACHES

A major problem that arises in surveying the results of studies of the economic effects of military spending in developing countries is the variety of such studies. They vary in the questions asked, the methods used, the sample of countries, the time period and in their theoretical underpinnings. As a result, in developing the empirical work there are so many auxiliary assumptions that have to be made that tests of particular hypotheses can become tests of the assumptions made and so comparisons of the studies can be at best difficult and at worst meaningless. Given such problems it is useful to consider some of the methodological and theoretical issues involved as prior to a review of the studies. While the main concern of the research we are interested in has been to investigate the relation between military spending and development, in applied work this is usually restricted to economic growth rather than development because of the problems of defining and measuring development. The former is, of course, only a necessary condition for the latter and the starting point for any such analysis should really be some theoretical understanding of the links between the two (Brauer (1993), Graham et al (1986)). Similarly, it is important to recognise that military spending is only one aspect of militarism in a society and is only a measure of inputs rather than output (Smith, 1983).

To interpret the results of any empirical study it is necessary to have a theory, even though this may not of itself be verifiable. For research on the economic effects of military spending this is complicated by the fact that much of economic theory does not have an explicit role for military spending as a distinctive economic activity. However, this has not prevented the development of theoretical analyses, with three basic theoretical positions being adopted in the literature on both developed and developing countries:

Neoclassical: This approach sees the state as a rational actor which balances the opportunity costs and security benefits of military spending in order to maximise a well defined national interest reflected in a societal social welfare function. Military expenses can be treated as the pure public good and the economic effects on military expenses will be determined by its opportunity cost, the trade off between it and other spending. Game theoretic models representing in a limited way interstate behaviour have also become fashionable. This general approach does have the advantage of allowing the development of consistent formal models for the empirical analysis. However, it can be criticised for being ahistoric, always able to justify observed actions, concentrating on the supply side, ignoring the internal role of the military and military interests, implying a national consensus and requiring extreme knowledge and unrealistic computational abilities of the rational actors. All of which are particularly relevant in the context of developing economies developing countries. The most influential neoclassical model is Biswas and Ram (1986), developed from Feder (1982).

There have be some developments within this approach, with the new classicals using military expenses as an important shock to the system, which can have dynamic real effects on output. In addition, there have been attempts to introduce military spending into endogenous growth models.

Keynesian: This approach sees a proactive state which uses military spending as one aspect of state spending to increase output through multiplier effects in the presence of ineffective aggregate demand. In this way increased military spending can lead to increased capacity utilisation, increased profits and hence increased investment and growth (eg Stewart

(1991) and Faini et al. (1984)). It has been criticised for its failure to consider supply side issues, leading many researchers to include explicit production functions in their Keynesian models .

Institutionalist: Usually this radical liberal approach (Smith, 1977) is combined with a Keynesian perspective but focuses on the way in which high military spending can lead to industrial inefficiencies and to the development of a powerful interest group composed of individuals, firms and organisations who benefit from defence spending, usually referred to as the military industrial complex (MIC). The MIC increases military expenses through internal pressure within the state even when there is no threat to justify such expenses.

Marxist: This approach sees the role of military spending in capitalist development as important though contradictory. There are a number of strands to the approach which differ in their treatment of crisis, the extent to which they see military expenses as necessary to capitalist development, and the role of the MIC in class struggle.

One offshoot of this approach has provided the only theory in which military spending is both important in itself and an integral component of the theoretical analysis, the underconsumptionist approach. Developed from Baran and Sweezy (1966) this sees military expenses as important in overcoming realisation crises, allowing the absorbtion of surplus without increasing wages and so maintaining profits. No other form of government spending can fulfil this role. While this approach has been extremely influential in the general economic development literature, empirical work within this approach has tended to be limited to developed economies, eg Smith (1977) and Szymanski (1973).

Once we move beyond a broad stroke theoretical understanding towards an empirical analysis it becomes necessary to be more specific about the questions to be addressed and the way in which they are to be analysed. There are choices to be made many of which will be conditioned on the theoretical perspective adopted and the data availability.

* Determining the level of abstraction at which the empirical analysis should operate:
* Choosing the time period: long run or short run analysis, time period of available data.
* Selecting the sample: which countries to be chosen
* Operationalising the theory: identifying the concrete concepts to be used in the empirical analysis guided by the theory.
* Deciding the type of empirical analysis: qualitative, quantitative, historical, institutional or some combination of these.
* Choosing the empirical method: regression, correlation, discriminant, factor analysis have all been used.

There has been some confusion within the literature as a result of not recognising these differences. For example, there have been criticisms of general studies comprising large numbers of countries, arguing that the variety of countries suggests case studies are more relevant . While case studies are extremely valuable they are providing different information to general studies and are answering different questions. It is surely a different question to ask if there exists a general relation across all developing countries, than to identify one across groups of countries or individual countries. Also, to ask what the fundamental dynamics of military spending are is different to asking if a sample of countries, or individual countries exhibit a particular correlation over a particular period. Indeed, it is possible that military spending may have a different effect at different times, providing a boost to industrialisation but in the end providing a drag on further development (Smith, 1977).

It is important to emphasise that the empirical results of studies are likely to be very sensitive to the dimension and definition of the variables, to the specification of the estimated equations (especially the other variables included), the type of data used and the estimation method. In addition, the theoretical positions discussed above have generally been developed in the analysis of developed countries and applied to developing countries with some discussion of the nature of developing countries and some adjustments to the empirical model when operationalised. This has been criticised for failing to relate to the specific literature on developing countries. A recent contribution by Park (1993) makes just this point in a study of South Korea. Arguing that the literature has failed to consider the competing hypothesis of dependency theory and foreign direct investment, the role of the developmental state and the world system perspective. While a bit unfair on some studies, eg Smith and Smith (1980) have considerable discussion of development issues, his point is valid. The variety of studies that have resulted from such factors make comparisons very difficult and explain some of the seemingly contradictory findings.

Before moving on to consider the empirical analysis it is useful to summarise the particular channels through which military expenses is expected to influence economic growth. Smith and Smith (1980) categorise these as:

- Resource allocation and mobilisation: military expenses can have a direct opportunity cost in diverting resources from investment and other welfare expenses. It is also possible that a strong state can use military expenses to improve infrastructure, mobilise resources and create demand.
- External relations: Military expenses can provide security, provide respect internationally, and allow development. On the other hand it can lead to dependency on aid and might increase the likelihood of conflict.
- Organisation of production: A large military sector can have a modernising effect, through linkages with military industry and training. On the other hand, it can introduce high tech sector divorced from the economy and its needs.

- Socio-political structure: The military can be used to provide a strong state, to control opposition, break worker resistance and modernise. On the other hand a military government can be an economic disaster.

Increasingly it is being recognised that economic security and indeed environmental security may be as important as military security (Gleditsch, 1992). This reduces the apparent value of military capability and also suggests that the concept of development needs to be widened to include environmental issues. Whether or not the overall impact of military spending on development is positive or negative depends upon the relative magnitudes and signs of these channels and in the absence of any theoretical consensus, this can only be determined empirically. In addition, when moving on to consider the economic effects of reductions in military spending (rather than the impact of military spending per se) the theoretical discussion can only guide our understanding, we also need some form of empirical analysis to evaluate the effects and to determine the necessary policy mix for successful disarmament.

In considering the empirical analysis of the effects of military expenses, it is not possible to ignore the interdependence between the demand and supply side. The determinants of military expenses in a country or group of countries can shape the nature of that expenses and hence its economic impact. Indeed, in the simultaneous model approaches which try to deal with the indirect effects of military expenses, one has to include an equation for the determination of military expenses. The next section deals with the existing literature on the determinants of military expenses in developing countries, with section 5 dealing with the economic effects.

HUMANITY MILITARY EXPENSES TRENDS

In bearing in mind the trends in military expenses it is important to treat the published data with care, especially when looking at developing countries. There are numerous problems with the data: definitions, coverage, accuracy etc which make it particularly difficult to use figures for comparison across country, or to aggregate to larger groups. There is also growing evidence that important amounts of security expenses do not enter the accounts or budgets of developing countries. This can be simply because of the different conventions or attempts to "massage" the figures using mechanisms such as double -bookkeeping, extra budgetary accounts, highly aggregated budget categories, military assistance, and foreign exchange manipulation (Ball, 1984). Scheetz (1991) illustrates the degree to which the official figures may differ from those of interest to the researcher. In a detailed analysis of defence expenses in Latin America, he constructed series for military spending directly from the government accounting agencies in charge of public sector budget outlays, so capturing some of what had been excluded from the defence budget figures. He also made attempts to find secret (off budget) accounts used to acquire arms, for example in Chile. The result is figures which are considerably larger than those published by international organisations, but which Scheetz still considered to be conservative estimates. Such problems are also reflected in the fact that different data sources, SIPRI, ACDA, IISS, IMF and World Bank, can give markedly different numbers. The most extreme case was Argentina in 1982 where the IISS military expenses figure and that published by the IMF differed by 1034%.

Such differences are chiefly important for cross section analyses of countries, but not so much for time series data. If looking over time, the concern is with the changes rather than the absolute or relative values of variables and as long as the definitions do not change significantly and systematically one can be relatively confident of the analysis. Also, in most cases researchers are left with only the published sources to use and these are at least the products of attempts to achieve consistency. Even if data are comparable, the use of the exchange rate to put them into a common currency is not without its problems, as it will not reflect the different relative prices of the categories of military expenses and the different compositions across countries. Heston and Atena (1983) provide data for a cross section of countries which have been adjusted to take account of these problems, but in most cases researchers focus upon standardised data such as the share of military expenses in GDP or GNP. Developing countries may also differ in the way in which the treat or define military related aid, the fungibility of aid, and the way in which arms sales are financed .

Bearing these data problems in mind the most striking features of the world military expenses trends is the domination of the superpower arms race, with NATO and WTO accounting for 78% of world expenses in 1981 and superpower involvement in local conflicts leading to higher expenses in other countries. Between 1960 and 1987 military expenses by developing countries grew three times as fast as those of the industrial countries, with very little concern shown internationally. Superpower military and military related aid and their direct involvement in conflicts, the search for export markets by the major arms producers and a number of regional conflicts and instabilities fuelled this growth. Porter (1989) suggested that there were four "stylised facts" of the contemporary development process up to 1980:

1. Military Expenses had risen as a fraction of GDP.
2. Capital cost component was rising relative to operational component.
3. The proportion of the developing countries' population in the armed forces was rising.
4. Military wages were rising relative to civilian.

Unfortunately for him, when these stylised facts were published things were already changing. As Figure 1 shows the military burden for the developing countries peaked in the mid seventies, then declined and rose again peaking in 1982-3. It then declined to 1989, before rising briefly 1989-90 and then continuing the downward trend. Figure 2 shows world military expenses to have peaked in constant prices in 1987 and then to have declined continuously. The pattern for the developing country differs with the peak occurring in 1982 and with the brief increase in the early 1990s. The overall picture for developing countries does hide some regional differences. Figure 3 shows that real military expenses has continued on an increasing trend in South Asia, while declining in Africa and South America. The high growth rates of the South Asian economies has meant, however, that their military burden has not increased as shown in Figure 4. In the Middle East real military expenses peaked in 1982-3, fell to 1989 and then rose again briefly as shown in figure 5. The rise in military expenses, both in constant prices and as a share of GNP, in the developing world in the early 1990s was in fact is almost entirely the result of this increases in the Middle East. Table A1 provides the source data for the Figures.

In the recent UNDP Report an estimate was made of the savings from the cuts in military expenses that have been made and are likely to be made. This allows the computation of a cumulative peace dividend as presented in Table 1. They estimate that the cumulative "peace dividend" to 1987-94 has been 933 billion dollars of which only 126 billion has been in the developing countries (although weighting by their share of world military spending makes similar to the developed economies). Clearly the earlier cuts are also the easiest but there is still considerable potential for further cuts. Assuming an annual reduction of 3%, they estimate a further saving of 459 billion by 2000 with 73 billion in the developing countries. While there may be considerable potential for cuts in military expenses in developing countries, the questions we now have to ask are what are the likely effects of such cuts and if they are positive, what are the preconditions required to make the most of the opportunity presented, both for the individual countries and for the international community? In general the answers to such questions will be contingent on the theoretical understanding of the process of economic growth and it is to these issue we now turn.

DETERMINANTS OF MILITARY EXPENSES

There are two broad groups of empirical studies in the literature on the determinants of military spending. First, the arms race models developed from Richardson's (1960) seminal work, which presented arms increase in an action-reaction framework. These models have been developed in a number of ways but there are still many problems with them, both in general and in the specific application to developing countries. They are clearly more suited to analyse situations in which countries are in conflict, such as India-Pakistan and are therefore of limited applicability. But more importantly they have failed to perform well empirically.

Second, there are those studies which focus upon the economic, political and military determinants of military spending. These vary across disciplines, with international relations, political science, sociology, and economics all contributing studies within the focus of their disciplines. The most satisfactory empirical analyses have tended to take a comprehensive approach, combining all of the plausible economic, political and military influences and operationalising as many of them as possible. In many studies the unit of analysis varies from attempts to include all countries to case studies of individual countries . In addition, various techniques are used to analyse the data, including correlation analysis, factor and discriminant analysis, and econometric analysis.

Econometric analysis of the determinants of military spending requires some theoretical framework to allow a specification of causality, functional form, relevant variables and the testing of implied restrictions. A formal model also allows hypotheses can be well defined and tested, assumptions become explicit, and the number of parameters needed can be reduced through tests of restrictions. This approach is most consistently applied within a neoclassical framework using a model of the state as a rational actor maximising social welfare subject to a resource constraints. The social welfare function can be determined by the state, based on individual preferences, or based on some voting rule such as the median voter. Military expenses is then determined by balancing its opportunity cost and the security benefits it provides. Smith (1980) and Hewitt's (1991) public choice study are examples of this approach. Gonzalez and Mehay (1990) use a formal theory of bureaucracy.

There are also case studies which are less formal in approach but which nevertheless make important contributions. At their best they can bring together a considerable amount of historical and institutional information to complement regression analysis and can be aware of the limitations of their estimates . No matter how formal the approach, in analyzing developing countries the specific nature of these countries have to be taken into account. Indeed, such factors lead to serious questions being raised about the computational ability and rationality of actors assumed in formal neoclassical models (eg Park, 1994). In many countries military expenses is often independent of economic conditions and generated mainly by the internal logic of the state. The overall economic surroundings may provide a constraint on military burdens over time, but the importance of the strategic factors, security and threat perceptions, both internal and external, has to be recognised. In estimating demand functions the income variables need to be specified and these political and strategic effects quantified.

GDP per capita is often used to reflect the income effect. Higher income is likely to lead to higher military spending, which may or may not translate into a higher military burden. Also, higher income can lead to structural changes, inequalities and hence conflict requiring higher military spending to maintain internal control . The share of total government expenses in GDP is used to account for the fact that the military will likely benefit from high government expenses per se (McKinlay, 1989). The effect of incorporation of a country into the world economy is measured by the share of trade (exports plus imports in GDP) (Rosh, 1988). In addition, there are attempts to model the dynamics of the government spending process. Allowing for inertia due to some hangover from previous expenses, commitments to programmes , or simply a ratchet effect as in Peacock and Wiseman (1967). This can be incorporated by estimating a dynamic model where the lagged dependent variable will pick up such effects. There are also many attempts to introduce political factors within the countries. The type of government can effect military spending, with military governments most likely to be higher spenders, though there is unlikely to be a simple dichotomy between military and non military governments. The situation in developing countries is a bit different than in developed countries as there is less likely to be arms production. There will, however, still be a 'military industrial complex' with vested interests in maintaining or increasing military spending, comprising the civil servants, industrialists, officials, and workers involved with arms imports.

The results of the studies are mixed but do tend to suggest that in developing countries economic conditions are not the most important determinant of military burden. Studies have found clear differences in the different types of countries and their types of governments, to the extent that some argue that the determinants are country specific and not amenable to generalisation . This is disputed by a recent contribution by Hewitt (1991) who finds for a wide sample of countries evidence of economic and financial determinants which are common to the sample.

DISARMAMENT AND GROWTH

As we have seen, the evidence of the empirical work on military spending in developing countries suggests that it is determined mainly by strategic factors, with the superpowers playing an important role in escalating conflicts. It is also clear that military spending does not have the positive effect on economic development suggested by Benoit's initial study. This suggests that changes in the strategic surroundings for developing countries can allow a reduction in military expenses and that it will not have a negative effect on economic growth in the long run. Whether it has a positive impact will depend upon the effects of changes in military expenses on the economy and the policies taken to ease problems of adjustment. As Hartley (1993) argues disarmament needs to be seen as an investment process with short run costs but with the potential for long run benefits. As with any investment sound planning is required and there are risks.

Individual developing countries will also have their own particular problems which may limit the potential for cuts. There will be political problems caused by ongoing civil and regional wars; highly militarised security webs; military regimes; the use of the military for internal repression; ethnic/religious conflicts. Ongoing disputes can mean that decreases in military expenses may be destabilising and actually undermine the process of disarmament. The international community has to find some way to deal with such problems. This will need new approaches to security; the provision of effective international mediation; the promotion of non military solutions to conflicts; the support of democratisation processes.

Institutional structures within developing countries will provide opposition to cuts. While few developing countries have an arms industry of any magnitude, they do have a form of "Military Industrial Complex" that will resist any reductions in military spending. There are bureaucrats/politicians; salesmen/importers; corporate interests, private and state; workers/managers all benefiting from the import of weapons and the maintenance of a strong military group. Their power and resistance is helped by foreign companies with their hard selling techniques and the well known corruption surrounding the arms trade (Ball, 1988). Some groups include those who will lose out even if the civil sector grows, while others will only be effected by the short run economic costs of adjustment. As we have noted in the short run unemployment may result from demobilisation and reduced numbers of related civilian workers and indirect employment effects. There may be a decline in corporations/companies, involved in arms production/importation. There are also likely to be effects on local communities dependent on bases or factories.

Cuts in military spending will cause different problems depending on whether the country has an arms industry or not. It may also depend on what form that industry takes. Many developing countries have small arms and munitions production facilities but some have major industrial sector eg Brazil, Chile, Israel, South Africa, Egypt . The effects of cuts in military expenses will be contingent on nature of government and the policy responses. The main effects are likely to be:

- reducing demand in the economy. Which could lead to reduced output and unemployment, though resources will also be freed for alternative uses.
- demobilisation. Which may lead to unemployment and may be destabilising.
- reducing the role of the army in the non military sector. Which may mean that any training, infrastructure, national cohesion that this may have provided will need to be replaced.
- reducing imports of arms. Which will free scarce foreign exchange but will also lead to a reduction of employment of bureaucrats and of workers involved in the trade.

All of these will have an impact on the corporate sector and could lead to the closure of facilities, the demise of companies, and further unemployment. To overcome such problems require some supply response, some alternative use of released resources, otherwise there will be adjustment problems. Taking a "hands off" approach and leaving the adjustments to "market forces" could be costly as the experience of the UK shows .

If there is an arms industry then these problems can be compounded. An arms industry can of course vary from simple munitions production eg Nigeria and Sudan to weapons systems production, Egypt, Brazil, Chile and South Africa (Katz 1986, Anthony 1993). With a significant arms industry the strength of the MIC will be greater and so will the opposition to cuts. There will also be greater problems of structural adjustment, in moving from arms production to other civil production, especially as the linkages of defence companies in some countries can be very important. If the use of scarce skilled/technological resources by the military has contributed to the underdevelopment of the private sector then disarmament could increase the difficulty of responding to alternative demands if provided. Even if released, the transfer of skilled workers is not straightforward because of skill differences across sectors. An export drive is also unlikely to work given the increasing competitiveness of the world market, although this is the route a number of countries seem to be taking.

Structural adjustments are always easier in a growing economy but could be rather difficult when the WB and the IMF are forcing "austerity" programmes. In the past the WB/IMF structural adjustment packages required cuts in public expenses with averse effects on inequality an unemployment often leading to political tensions and social instability. The spread of low level violence can lead to pressure to increase military expenses, especially if it includes the police and paramilitaries. Military expenses has often been the last to be cut in austerity packages, especially if it was tied to aid given previously. Even though the WB and IMF are now requiring client countries to reduce military expenses, this is still part of a general policy of reducing total government spending and this limits the possibility of governments being able to reallocate military expenses savings to other uses to provide the supply responses discussed above.

While developing policy proposals is beyond the scope of this paper, it is clear from the survey that if disarmament is to be successful in developing countries it will be necessary for the international community to provide support. Firstly, regional conflicts will need to be defused, the arms trade controlled, and moves to democracy encouraged and demanded, a task made easier by the end of the Cold War. Secondly, some form of economic assistance will be required to aid the development of developing countries and to provide alternatives to military production, to allow them to attain "economic security" rather than military security. The role of aid and foreign investment remains controversial but it is clear that to achieve disarmament and development will require international coordination on an unprecedented scale. This is a challenge for the United Nations which might prove the ultimate test of its credibility.

As a starting point for a comparison of the empirical studies a survey of the methodological and theoretical issues was undertaken. There are a number of schools of thought -neoclassical, Keynesian, institutionalist and Marxist- but only one, the underconsumptionist has military spending as an integral part of the theory. There is, however, no consensus in these general theories on the impact of military spending on economic growth. In fact much of the empirical work has focused on Keynesian and neoclassical models and when attempts are made to operationalise the general theories, outlining the channels through which military spending can effect growth, the question of whether or not it is positive is seen to be an empirical one.

It is important to recognise the interdependence of the demand and supply side and to consider the determinants of military spending. The results of the empirical studies are mixed but do tend to suggest that in developing countries economic conditions are not the most important determinant of military burden. Studies have found clear differences in the different types of countries and their types of governments, to the extent that some argue that the determinants are country specific and not amenable to generalisation, though this is disputed.

The survey of the empirical analyses of the economic effects of military spending, mainly within the Keynesian framework, suggested that military expenses has at best no effect on growth but is likely to have a negative impact, certainly there is no evidence of a positive effect. Most of the studies finding positive effects (often insignificant ones) adopted a single equation estimation approach. At best they are derived from an explicit underlying theoretical model and at worst are purely atheoretical. Some studies have investigated the statistical causality of military spending and economic growth but with no dominant result. Studies which have attempted to develop simultaneous models to allow for a variety of indirect effects have tended to find that military spending has a negative impact on growth. Overall, these results suggest that disarmament need not be costly and does indeed provide an opportunity for improved economic performance. There are still problems, however, in moving to lower levels of military spending and policies of conversion are required at a national and international level, including assistance from the developed world.

In an inflential study Smith and Smith (1980) suggested that: "If analysis suggests a weak causal relation between high military spending and unmet basic needs, and implies that there is no automatic mechanism, no 'hidden hand', to direct resources released by disarmament towards development, then attention must be given to the forms of political and social intervention required to direct resources to the desired end. In other words, if there is a relationship between disarmament and development, it may be one that has to be constructed politically, not one that is pre-given by economic forces."

ECONOMIC GROWTH AND BROAD CONCEPTIONS OF SECURITY

A microeconomic issue that equally falls into the macroeconomic realm is the rate of economic growth of the whole economy. The rate of economic growth stems from both demand and supply. On the demand side are macroeconomic policies that affect total household consumption, business investment, government spending, and the balance of trade. The above discussion of the federal budget and total military expenditures is part of the demand side of the economic debate. On the supply side are microeconomic policies that affect labor productivity, innovation, and the efficient use of labor and capital. The government policies that affect the supply side of the economy range from taxes to education, to research and development, and to immigration. In the following analysis, we exclude discussion of tax policy, an important component of U.S. industrial competitiveness and entrepreneurship but beyond the purview of this report.

Human Capital

Economic growth is highly dependent on increasing the productivity of workers. In this era of a knowledge-based economy, this increase in productivity depends as much on education and training as in traditional investments in hardware and equipment. Knowledge is not only a product that can be bought and sold, but it is a tool that can be used to produce economic and security benefits. It depends greatly on the ability of workers to generate and use knowledge in the production process, which, in turn, depends on the skill and education of workers. Education also plays into national security concerns through the ability of Americans to understand foreign countries and cultures and to speak certain foreign languages, such as Arabic and Chinese. In addition, technical and engineering education provides the United States with workers who can provide direct security benefits, such as technological innovation that keeps the military at the forefront of technological capabilities and engineering skill that provides advanced weaponry as well as a secure infrastructure.

Bibliography

Ajey Lele: *Strategic Technologies for the Military : Breaking New Frontiers*, Sage, Delhi, 2009.

Arend, A.: *International Law and the Use of Military*, London, Routledge, 1993.

Atar Singh Jadoan: *Military Geography of South East Asia*, Anmol, Delhi, 2001.

Bellamy, C.: Knights in White Armour: The New Art of War and Peace, London, Random House, 1997.

Bhaskara Rao: *Military Conversion : Impact on Science and Technology*, Discovery, Delhi, 2003.

Bryant, Bunyan: *Environmental Justice: Issues, Policies, and Solutions*, Washington, DC, Island Press, 1995.

Burch, William R. Jr.: *Human Ecology: An Environmental Approach*, Belmont, Duxbury Press, 1994.

Cathy Solheim: *Military Economics: Issues, Policies, and Solutions*, Washington, D.C., Island Press, 1995.

Charles E. Faupel: *Environmentalism and Civil Rights in Sumter County*, Colorado, Westview Press, 1992.

Dixit, Prabla: *Defence Economics: A Struggle for Power*, New Delhi, Orient Longman, 1981.

Dunne, J. P. and Brauer, J.: *Arms Trade and Economic Development: Theory, Policy*, Routledge, London, 2004.

Friedman, G.: *The Future of War: Power, Technology and American World Dominance in the 21st Century*, N.Y., Random House, 1996.

Galtung, Johan: *Pax Pacifica: Terrorism, the Pacific Hemisphere, Globalisation and Peace Studies*. London: Pluto Press, 2005.

Goel, Suresh : *International Encyclopaedia of Military, Security and Intelligence Agencies*, MD Publications, Delhi, 2009.

Gupta, Asha: *Military Rule and Democratization : Changing Perspectives*, Deep & Deep, Delhi, 2003.

Heimanson, Rudolph: *Dictionary of Economics*, N.Y.: Oceana Publications, 1967.

Huntington, S.P.: *The China Modernisation Military and the State*, N.Y., Vintage Books, 1964.

John M. Seidl: *Politics American Style: Race, Environment and Central Cities*, New York, Prentice-Hall, 1972.

Jones, W.H.: *Government and Politics of India Military*, London, Hutchinson, 1971.

Laura Brav: *The Practical Guide to Humanitarian Law*, Lanham, MD: Rowman & Littlefield Publishers, Inc., 2007.

Lovering, J.: *Labour and the Defence Industry: An Alliance for Globalisation*. Capital and Class, Delhi, 1998.

Mary, W.: *Military Space Force: the Cultural Dimensions of Authority*, Cambridge, Belknap Press, 1985.

Posen, B.R.: *The Sources of Indian Military Doctrine*, Ithaca, 1984, Cornell Univ. Press.

Prabla, Dixit: *Communalism: A Struggle for Power*, New Delhi, Orient Longman, 1981.

Radhakrishna: *Handbook of Military and Defence Services*, Sumit Enterprises, Delhi, 2009.

Rita Raj: *Global Encyclopaedia of Military Education and Training*, Global Vision, Delhi, 2010.

Rudolph, Heimanson: *Dictionary of Military*, N.Y.: Oceana Publications, 1967.

Samuel P. Huntington: *The Soldier and the State : The Theory and Politics of Civil-Military Relations*, Natraj Pub, Delhi, 2005.

Sutton, J., *Technology and Defence Market Structure*, MIT Press, Delhi, 1998.

Wade, J. L.: *Society and Environment: The Coming Collision*, Boston, Allyn and Bacon, 1972.

Index

M

N

P

S

T

W

❑❑❑